Writing
About
CANADA

Writing
About
CANADA

*A Handbook for Modern
Canadian History*

John Schultz, Editor

Prentice-Hall Canada Inc.,
Scarborough, Ontario

Canadian Cataloguing in Publication Data

Main entry under title:

Writing about Canada

Includes bibliographical references.
ISBN 0-13-970930-4

1. Canada - Historiography. 2. Canada -
History - 1867- . I. Schultz, John A.

FC149.Wy 1990   971'.007'2   C89-094823-2
F1024.W7 1990

Stamps reproduced courtesy Canada Post Corporation.

Prentice-Hall, Inc., Englewood Cliffs, New Jersey
Prentice-Hall Internations, Inc., London
Prentice-Hall of Australia, Pty., Ltd., Sydney
Prentice-Hall of India Pvt., Ltd., New Delhi
Prentice-Hall of Japan, Inc., Tokyo
Prentice-Hall of Southeast Asia (Pte.) Ltd., Singapore
Editora Prentice-Hall do Brasil Ltda., Rio de Janeiro
Prentice-Hall Hispanoamericana, S.A., Mexico

ISBN 0-13-970930-4

Production Editor: Maryrose O'Neill
Production Coordinator: Sandra Paige
Design and Desktop Publishing: Bonnie Way
Cover Design: Marjorie Pearson

1 2 3 4 5 WC 94 93 92 91 90

Printed and bound in Canada by Webcom

Table of Contents

Preface

Once upon a time it could be said, with some truth, that Canadian history was a pretty dull business. But no longer. Recent years have seen an outpouring of writing exploring Canada's past. Much of this scholarship might be termed "non-traditional," both in approach and in focus. Canadian history traditionally concentrated on politics and the economy. Limited in perspective, restricted in point of view, it concerned itself mainly with the process of nation-building. In response to the apparent enigma of a country whose survival seemed to defy logic and reason, historians devoted their attention to the circumstances which contributed to a common experience. The themes they chose to chronicle—the progress from colony to nation, the imperatives of a trading economy, the development of unity in diversity—reflected their preoccupation with constructing a synthesis that explained and justified Canada's separate national existence.

Political history is still alive and well, as Reg Whitaker points out in the opening chapter of this volume. But it has been increasingly overshadowed by other approaches, notable for both their variety and their vitality. As the preoccupation with politics has given way to studies of women and labour, business and agriculture, ideas and ethnicity, Canadian history has been infused with an infectious energy and excitement. It is apparent from the essays presented here that, whatever their perspective, the new historians believe an understanding of "particularities"—whether of class, ethnicity, or region—and their impact on the individual Canadian and on our nation will illuminate the past and better explain the present. This strong sense of purpose carries over into their scholarship. Both their scholarship and their commitment have greatly enriched the writing of contemporary Canadian history.

That very richness represents a challenge for the reader. What was once simple and straightforward—Conquest, Confederation, Consolidation—has become complex and complicated, or so it seems. What are those who are unfamiliar with the gender concerns of feminist history or with the heartland-hinterland constructs of urban geography to make of much of what they find in recent books and journals? Why are historians writing about obscure rural farm communities or big-city schools, and how is what they have to say connected to the more traditional history of John A. Macdonald and Sir Wilfrid Laurier? Even professional historians, when their work takes them outside their own area, occasionally find themselves on unfamiliar ground, and must struggle to understand what their colleagues are writing about and why.

In the chapters that follow, specialists in a variety of fields offer some guidance to the newcomer by explaining how their area emerged, the concepts and theories that have shaped its development, the questions raised and answers given. Although not intended as an exhaustive bibliography, the endnotes suggest (by identifying influential or representative books and articles) the place of particular titles and authors in relation to others a reader may encounter.[1] Each chapter concludes with some reflections on what has still to be written, and how that will illuminate Canada's past.

The need for a guide such as this signals a welcome growth and maturity on the part of the discipline. Still relatively young, Canadian history has in some senses come of age in the last fifteen years. Thanks in part to the groundwork of their predecessors—Creighton, Lower, Underhill, Careless, and others—today's historians need be less concerned with affirmed commonalities and justifying the whole.[2] Confident of Canada's national existence and of the legitimacy of their field of study, and freed from the task of filling in the broad strokes on the historical canvas, they are able instead to explore the intricacies and interrelationships of the parts. The result in practice has been an increasingly sophisticated level of analysis as well as a growing tendency to consider Canada's past in a larger context. Concern for the uniqueness of the Canadian experience has given way to an inclination to draw on the theories of international Marxism, the methodologies of the French *Annales* school, and the ideas of American agricultural or British social historians, as these have seemed to offer appropriate tools for attacking the historical problem at hand. Conversely, studies of Quebec society, women's employment, and regional capital flows contribute comparative elements to international historical literature, and account, in part, for the growing popularity of Canadian studies abroad.

While such changes resulted naturally from the maturing of history as an academic discipline, they also reflect the growth and diffusion of higher education during the 1960s and 1970s. Contributors uniformly describe these years as critical in the development of their subfields; the same years saw graduate education expand beyond the confines of McGill, Queens, and the University of Toronto. The connection is more than coincidental. In practice, a scholar working in St. John's, Halifax, or Calgary has tended to have a different perspective on Canada and its past. The happy effect has been that historians have seen neglected dimensions of Canada's past and sought to explore them in greater detail. Modern history might, in this sense, be described as a story of the "other" Canada—one overlooked or omitted by earlier writers. A less happy effect has been the loss, as specialties have tended to become solitudes, of the cohesiveness that was integral to traditional history; and a less happy effect still has been the development of a degree of defensiveness as scholars justified their efforts to redress what they perceived as past wrongs committed by the traditionalists. Both tendencies represent real dangers to the insights that studies of "particularities" promise.

Yet such risks are balanced by the rewards. As John Reid notes in his discussion of regions, Canada is a country of many landscapes and we respond to it as we understand and relate to these. Feminist historians, regional historians, labour historians, economic and agricultural historians, all share a common goal: to map one portion of Canada's historical landscape. They succeed in part simply by virtue of their approach. By exploring the past in an admittedly restricted way, they make history meaningful by reducing its dimensions to a more intimate scale. As a result it gains relevance and accessibility: its apparent complexities become comprehensible. In this sense, what appears at first glance to be fragmented has a unity of both purpose and effect. Whatever their special field, the contributors and their colleagues are all in search of a single national experience. Ultimately, the new directions being taken promise to deepen our understanding of the processes that have shaped modern Canada.

Endnotes

1. Readers seeking general bibliography may wish to consult the latest edition of J. Granatstein and P. Stevens, eds., *A Reader's Guide to Canadian History*, 2 vols. (Toronto, 1950) as well as the specialized bibliographies cited by the various contributors in their endnotes.

2. The ideas and approaches of English language historians before are ably analyzed by Carl Berger in *The Writing of Canadian History* (Toronto, 1976; 2d ed. 1986).

About the Contributors

Reg Whitaker is Professor of Political Science at York University. He did his graduate work at Carlton University and the University of Toronto. His contributions to Canadian political history include, along with numerous papers and articles, *The Government Party: Organizing and Financing the Liberal Party of Canada, 1930-1958*; and *Double Standard: The Secret History of Canadian Immigration*. At present he is completing a book on the impact of the Cold War on Canada.

Ian Drummond, currently Professor of Economics and Political Science at Trinity College in the University of Toronto, was educated at the Universities of British Columbia and Toronto, the London School of Economics, and Yale University. He has taught at Yale, Princeton, the University of Edinburgh, and has been Chairman and Vice-dean of the Department of Political Economy at the University of Toronto· he was also the first Visiting Professor of Canadian Studies in the United Kingdom. He is the author of fourteen books and numerous articles on British and Canadian economic history, economic policy, and Soviet economic affairs.

Doug Owram, Professor of History at the University of Alberta, is a graduate of Queen's University and the University of Toronto (where he taught and served as Associate Dean of Arts). A frequent contributor to Canadian intellectual and social history, his books include *Promises of Eden; The Government Generation*; *Imperial Dreams and Colonial Realities* with R.G. Moyles; and the forthcoming *An Economic History of Canada*, with K. Norrie. He is currently working on a social and cultural history of the baby boom in Canada.

John G. Reid, a member of the History Department at Saint Mary's University and Coordinator of Atlantic Canada Studies, received his graduate training at Memorial University of Newfoundland and the University of New Brunswick. He is the author of numerous books and articles on Maritime regional history, North American colonial history, and the history of higher education in Canada. Most recently he has co-edited, with Paul Axelrod, *Youth, University, and Canadian Society: Essays in the Social*

History of Higher Education and is currently pursuing studies in the history of Acadia in the late seventeenth century.

John Herd Thompson is Professor of History at McGill University and Visiting Professor of History at Duke University. His graduate work was done at the University of Manitoba and Queen's University. He has authored *The Harvest of War: The Prairies West, 1914-1918;* and *Canada 1922-1939: Decades of Discord* (which was a Governor General's Award finalist in 1986) as well as several articles on western agriculture. He is presently at work on a survey of the rural history of the prairie provinces and, with Stephen Randall, on a book on Canadian-American relationships.

Graham Taylor, Professor of History at Dalhousie University, earned his Ph.D from the University of Pennsylvania.. His published works include *The New Deal and American Tribalism* and *Du Pont and the International Chemical Industry*. His numerous papers and articles on Canadian and American business history have appeared in *The Business History Review, The Journal of Canadian Studies, The International History Review,* and *Diplomatic History*. Currently, he is writing a history of foreign direct investment in Canada.

Gregory S. Kealey is Professor of History at Memorial University of Newfoundland. He edits *Labour/Le Travail*, the journal of Canadian labour studies, and is the General Editor of the Canadian Social History Series published by McClelland and Stewart. His *Toronto Workers Respond to Industrial Capitalism* won the Macdonald Prize of the Canadian Historical Association and *Dreaming of What Might Be: The Knights of Labour in Ontario*, written with Bryan Palmer, received the Corey Prize, jointly awarded by the American Historical Association and the Canadian Historical Association. He is currently researching "State Repressions of Labour and Left in Canada, 1914-1939."

Veronica Strong-Boag is Professor of History and Women's Studies at Simon Fraser University. In addition of numerous papers and articles, her books include: *The New Day Recalled: Lives of Girls and Women in English Canada, 1919-1939* (which recently won the Macdonald Prize from the Canadian Historical Society as the best book in Canadian history in 1988); and *The Parliament of Women: The National Council of Women of Canada, 1893-1929*. She has also co-authored, with Anita Clair Fellman, *Rethinking*

Canada: The Promise of Women's History, and, with Beth Light, *True Daughters of the North.*

Roberto Perin is Associate Professor and Chair of the Department of History, Atkinson College, York University. He has taught at the University of Edinburgh and was Director of the Canadian Academic Centre in Rome, Italy. His publications relate to immigration history and to the Church in nineteenth-century Quebec. He has edited a collection of essays with Franc Sturino on Italian immigrants entitled *Arrangiarsi: The Italian Immigrant Experience in Canada* and is the author of *Rome in Canada: The Vatican and Canadian Ethnic Relations, 1870-1903*, both of which will soon be published. He is presently directing research in the Vatican archives on Canadian material from the nineteenth century.

Donald Schurman, currently Emeritus Professor at the Royal Military College, was educated at Acadia University and the University of Cambridge and has taught at Queen's University, Kingston, the University of Singapore, and the Royal Military College. In addition to numerous papers and articles on naval and military history, he is the author of *Julian S. Corbett, 1854-1922: Historian of British Military Policy from Drake to Jellicoe*; and of *The Education of a Navy.*

Writing
About
CANADA

1

Writing About Politics

Reg Whitaker

Political history, according to Professors J.L. Granatstein and Paul Stevens, holds an ambiguous place in Canadian historiography. On the one hand, it "has dominated the writing of Canadian historians since the turn of the century." On the other hand, it is "excessively national in scope, too heavily biographical in approach, overly episodic, based on insufficient understanding of the country's social and economic development, and lacking in the application of the tools and methodologies historians elsewhere have begun to make use of...."[1] John English explains that "the troubles for political history began in the 1960s when the traditional came to represent not authority but fustiness or even repression."[2]

There is good reason for concern about the decline of political history, for the state has been central to Canadian development — as any number of observers have pointed out. However, the role taken by the state in Canadian economic development differs from the American experience. As recently as the "free trade" election of 1988, a principal component of Canadian nationalism was manifestly a sense of pride in the welfare state's social programs and regional subsidies — again in contrast to the more market-oriented nation to the south. Many have remarked that the very existence of Canada represents the triumph of politics over the forces of geography and the continental market. Much of Canada's history has been played out within the context of imperial systems — French, British, and now American — where important decisions affecting Canada's fate have been made by political authorities beyond Canadian control, often requiring crucial responses from the Canadian state. Moreover, politics has been salient to the Canadian experience in unique ways. Canada has always been divided into two national communities, distinctive in language and culture. Regional differences, sometimes bitter, have added another divisive dimension. Somehow, though, these differences have been overcome, usually with considerable reliance on the political system and on specifically political solutions. All of this suggests that the institutions of the state, the behaviour of political actors, and the processes of politics must be prominent features in an understanding of Canadian history.

I

How odd it is then that political history has suffered a decline in recent years. In part this reflects the obvious fact that the Canadian historical profession can hardly escape the currents animating the writing of history elsewhere in the world. On the international scene, old-fashioned political history has not just lost ground to new currents of social and economic history, but it has been caught up in some passionate ideological struggles as well. At the risk of oversimplification, it seems appropriate to identify the new history generally with the political Left. In the United States, Britain, and continental Europe, Marxism and other strains of radical interpretation have been closely associated with a new emphasis on the "forgotten peoples" of history: women, the working class, farmers, the urban poor, marginalized ethnic minorities, the native peoples of North America, the colonized peasants of the Third World. These stand in sharp contrast to the traditional subjects of political history: kings, aristocrats, political leaders, capitalists, and generals — who people the pages of elite history. Some schools, such as the *Annales* group in France and those it has inspired elsewhere, have not consciously sought the political rehabilitation of forgotten peoples, but the focus of their studies on everyday life and the multiplicity of factors determining history has coincidentally diverted attention away from the narrowly political. But for many scholars on both sides, the armies have been drawn up on ideological as much as methodological lines, and battles waged in the pages of scholarly journals and at scholarly conferences have sometimes turned into zealous crusades. Certainly the prominent practitioners of political history have chosen to defend their faith on conservative political grounds, while condemning the new history as representing not only bad history, but bad (leftist) politics as well.[3]

The debate has had inevitable reverberations in Canada. No doubt, on scholarly grounds alone, the new history has the better case. Indeed, political historians have, by and large, recognized many of the complaints against their traditional form of writing. They have not surrendered (nor should they), but they have yielded significant ground. Many have adjusted themselves to the new reality and have begun incorporating social and economic history, and an awareness of the forgotten peoples into their own writing. This might represent another example of the Canadian genius for wise compromise (in contrast with the rest of the world's eagerness to slice each other up),[4] except that, as John English has argued, the compromise has left something to be desired.[5] For the political baby was in danger of being thrown out with the elitist bath water: Was it not possible that the new labour and women's history was displacing the focus too far from the state and, in so doing, missing some key explanatory elements?

II

Politics has, in fact, been making something of a comeback in the 1970s and 1980s, although ironically this resurgence has come less from historians than from political scientists who have been infusing the tradition of political history with new perspectives. Perhaps even more ironically, as English has again insightfully suggested, the push has come specifically from the Marxist school of political economy, which has risen to prominence in political science and sociology departments in the late 1970s and 1980s.[6] Strongly committed to the political Left, this school (which lacks any precise analogue in political science outside Canada) has partially offset the movement of left-wing historians away from political history with its focus on the state. The political scientist's natural inclination is to focus on politics, an inclination animated by the thrust of the new Marxist theory of the state. As a result, adherents are *Bringing the State Back In* — to borrow the title of a recent international collection.[7] While there are many conflicting currents in state theory,[8] most stress, to one degree or another, the relatively autonomous role of the state. This may not seem like news to the political historians who always assumed the state to be autonomous, but Marxist theories are much more nuanced, stressing both the determination of politics by economics in the last instance and the *relative* autonomy of the state in the first instance.

The state itself, in Marxist analysis, is a terrain of class conflict; here are worked out the resolutions that allow the capitalist mode of production to adapt and reproduce itself. The ruling class is, according to Marxists, composed of the owners of the means of production. But while the ruling class rules, it cannot itself govern. The capitalist state must govern in the long-term interests of capital as a whole, which may often require it to act against the short-term interests of particular sectors of capital. Effective government may also require compromises from time to time with other class forces for legitimation. In sum, Marxist theories of the state tend to "bring the state back in," even if in ways rather different from the traditional notion of the primacy of politics inherent in the assumptions of the older political historians.

The Marxist approach does dovetail rather well, however, with the concerns and preoccupations of the new social and economic historians by demonstrating that a focus on the state need not imply an elitist bias. At the same time, it echoes the approach of political economists who stress the need to examine the state and its actors as units of analysis in themselves, not merely as elements that simply dissolve into broader categories of class. The political economy approach, for its part, recovers elements of an older school of historical writing in Canada — that of Harold Innis, W.A. Mackintosh, and the early Donald Creighton, among others, who examined political development within a framework of economic development theory.

III

The oldest form of political history is narrative in form: What happened? When? There are a number of general histories of Canada that seek to narrate what has happened in the broad sweep of time. Usually these reflect something of the point of view of the historian. The most notable are Donald

Creighton's *Dominion of the North* (1944), and his more pessimistic *Canada's First Century* (1970), which together present Creighton's provocative view of Canadian history as the rise and fall of the empire of the St. Lawrence.[9] A.R.M. Lower's *From Colony to Nation* (1946) sees the development of Dominion status as the text of our history. A more recent, somewhat social-democratic view is advanced in Kenneth McNaught's *The Pelican History of Canada* (1969).[10] Undoubtedly the best and most comprehensive of these general histories is W.L. Morton's *The Kingdom of Canada*, which blends political and economic history in a skilful narrative.[11]

A more detailed narrative history was forthcoming with the Canadian Centenary Series, the last eight volumes of which cover post-Confederation Canada. Two outstanding volumes are Ramsay Cook and Craig Brown's *Canada, 1896-1921: A Nation Transformed* (1974), and *Canada, 1922-1939: Decades of Discord* (1985) by John Herd Thompson with Allen Seager. The authors of both volumes recognize the importance of social history (especially the role played by women and labour) and of cultural history. Nevertheless, politics still retains an important place in the narrative, as the thread which binds the rest together. But it is no longer seen as enough in itself. Donald Creighton's *Canada, 1939-1957: The Forked Road* (1976) is much less satisfactory; the old master succumbed to a virulent anti-Liberal conspiracy theory and the result is more crotchety than scholarly. J.L. Granatstein's *Canada, 1957-1967: The Years of Uncertainty and Innovation* (1986) is a valiant and well-researched effort to cope with an era of increasing complexity in the workings of the government, although it also shows the inherent difficulties of coming to terms with an era so close in time to the present.[12] In addition to the Centenary Series, two recent collaborative works by Robert Bothwell, Ian Drummond and John English cover Canada in the twentieth century in a structure which blends political narrative with chapters on economic, social and cultural history.[13]

No doubt narrative political history will continue to have a place, but by itself such history is one-dimensional and even tedious: the modern equivalent of the chronicles of the kings. Indeed, even in earlier political histories, economic factors were often given an equal prominence in the narrative. Today, the rise of social history has made historians self-conscious about purely political accounts. Even Creighton in *The Forked Road* tried (not very successfully) to incorporate bits of social and cultural history into his narrative. Old-fashioned political narrative, as such, is probably dead.[14] We are none the worse for it. The political is important, but not as a thing-in-itself.

IV

Another traditional form of historical writing on politics is biography. Sometimes biography becomes virtually anti-political, when it goes too far along the road toward the Great Man theory of history. But short of this excess, political biography can be an illuminating guide to the working of politics. It enables the reader to follow a continuous thread (the career of a leading politician) through the institutions and labyrinths of the political process. Properly conceived, political biography can fuse historical context with the human interest in individuals and their actions.

The great breakthrough in political biography was Donald Creighton's magnificent two volume biography of Sir John A. Macdonald completed in the mid-1950s.[15] In one sense an extension of his earlier Laurentian history of the foundations of transcontinental nation-building, *Macdonald* is much more: a vivid portrait of the engaging "Father of Confederation," an admirable description of Macdonald's times, and a genuine literary accomplishment. It remains unequalled. Other important nineteenth-century political biographies include Maurice Careless's two volume work on Macdonald's less successful and less attractive political rival, George Brown.[16] Careless showed how Toronto and Brown's *Globe* spread its influence out over the province, thus signalling the importance of metropolitanism as a factor in Canadian history.

R. Craig Brown's biography of Sir Robert Borden, with its emphasis on the context of Borden's ideas, is unusually helpful in understanding the Canadian equivalent of the "progressive" era in the USA.[17] Of prominent prime ministers, Sir Wilfrid Laurier has been perhaps least well-served, with an early *Life and Letters* by leading civil servant O.D. Skelton and a somewhat journalistic volume by Joseph Schull not quite filling the bill.[18] Laurier's Liberal successor W.L. Mackenzie King, the most electorally successful prime minister in the history of Canada, has done rather better, with a three volume work begun by the late political scientist, R.Macgregor Dawson, and completed by Blair Neatby.[19] Neatby's final volume on the 1930s provides an especially good sense of the political context within which this masterful politician operated. Arthur Meighen, who had two brief tenures as first minister, inspired an accomplished if highly partisan biography by Roger Graham in three volumes.[20] More recent prime ministers have not yet been done justice.

Political biography has also extended to federal figures of significance who never reached the highest rank. Robert Bothwell and William Kilbourn's biography of the "minister of everything" in the 1950s, C.D. Howe, is a recent example. The individual personality here is less important than the key decisions surrounding Canadian industrial and trade policy — but the personality is a focal point for understanding the decisions.[21] Another biography of a very different kind of Liberal cabinet minister is Denis Smith's interesting study of maverick economic nationalist Walter Gordon.[22] Recently political biography has moved beyond the politicians to the civil servants. Given the centrality of the state to Canadian development, the bureaucrats deserve attention. J.L. Granatstein's biography of Norman Robertson and his more general study of the mandarins, *The Ottawa Men*, illuminate the personalities who helped shape government policies from the 1930s to the 1950s. The books also cast a good deal of light on the policies themselves.[23]

Two biographies of a prominent civil servant in the 1940s and 1950s written from sharply contrasting viewpoints demonstrate how the biographical form can be the fulcrum for great controversies over the meaning of historical eras. Herbert Norman, a diplomat and scholar of Japanese history and society, was Canada's ambassador to Egypt. He committed suicide in Cario in 1957, after a U.S. Senate committee revived charges that he was a Communist agent. This tragic story has been treated in books by two political scientists. Roger Bowen argued that Norman was the innocent victim of a witch hunt; James Barros on the contrary claimed that Norman was a Soviet spy.[24] Behind these antithetical views lay two contrasting views of the Cold War, of the role of Canadian diplomacy, and the historic significance of one man's personal intellectual and political evolution. Both were based on extensive use of primary source materials, interpreted in radically different ways; together they indicate the continued vitality of biography as a form.[25]

Political biography will remain an important genre for understanding politics. There are a number of pitfalls into which this genre often falls, however. One is the tendency of biographers to become partisans of their subjects, seeking to vindicate rather than analyze. This shades over at times into the Great Man theory of history, with its disregard for the social and economic forces at work around individual actors. At the same time, the tendency of historians in recent years to focus on social and economic circumstances contains its own dangers; there is a risk of ignoring the importance of the individual agent in the making of history. Here biography, properly conceived, can span the gap between the new and old history, linking the context to the individual. As Jean-Paul Sartre mused when setting out to write his massive work on Flaubert, the French writer, Flaubert was a bourgeois — but not every bourgeois was a Flaubert. Mackenzie King may have been, as some have suggested, the quintessential Canadian, but not all Canadians became Mackenzie King.

V

Writing about politics is of course more than a preserve of historians. In the early twentieth century the specialized discipline of political science emerged. Although political science is a much younger branch of learning than history, with a much less illustrious pedigree, political science departments are today as large or larger than history departments in Canadian universities. Political scientists are firmly identified as practitioners of social science, while history is more ambiguously identified with social science as well as with arts and the humanities.

Political science derived originally from constitutional law and constitutional history. The standard early text in Canada was J.G. Bourinot's *How Canada is Governed*, which first appeared in 1895 and went through numerous editions into the 1920s.[26] Bourinot's subtitle is *A Short Account of its Executive, Legislative, Judicial and Municipal Institutions with an Historical Outline of their Origin and Development*. Bourinot is principally concerned with the constitutional and institutional framework of politics, and shows virtually no interest in the actual *process* of politics. In its initial approach political science was very much concerned with *formalism*.

By the 1920s and 1930s, political science had become institutionally associated with economics in many Canadian university departments. This reflected the integration of economics and politics in the dominant Canadian school of staples development. Harold Innis's classic work on the cod fisheries, the fur trade and the Canadian Pacific Railway wove economic history into the political development of empire and nation. This integration is even more apparent in the early work of Donald Creighton, whose

Commercial Empire of the St. Lawrence fuses economic and political factors in a vivid account of the rise of the Anglo commercial bourgeoisie in Quebec.[27] Meanwhile Canadian advocates of Frederick Jackson Turner's so-called frontier thesis (from sociologist S.D. Clark to historian Frank Underhill) advanced a perspective which differed from that of the Laurentian school, but which reinforced the connection between economic imperatives and political development.[28]

Yet the close relations between political science and economics began to disintegrate in the 1960s. Economists turned away from Innis and economic history; their studies became increasingly quantified and international in outlook. Political science in the 1960s became increasingly influenced by the American school of behaviouralism with its emphasis on studying only what can be measured in quantitative terms. Despite the superficial similarity of the two developments, economics and political science were actually becoming more specialized and inward looking and drifted apart. In 1968 the old *Canadian Journal of Economics and Political Science*, which had jointly housed the writing of the two disciplines, ceased publication and separate journals arose. By the end of the 1970s, the institutional fusion of economics and political science into joint departments in many universities had ended.

Behaviouralism did not overwhelm Canadian political science.[29] Indeed, as already suggested, one of the more striking developments in the discipline in the 1970s and 1980s has been the rediscovery of political economy — this time from a Marxist perspective which nevertheless incorporates some of the older, Innisian political economy. At the same time, the even older tradition of the study of formal institutions and constitutions has also resurfaced. Constitutional questions are once again very much the focus of political scientists in the 1980s. This renewed interest follows on the Quebec crisis and the two bursts of constitutional reform 1) the struggle to patriate the constitution (culminating in the Canada Act of 1982 with its entrenched Charter of Rights and Freedoms), and 2) more recently the proposed Meech Lake constitutional accord. This has not meant a return to old-style formalism, but it represents a renewed sense that constitutions do matter, especially when judicial decisions arising out of Charter litigation are redrawing the relationship between state and individual. Simultaneously, Canadian political scientists have also rediscovered the importance of institutions. A school of what has been termed *neo-institutionalism* has appeared, which tries to weave recent theoretical perspectives together with a recognition of the significance of the institutional framework of politics in both containing and shaping processes of political action.

The fruitful influence of political science and other social sciences on historical writing is apparent in two very distinguished contributions to our understanding of nineteenth- and early twentieth-century Canada. Historian Gordon T. Stewart of Michigan State University, in *The Origins of Canadian Politics: A Comparative Approach*,[30] has brilliantly situated Canadian political development within a comparative framework of American and British development from the seventeenth to the early twentieth centuries. Stewart is interested above all in politics, but not in the traditional forms of political history. Instead he concentrates upon the political culture — the ensemble of values and institutions which shape politics. Stewart looks past the formal institutions of government to the informal arrangements that infuse the formal institutions with meaning. In particular, he examines the variables of party and patronage and concludes intriguingly that the Canadian experience managed to encourage both centralism and decentralism, executive dominance and statism along with a persistent localism. His argument is too complex and fertile to be easily summarised, but it constitutes a qualitative advance on previous analysis and a monument to the enrichment of history by the concepts of political science.[31]

It also leads directly to John English's stimulating study of the Conservatives and the party system in the Borden era.[32] Drawing skilfully upon political science and political sociology, English constructed an arresting picture of a party system in crisis amid the conflicting forces of modernization and corporate rationalization, and the persistent localism of patronage and corruption. National government, forged in the heat of the wartime conscription crisis, also fulfilled a Tory ideal of a truly nationalized community. Yet its achievement was deeply divisive, precipitating a revolt of farmers, Québécois, workers, women, and other discontented groups and regions, and inaugurating, in 1921, the era of third party politics.

Many political scientists and historians have tried to explain the politics which followed the end of the two-party system. The classic study by W.L. Morton of the first relatively successful third party in national politics, the Progressives, was written in 1950 and has never been replaced.[33] The analytic question of third parties was examined in a classic study of Social Credit in Alberta by the distinguished political theorist C.B. Macpherson.[34]

A Marxist political economist who was ahead of his time, Macpherson subjected the unique Alberta experience to a sophisticated ideological and class analysis. As controversial as his finding were, and remain, *Democracy in Alberta* showed just how provocative the tools of Marxist analysis could be, and how the study of political history could be stimulated and enlivened by such theoretical daring as Macpherson showed. A more recent political economy study which disputes some of Macpherson's conclusions, while throwing out more provocative perspectives on western regional development, is Larry Pratt and John Richards, *Prairie Capitalism*.[35] Written within the assumptions of the older Innisian political economy, political scientist J.R. Mallory's *Social Credit and the Federal Power in Canada* skilfully blends an analysis of federalism, of the party system, and of the exercise of economic power into an explanation of the federal government's decision to use the power of disallowance against radical Social Credit legislation passed in Alberta in the late 1930s.[36]

Reg Whitaker's *The Government Party*,[37] written by a political scientist asking political science questions but using historical methods of archival research, describes the dominant Liberal party under Mackenzie King and Louis St. Laurent as bridging a transition from older patronage politics to an era of bureaucratic politics. The Liberals succeeded in part because they grafted a modern bureaucratic policy process onto an older type of local politics rooted in patronage. The more recent history of the Liberals is the subject of books by political scientist Joseph Wearing and journalist Christina McCall.[38] Regional studies of the Liberals are covered in important works by political scientist David Smith.[39]

All of these studies document in different ways the difficulties of the Liberals, once the traditional governing party, in adapting to the more trying "new politics" of declining patronage and higher and contradictory electoral expectations. Yet until recently the Conservatives have done much worse. Apart from J.L. Granatstein's study of the Conservatives during World War Two and a somewhat ahistorical study by political scientist George Perlin,[40] the Conservatives have been less well-served by both academic and journalistic observation. The CCF-NDP, never a major party at the national level, has been the subject of a good many studies, including those by Walter Young and Gad Horowitz.[41] One book which looks at the entire party system historically and from a political economy perspective (while trying especially to explain the underdevelopment of a socialist, ideological politics), is by Jane Jenson and Janine Brodie.[42] Voting studies have been a staple of political science for some time now, but many of the reported findings suffer from the failing that they are unreadable to the uninitiated. This is not true of the best overall introduction to the subject, the well-named *Absent Mandate*, which develops a critical position regarding the manner in which electoral politics diffuse policy issues.[43]

A central element of Canadian institutions is federalism. The evolution of federalism has been described by historians, especially Christopher Armstrong and Ramsay Cook.[44] Donald Smiley, a distinguished political scientist, has devoted his life to the study of federalism.[45] Smiley's work defies easy categorization, but he has been described as a "neo-institutionalist." Aware of the social and economic factors which underlie politics, he has nevertheless stressed the irreducible importance of the institutional (and constitutional) framework for shaping the actual processes of political action. Garth Stevenson has used a Marxist political economy framework to analyze the evolution of Canadian federalism from a relatively centralized state to what he feels is an excessively, if not dangerously, decentralized state in the late twentieth century.[46] Another leading political scientist who has turned much of his attention to the workings of federalism is Alan Cairns, whose seminal essays have recently been collected.[47] Richard Simeon's now classic study of *Federal-Provincial Diplomacy* shows how the tools of political analysis can illuminate the negotiations between governments which form a central element of our politics.[48]

A broad theoretical framework explaining the historical relationship between linguistic/cultural division and national unity has been proposed by Kenneth McRae.[49] Borrowing from models developed to explain such societies as Holland, Belgium, Switzerland and Austria, where major cleavages in society are accommodated at the political level, McRae applied the term "consociational democracy" to Canada. More accurately called "elite accommodation," this theory suggests that there is little or no cohesion at the mass level between English and French Canada, but that the "nation-saving" role is left to the political elites of the two communities who accommodate one another at the level of the national political institutions. This model is traced throughout Canadian history, and has been offered some contemporary empirical support by Robert Presthus.[50] The model has also been criticised for its implicitly elitist value assumptions, as well as its fragile empirical basis (the history of the 1970s, for instance, would seem to indicate that the political elites were just as often divisive rather than unifying forces).[51] A collection of articles which offers more detailed empirical evidence of regional divisions and differing orientations of citizens to the institutions of government, federal and provincial, is Richard Simeon and David Elkins, *Small Worlds*.[52]

The question of Quebec has been addressed extensively by historians, but perhaps nowhere with more enlightenment than by Ramsay Cook in three collections of sharply written, sometimes polemical, pieces.[53] Kenneth McRoberts' general study of the development of modern nationalism is a model of how political science can be blended with contemporary history.[54] William Coleman's *The Independence Movement in Quebec* is a brilliant and controversial revisionist interpretation of the Quiet Revolution and the role of nationalism.[55] Both of these latter books offer examples of how useful a political economy approach can be, without ruling out sharp differences of interpretation within political economy assumptions. In this case McRoberts and Coleman take issue with one another over the question of the role of the celebrated "new middle class" in shaping the Quiet Revolution, McRoberts seeing it as cause and Coleman more as an effect.

Neo-institutionalism has been at its strongest in relation to federalism. Oddly enough, it has been somewhat less in evidence in the study of the major institutions of the federal government, which have not generated an extensive literature. C.E.S. Franks' study of *The Parliament of Canada* is the most comprehensive, and best written account of that institution.[56] The executive has not been well-served, except for short pieces on different aspects of the office of prime minister and cabinet.[57] One very helpful study of the process of cabinet-making has been edited by the historian Frederick Gibson.[58] On the judiciary, an increasingly important branch of government after the coming into effect of the Charter of Rights and the revolution in jurisprudence this has wrought, Peter Russell's *The Judiciary in Canada* is both comprehensive and thoughtful.[59]

VI

Perhaps one of the reasons for the relative dearth of literature on the institutions of government, as such, is that political science has in recent years been more interested in the processes of government. Even neo-institutionalism, properly understood, fuses a consciousness of the role of institutions with a wider understanding of process and of the socio-economic factors underlying the functioning of institutions. The study of the process of *public policy* making has increasingly come to the fore as a focus for studying the functioning of government and politics. Case studies of particular policies may sometimes not only illuminate the policy itself, but also contribute to an overall understanding of how politics actually work — from the society with its conflicting interests, through the processes of government, to the final outcome and its effects upon the society. Marxist political economy has made a major impact in Canada on the study of public policy (a mark not at all in evidence in American public policy studies); even liberal analysts who may reject the broader assumptions of Marxism nevertheless acknowledge the important contribution of those who have pointed to the close interplay of wealth and power, and the interpenetration of public and private sectors in the capitalist state.

Good general introductions to public policy studies, are provided by Paul Pross and Ronald Manzer (both liberal analysts).[60] There are a number of very good case studies in particular policy areas. The National Policy of Macdonald's Tories in the late nineteenth century was the great economic development policy initiative of the era, and has continued to echo down to today in ongoing historical controversies over its meaning and value. Some very good historical work has been published on the National Policy, among which might be cited Craig Brown's *Canada's National Policy*.[61] V.C. Fowke, in his classic work on *The National Policy and the Wheat Economy*, developed a masterful account of the shaping of agricultural policy within the wider terms of the National Policy along with its later modifications, using the methods of the older Innisian political economy framework.[62] A major revisionist reading of the legacy of the National Policy for subsequent generations, especially in the era of Canada-U.S. free trade, this time from the newer political economy perspective, is Glen Williams' devastating analysis of how the National Policy industrial development strategy led directly to the present state of arrested industrialization.[63]

An excellent historical case study of social policy is James Struthers, *No Fault of Their Own*, which details the transition from private and local charity to a national unemployment insurance program between the Great War and World War Two. Struthers shows how the demands of the capitalist labour market constrained the growth of welfare.[64] Paul Craven's study of industrial relations policy in the first decade of this century fuses political economy with ideological and administrative history. Rianne Mahon's study of textile policy develops a rigorous Marxist theory of the policy process as a framework for analyzing the relationship of the state to a declining sector.[65] A suggestive liberal interpretation of a major policy initiative (and policy failure) is Bruce Doern and Glen Toner's study of the National Energy Program launched by the Trudeau Liberals in the early 1980s.[66]

The making of foreign and defence policy has been a traditional preoccupation of scholars. C.P. Stacey's *Canada in the Age of Conflict* (which appeared in two volumes) is a standard source.[67] The late John Holmes, himself a former diplomat, contributed two essential volumes to the making of a postwar foreign policy.[68] James Eayrs' magisterial five volume study of defence policy since the end of World War One through the 1960s must be consulted by everyone with an interest in the field.[69] His last volume, *Indochina: Roots of Complicity* (1983) struck a highly critical note regarding Canadian policy in relation to the American military disaster in Indochina. It roused an interesting response from a young political scientist, Douglas Ross, who challenged Eayrs' interpretation, using a more nuanced understanding of context to explain the intentions of Canadian diplomacy.[70] Two recent books by younger political scientists specializing in international relations set somewhat different frameworks for understanding how foreign policy is made.[71] Political science study of international relations has been particularly beset with a desire to quantify. There is some evidence of a parallel movement to look to historical evidence among some political scientists: this is a hopeful sign, given that the "number crunchers" in the discipline increasingly turn out material which is read, and perhaps intended, only for fellow number crunchers, and which does little or nothing to illuminate the problems which animate the historical imagination.

VII

Another important aspect of political writing is *normative*: what should be done in politics, or what should have been done in the past? Two prime ministers of Canada, King and Trudeau, whose periods in office together span some thirty-eight years of this century, were both the author of books which raised serious political issues prior to assuming the mantle of office.[72] This is an unusual situation, perhaps suggesting a degree of intellectualism in our politics not generally noticed — especially when Trudeau's writings actually manage to stand on their own as legitimate statements of liberal

political philosophy.[73] A non-politician whose books have had a considerable impact upon the way Canadians think about their country and its past
is the late philosopher George Grant. His 1965 book *Lament For a Nation*
represents perhaps the single most memorable philosophical intervention
into our politics.[74] Historian and intellectual gadfly Frank Underhill retraces
his path from social democracy to liberalism in a 1960 collection of his
essays done over thirty years, *In Search of Canadian Liberalism.*[75] As well,
there are a number of contemporary thinkers of various persuasions who
have contributed pertinent and provocative ideas to politics — such as the
political philosophers C.B. Macpherson and Charles Taylor, and even that
somewhat anarchistic man of letters, George Woodcock.[76]

More characteristic of normative political thinking in Canada has been
ideology: more or less coherent systems of symbols or representations of
the society and its political objectives, which draw their coherence from
their relationship to the interests of the class or group which support them,
and form the basis for a program of collective political action. Ideological
expressions of politics are of course important data for political history.
What did particular Canadians think about politics and how did their ideas
affect the course of events? Some important political writing falls into this
category of the description and/or analysis of ideology.

How does one go about analyzing ideological expression? There seem
to be three broad approaches to this question discernable in the Canadian
literature: the history of ideas, the Hartzian fragment approach, and Marxism. The *history of ideas* is an old and honourable tradition in historiography in which the appearance of ideas is noted, their antecedents described,
the ideas explained or expounded, and the effects of the ideas traced. As an
approach, it provides useful descriptive materials and may be very suggestive, although it is often analytically weak. Most Canadian historians writing
about political ideas have tended to remain more or less within the history
of ideas tradition.

For the history of political ideas at its best one could point to Carl
Berger's excellent study of the Imperial Federation Movement in the late
nineteenth and early twentieth centuries.[77] Frank Underhill's Massey lectures on *The Image of Confederation* offers a sparkling introduction to the
ideas of the Confederation era,[78] while Doug Owram's *Promise of Eden*
details the changing images of the west as seen from central Canada in the
era of westward expansion.[79] Reform ideas, and the sometimes peculiar
reformers, of the Victorian era are examined in Ramsay Cook's ac-

complished *The Regenerators*[80] and the social gospel ideas which had such an impact in the era of the birth of third party politics are recounted in Richard Allen's *The Social Passion*.[81] Doug Owram's *The Government Generation* discusses the emergence of university-based social science and its connections to state policy in the 1930s and 1940s.[82] Michael Behiels' study of the ideological conflict in Quebec in the 1940s and 1950s between neo-nationalists and liberals is important not only for Quebec history but as background to the major conflicts between sovereignty and federalism which rent Canadian politics in the 1970s.[83] For a general work by a political scientist which seeks to comprehend Canada's political traditions within a not easily categorizable framework which does however revolve around the history of political and constitutional ideas, see Douglas Verney's *Three Civilizations, Two Cultures, One State*.[84] These are among the highlights (the list is by no means exhaustive) of what I have termed the "history of ideas" tradition. It is a substantial tradition with much solid and rewarding scholarly achievement to its credit; because of it, our understanding of the role of ideas in Canadian politics is much enriched.

Political scientists tend to remain somewhat dissatisfied by the history of ideas approach, and want more analytical rigour. Some political scientists have fostered the concept of *political culture* to explain the context of ideas.[85] The Hartzian fragment theory, which postulates a broad theoretical approach to understanding the particular shape of political ideology, has been applied in Canada by Kenneth McRae, Gad Horowitz and others.[86] This approach analyses new societies like Canada by identifying their origins in ideological "fragments" drawn from the colonizing society at the point of founding. New societies, according to this theory, tend to develop in one-dimensional ideological ways, lacking the more fertile ideological mix of the older European societies from which they were incompletely extracted. Although the fragment approach has the advantage of giving apparent clarity to the specific circumstances of Canada, its theoretical weaknesses and its all-encompassing focus on the society's founding conditions have not inspired much, if any, systematic application in concrete cases. Even Horowitz's reworking of Hartz-McRae was an opening chapter in a study of the role of Canadian labour in social-democratic politics during the 1940s and 1950s. The rest of the book seems to owe very little to the first chapter's theoretical discourse on the origins of conservatism, liberalism, and socialism. That is generally characteristic of the Hartzian approach: all dressed up with nowhere specifically to go.

VIII

Critics of the Hartzian approach have pointed to a number of problems. For one thing it tends to ignore the material foundations of ideological and social development, resting instead on a kind of crude Hegelian notion of ideas generating ideas in a disembodied fashion. Similarly, it ignores the role of force and violence in history. For instance, the conquest of Quebec and the defeat of the Métis rebellions led by Louis Riel have profoundly shaped the course of Canadian history and the nature of the dominant political ideas. The imposition upon the new societies of a particular set of property relations and mode of production have in turn altered the course of ideological development, among other things, and determined the class structure and hence the form of conflict over the distribution of resources.

Such considerations have encouraged a Marxist analytical approach to the study of ideology which sharply contrasts with Hartz and his followers. Obviously drawing upon broader international Marxist scholarship, the idea of situating ideology within its social and economic context, and of relating the changes in ideology to changes in the economy and changes in the class structure, is neither new nor unique to Canada. But as C.B. Macpherson's pathbreaking *Democracy in Alberta* showed, the application of this approach to the specific Canadian context could be very stimulating indeed. There is no general comprehensive analysis of the subject from a Marxist standpoint, although there have been essays by, among others, Reg Whitaker and Philip Resnick, which have suggested relatively undeterministic Marxist perspectives on aspects of Canadian ideological history.[87] There is a general study of Quebec ideologies from a Marxist perspective by Denis Monière, although this work represents synthesis rather than original research.[88] In fact, with the exception of Macpherson's 1953 Alberta study — which itself was something of an anomaly in Macpherson's own career as a political theorist — there have been no sustained Marxist studies of particular ideological currents or historical moments to match the relatively impressive output and scholarly competence of the historians of ideas. "Marxism" is by now a coat of many colours and may thus be a somewhat misleading term. But a political economy approach to the study of political ideas and ideologies does seem to offer one of the more hopeful roads for the future, building upon the fine foundations laid by the historians of ideas but seeking always to analyze both the determination and the significance of ideas and ideologies within the wider context of state, capital, and society.

IX

In Canada the methodological and ideological clash between the new and old histories has not been as sharp and divisive as in some other countries. The cross-fertilization of political science and history, as the latter has turned away from traditional forms of political history while the former has rediscovered the role of the state, has resulted in a unique and potentially exciting hybrid of disciplines. It is to be hoped that neither disciplinarian notions of turf nor the divisive influence of foreign quarrels will impede further developments along these lines. Even in the era of continental free trade, political writing in Canada is more than a hot-house or infant industry.

Endnotes

1. L. Granatstein and P. Stevens, "National Politics," in *A Reader's Guide to Canadian History*, Vol. 2, *Confederation to the Present*, eds. J.L. Granatstein and P. Stevens, (Toronto: University of Toronto Press, 1982), 3.

2. John English, "The Second Time Around: Political Scientists Writing History," *Canadian Historical Review* 67:1 (March 1986), 1.

3. Perhaps the most strident statement of this conservative reaction in a popular forum can be found in Gertrude Himmelfarb, "Denigrating the Rule of Reason," *Harper's* (April 1984), 84-90.

4. "E.P. Thompson Vs. Harold Logan: Writing About Labour and the Left in the 1970s," *Canadian Historical Review* 57 (1981), 141-68; and Bryan Palmer, "Listening to History Rather Than Historians: Reflections on Working Class History," *Studies in Political Economy* 20 (Summer 1986), 47-84.

5. English, "The Second Time Around," 4.

6. The main scholarly expression of this school is the journal *Studies in Political Economy*, significantly subtitled *A Socialist Review*, which began publication in 1978. A key work is Leo Panitch, ed., *The Canadian State: Political Economy and Political Power* (Toronto: University of Toronto Press, 1977). See Daniel Drache and Wallace Clement, eds., *The New Practical Guide to Canadian Political Economy* (Toronto: Lorimer, 1985) for a bibliographical guide.

7. Peter B. Evans, Dietrich Rueschmeyer, and Theda Skocpol, eds., *Bringing the State Back In* (Cambridge: Cambridge University Press, 1985).

8. For an American summary, see Martin Carnoy, *The State and Political Theory* (Princeton: Princeton University Press, 1984). A Canadian view can be found in Murray Knutilla, *State Theories: From Feminism to the Challenge of Feminism* (Toronto: Garamond Press, 1987).

9. Donald Creighton: *Dominion of the North: A History of Canada* (Toronto: Macmillan, 1944); *Canada's First Century (Toronto: Macmillan, 1970)*.

10. Kenneth McNaught, *The Pelican History of Canada* (Harmondsworth, Middlesex: Penguin, 1969).

11. W.L. Morton, *The Kingdom of Canada: A General History from the Earliest Times* (Toronto: McClelland and Stewart, 1963).

12. All of the titles in this series were published by McClelland & Stewart, Toronto.

13. Robert Bothwell, Ian Drummond, and John English, *Canada Since 1945: Power, Politics and Provincialism* (Toronto: University of Toronto Press, 1981); and *Canada: 1900-1945* (Toronto: University of Toronto Press, 1987).

14. Donald Creighton, *Canada, 1939-1957: The Forked Road* (Toronto: McClelland and Stewart, 1976).

15. Donald Creighton, *John A. Macdonald*, 2 vols. (Toronto: Macmillan, 1952 and 1955).

16. Maurice Careless, *Brown of the Globe*, 2 vols. (Toronto: Macmillan, 1959 and 1963).

17. R. Craig Brown, *Robert Laird Borden: A Biography*, 2 vols. (Toronto: Macmillan, 1975 and 1980).

18. O.D. Skelton *The Life and Letters of Sir Wilfrid Laurier*, 2 vols. (Toronto: Oxford University Press, 1921); Joseph Schull, *Laurier: The First Canadian* (Toronto: Macmillan, 1965). But see Blair Neatby's *Laurier and a Liberal Quebec: A Study in Political Management* (Toronto: McClelland & Stewart, 1973) which looked to the political side of Laurier's leadership.

19. R. Macgregor Dawson, *William Lyon Mackenzie King: A Political Biography, 1874-1923*, Vol. 1 (Toronto: University of Toronto Press, 1958); H. Blair Neatby, Vols. 2 and 3 (Toronto: University of Toronto Press, 1963 and 1976).

20. Roger Graham, *Arthur Meighen*, 3 vols. (Toronto: Clarke, Irwin, 1960-1965).

21. Robert Bothwell and William Kilbourn, *C.D. Howe: A Biography* (Toronto: McClelland & Stewart, 1979).

22. Denis Smith, *Gentle Patriot: A Political Biography of Walter Gordon* (Edmonton: Hurtig, 1973).

23. J.L. Granatstein: *A Man of Influence: Norman A. Robertson and Canadian Statecraft, 1929-68* (Ottawa: Deneau, 1981); *The Ottawa Men: The Civil Service Mandarins 1935-1957* (Toronto: Oxford University Press, 1982).

24. Roger Bowen, *Innocence is Not Enough: The Life and Death of Herbert Norman* (Vancouver: Douglas & McIntyre, 1986); James Barros, *No Sense of Evil: Espionage. The Case of Herbert Norman* (Toronto: Deneau, 1986).

25.   This is not the place to judge the correctness of the interpretations; my views are set out in a lengthy critique of Barros in the *Canadian Forum* 66:763 (November 1986), 11-28.

26.   J.G. Bourinot, *How Canada Is Governed: A Short Account of Its Executive, Legislative, Judicial and Municipal Institutions* (Toronto: Copp, Clark, 1895).

27.   Donald Creighton, *Commercial Empire of the St. Lawrence, 1760-1850* (Toronto: Ryerson Press, 1937).

28.   S.D. Clark, *Movements of Political Protest in Canada, 1640-1840* (Toronto: University of Toronto Press, 1959).

29.   Reg Whitaker, "Confused Alarms of Struggle and Flight: English-Canadian Political Science in the 1970s,"*Canadian Historical Review* 60:1 (1979), 1-17.

30.   Gordon T. Stewart, *The Origins of Canadian Politics: A Comparative Approach*, (Vancouver: University of British Columbia Press, 1986).

31.   This is not to suggest that there are not some shortcomings in Stewart's argument, especially as it relates to twentieth-century developments which sometimes fail to follow the projection Stewart lays down: see Reg Whitaker, "Between Patronage and Bureaucracy: Democratic Politics in Transition," *Journal of Canadian Studies* 22:2 (Summer 1987), 55-71, especially 57-61.

32.   John English, *The Decline of Politics: The Conservatives and the Party System, 1901-1920* (Toronto: University of Toronto Press, 1977).

33.   W.L. Morton, *The Progressive Party in Canada* (Toronto: University of Toronto Press, 1950).

34.   C.B. Macpherson, *Democracy in Alberta: The Theory and Practice of a Quasi-Party System* (Toronto: University of Toronto Press, 1953).

35.   Larry Pratt and John Richards, *Prairie Capitalism: Power and Influence in the New West* (Toronto: McClelland & Stewart, 1979). For a less radical interpretation, see Roger Gibbins, *Prairie Politics and Society: Regionalism in Decline* (Toronto: Butterworth, 1980).

36.   J.R. Mallory, *Social Credit and the Federal Power in Canada* (1954. Reprint, Toronto: University of Toronto Press, 1974).

37.   Reg Whitaker, *The Government Party: Organizing and Financing the Liberal Party of Canada, 1930-1958* (Toronto: University of Toronto Press, 1977).

38.   Joseph Wearing, *The L-Shaped Party: The Liberal Party of Canada, 1958-1980* (Toronto: McGraw-Hill Ryerson, 1981); Christina McCall-Newman, *Grits: An Intimate Portrait of the Liberal Party* (Toronto: Macmillan, 1982).

39.   David Smith: *Prairie Liberalism: The Liberal Party in Saskatchewan, 1905-71* (Toronto: University of Toronto Press, 1975); *The Regional Decline of a National Party: Liberals on the Prairies* (Toronto: University of Toronto Press, 1981). Party patronage, very much the focus of the cited works by Stewart, English, Whitaker and Smith, is the subject of journalist Jeffrey Simpson's historically sophisticated *Spoils of Power: the Politics of Patronage* (Toronto: Collins, 1988).

40. J.L. Granatstein, *The Politics of Survival: The Conservative Party of Canada, 1939-1945* (Toronto: University of Toronto Press, 1967); George Perlin, *The Tory Syndrome: Leadership Politics in the Progressive Conservative Party* (Montreal: McGill-Queen's University Press, 1980).

41. Walter Young, *The Anatomy of a Party: The National CCF, 1932-61* (Toronto: University of Toronto Press, 1969); Gad Horowitz, *Canadian Labour in Politics* (Toronto: University of Toronto Press, 1968).

42. Janine Brodie and Jane Jenson, *Crisis, Challenge and Change: Party and Class in Canada Revisited* (Ottawa: Carleton University Press, 1988).

43. Harold Clarke, Jane Jenson, Lawrence LeDuc, and Jon Pammett, *Absent Mandate: The Politics of Discontent in Canada* (Toronto: Gage, 1984).

44. Christopher Armstrong, *The Politics of Federalism: Ontario's Relations with the Federal Government, 1867-1942* (Toronto: University of Toronto Press, 1981); Ramsay Cook, *Provincial Autonomy: Minority Rights and the Compact Theory, 1867-1921* (Ottawa: Queen's Printer, 1969). See also A.I. Silver's intriguing study of the evolution of Quebecers into French Canadians in the late nineteenth century, *The French Canadian Idea of Confederation, 1864-1900* (Toronto: University of Toronto Press, 1982).

45. See, among the voluminous corpus of Donald Smiley's work *The Federal Condition in Canada* (Toronto: McGraw-Hill Ryerson, 1987) — a completely revised version of his earlier text *Canada in Question* which had gone through three editions — and *The Canadian Political Nationality* (Toronto: Methuen, 1967).

46. Garth Stevenson, *Unfulfilled Union: Canadian Federalism and National Unity*, 3d ed. (Toronto: Gage, 1988).

47. Alan Cairns, ed. Douglas Williams, *Constitution, Government and Society in Canada* (Toronto: McClelland & Stewart, 1988). See also the extremely interesting collection edited by Cairns with Cynthia Williams for the Macdonald Royal Commission on the economy, *Constitutionalism, Citizenship and Society in Canada* (Toronto: University of Toronto Press, 1986).

48. Richard Simeon, *Federal-Provincial Diplomacy: The Making of Recent Policy in Canada* (Toronto: University of Toronto Press, 1972).

49. Kenneth McRae, ed., *Consociational Democracy: Political Accommodation in Segmented Societies* (Toronto: McClelland & Stewart, 1974).

50. Robert Presthus, *Elite Accommodation in Canadian Politics* (Toronto: Macmillan, 1973).

51. Reg Whitaker, "Federalism, Democracy, and the Canadian Political Community," in *The Integration Question: Political Economy and Public Policy in Canada and North America*, eds., Jon Pammett and Brian Tomlin, (Don Mills: Addison-Wesley, 1984), 72-94.

52. Richard Simeon and David Elkins, *Small Worlds: Provinces and Parties in Canadian Life* (Toronto: Methuen, 1980).

53. Ramsay Cook: *Canada and the French Canadian Question* (Toronto: Macmillan, 1966); *The Maple Leaf Forever: Essays on Nationalism and Politics in Canada*

(Toronto: Macmillan, 1971); *French Canadian Nationalism: An Anthology* (Macmillan: Toronto, 1969).

54. Kenneth McRoberts, *Quebec: Social Change and Political Crisis*, 3d ed. (Toronto: McClelland & Stewart, 1988).

55. William Coleman, *The Independence Movement in Quebec, 1945-1980* (Toronto: University of Toronto Press, 1984).

56. C.E.S. Franks, *The Parliament of Canada* (Toronto: University of Toronto Press, 1987).

57. The best pieces are collected in Thomas Hockin, ed., *Apex of Power: The Prime Minister and Political Leadership in Canada* (Scarborough: Prentice-Hall, 1977). See also Robert Jackson and Michael Atkinson, *The Canadian Legislative System,* 2d ed. (Toronto: Macmillan, 1980).

58. Frederick Gibson, *Cabinet Formation and Bicultural Relations: Seven Case Studies* (Ottawa: Queen's Printer, 1970).

59. Peter Russell, *The Judiciary in Canada: The Third Branch of Government* (Toronto: McGraw-Hill Ryerson, 1987).

60. A. Paul Pross, *Group Politics and Public Policy* (Toronto: Oxford University Press, 1986); Ronald Manzer, *Public Policies and Political Development in Canada* (Toronto: University of Toronto Press, 1985).

61. Craig Brown, *Canada's National Policy: A Study in Canadian-American Relations* (Princeton: Princeton University Press, 1964).

62. V.C. Fowke, *The National Policy and the Wheat Economy* (Toronto: University of Toronto Press, 1957).

63. Glenn Williams, *Not For Export: Toward a Political Economy of Canada's Arrested Industrialization* rev. ed. (Toronto: McClelland & Stewart, 1986).

64. James Struthers, *No Fault of Their Own: Unemployment and the Canadian Welfare State, 1914-1941* (Toronto: University of Toronto Press, 1983).

65. Paul Craven, *"An Impartial Umpire": Industrial Relations and the Canadian State, 1900-1911* (Toronto: University of Toronto Press, 1980). Rianne Mahon, *The Politics of Industrial Restructuring: Canadian Textiles* (Toronto: University of Toronto Press, 1984).

66. Bruce Doern and Glen Toner, *The Politics of Energy: The Development and Implementation of the NEP* (Toronto: Methuen, 1985).

67. C.P. Stacey, *Canada in the Age of Conflict*, Vol. 1 (Toronto: Macmillan, 1977); Vol. 2 (Toronto: University of Toronto Press, 1981).

68. John Homes, *The Shaping of Peace: Canada and the Search for World Order*, 2 vols. (Toronto: University of Toronto Press, 1979 and 1982).

69. James Eayr, *In Defence of Canada*, 5 vols. (Toronto: University of Toronto Press, 1964-1983).

70.   Douglas Ross, *In the Interests of Peace* (Toronto: University of Toronto Press, 1984).

71.   Kim Richard Nossal, *The Politics of Canadian Foreign Policy* (Scarborough: Prentice-Hall, 1985); David B. Dewitt and John J. Kirton, *Canada as a Principal Power* (Toronto: Wiley, 1983).

72.   W.L. Mackenzie King, *Industry and Humanity: A Study in the Principles Underlying Industrial Reconstruction* (1918, reprint Toronto: University of Toronto Press, 1973). Pierre E. Trudeau: *Federalism and the French Canadians* (Toronto: Macmillan, 1968); and *Approaches to Politics* (Toronto: Oxford University Press, 1970).

73.   Reg Whitaker, "Reason, Passion and Interest: Pierre Trudeau's Eternal Liberal Triangle," *Canadian Journal of Political and Social Theory* 4 (1980), 5-31.

74.   George Grant, *Lament for a Nation: The Defeat of Canadian Nationalism* (Toronto: McClelland & Stewart, 1965); for George Grant's work see also *Technology and Empire: Perspectives on North America* (Toronto: Anansi, 1969) and *English-Speaking Justice* (Sackville, N.B.: Mount Allison University, 1974).

75.   Frank Underhill, *In Search of Canadian Liberalism* (Toronto: Macmillan, 1960).

76.   C.B. Macpherson, *Democracy in Alberta*, 2nd ed. (Toronto: University of Toronto Press, 1962); Charles Taylor, "Alternative Futures: Legitimacy, Identity and Alienation in Twentieth Century Canada" in *Constitutionalism, Citizenship and Society in Canada*, eds. Alan Cairns and Cynthia Williams (Toronto: University of Toronto Press, 1985); George Woodcock, *The Rejection of Politics* (Toronto: New Press, 1972).

77.   Carl Berger, *The Sense of Power: Studies in the Ideas of Canadian Imperialism* (Toronto: University of Toronto Press, 1970).

78.   Frank Underhill, *The Image of Confederation* (Toronto: Canadian Broadcasting Corporation, 1964).

79.   Doug Owram, *Promise of Eden: The Canadian Expansion Movement and the Idea of the West, 1856-1900* (Toronto: University of Toronto Press, 1980).

80.   Ramsay Cook, *The Regenerators: Social Criticism in Late Victorian English Canada* (Toronto: University of Toronto Press, 1985).

81.   Richard Allen, *The Social Passion: Religion and Social Reform in Canada, 1914-1928* (Toronto: University of Toronto Press, 1971).

82.   Doug Owram, *The Government Generation: Canadian Intellectuals and the State, 1900-1945* (Toronto: University of Toronto Press, 1986).

83.   Michael Behiels, *Prelude to Quebec's Quiet Revolution* (Montreal: McGill-Queen's University Press, 1985).

84.   Douglas Verney, *Three Civilizations, Two Cultures, One State* (Durham NC: Duke University Press, 1986).

85.   David Bell and Lorne Tepperman, *The Roots of Disunity: A Look at Canadian Political Culture* (Toronto: McClelland and Stewart, 1979).

86.   Kenneth McRae, "The Structure of Canadian History," in *The Founding of New Societies*, ed. Louis Hartz (New York: Harcourt, Brace and World, 1964), 219-74;

Gad Horowitz, *Canadian Labour in Politics* (Toronto: University of Toronto Press, 1968). See also H.D. Forbes, "Hartz-Horowitz at Twenty: Nationalism, Toryism and Socialism in Canada and the United States," *Canadian Journal of Political Science* 20:2 (June 1987), 287-316.

87.   Reg Whitaker, "Images of the State in Canada," in *The Canadian State: Political Economy and Political Power*, ed. Leo Panitch (Toronto: University of Toronto Press, 1977), 28-68. For a recent example of Philip Resnick's work and some of the debate it has inspired, see his "Montesquieu Revisited, or the Mixed Constitution and the Separation of Powers in Canada," *Canadian Journal of Political Science* 20:1 (March 1987) with comments and reply, 97-130.

88.   Denis Monière, *Ideologies in Quebec: The Historical Development*, trans. Richard Howard (Toronto: University of Toronto Press, 1981).

2

Writing About Economics

Ian Drummond

An unkind observer once remarked that, thanks to the pioneering work of Harold Innis, Canadian economic historiography suffered from "premature synthesis."[1] Another observer has spoken of Innis's "dead hand."[2] Innis's insight was simple: where an economy was rich in natural resources yet scantily capitalized and thinly peopled, the development of what Innis called "staple products" — comparatively simple commodities that relied heavily on the natural resource endowment — would determine almost everything in national economic development: immigration, capital formation and capital import, living standards, urbanization, and industrialization. Canadian economic history, therefore, was a series of "staple sagas": first the fur trade and the cod fisheries, then the transatlantic trades in rough-hewn pine timber and masts, next the wheat of upper Canada and non-ferrous metals such as nickel, then the wheat of the western Canadian prairie and finally the timber of British Columbia. This is the sequence which W.A. Mackintosh first detected in the 1920s and later elaborated on in the late 1930s,[3] and which Innis adopted and propagated as an organizing scheme for the study and teaching of Canadian economic history.[4] For Innis the physical characteristics of each staple product could have important effects on political affairs as well as economic development. Innis saw the transatlantic trade in timber as creating excess shipping capacity on the western voyages, thus encouraging the inward movement of settlers, while at an earlier period the nomadic character of the fur trade was a barrier to agricultural settlement. But he also saw the creation of the Dominion of Canada as reflecting debt and transport problems which, in turn, reflected the developmental imperatives of earlier staple commodities and the anxieties of commercial communities that were based on these commodities. The Innis scheme involves a very large element of geographical determinism, not only for Canadian economic development but for the nation's political history. Innis certainly was a materialist, but it is difficult to see him as a Marxist, because his materialism and determinism were concerned with the physical characteristics of objects and of landscape, not with the social and class relations of production. What has happened to the economic historiography of Canada since Innis died in 1952? How much of Innis's vision has survived?

I

Innis's influence can easily be exaggerated or unjustly maligned. Admittedly, for forty-five years the textbooks first of his wife and then of his disciples, W.T. Easterbrook and Hugh Aitken, dominated the teaching of Canadian economic history in the nation's English-speaking universities.[5] Non-specialists still turn to these textbooks to discover "what happened in Canadian economic development." Later texts have not been able to break free entirely of the Innisian mold.[6] Innis's approach forms an important element in the work of Canada's "new political economists," who wish to explain the present shape of Canada's polity and economy by reference to the country's economic evolution.[7] On the other hand, new and quite separate elements — quantitative economic history, cliometrics, demographic history, labour history, Marxism and Thompsonianism, dependency theory, women's history, agricultural history, and self-conscious regional history — have all sprung up and flourished in the years since Innis's death. Thus, not only is there life after Innis, that life is so energetic and combative that it resembles a Hobbesian war of all against all. The new work is based upon a series of intellectual deposits, transmitted in various ways from the more fertile soils of the United States, Britain, and France.

The present situation, therefore, is paradoxical. MacIntosh and Innis were original and creative, and their work represents a genuine Canadian contribution to social science methodology, while the "staple approach" remains in all sorts of ways a necessary starting point for work on Canadian economic history. Yet that "approach" explains less and less of the nation's economic evolution.

Innis did not, in the usual sense, form or found a "school." His doctoral students were few, and most were people of one book or none. The two most creative and productive disciples, or "descendants," were W.T. Easterbrook, whose textbook is mentioned above, and V.C. Fowke, whose writings on the prairie wheat economy were seminal.[8] Some of the most promising Innisians gave themselves over to university administration, government advising, or political and cultural agitation.

Meanwhile a circulation of scholars and ideas was at work. In the sixties and early seventies, when immigrant historians and economists were numerous, there was bound to be a most un-Innis-like diversity of emphasis and approach: the immigrants generally knew little of Innis and cared less.[9] Hence the influence of Marxism, Thompsonianism, and dependency theory — elements foreign not only to Innis but to orthodox mainstream economics, and thus found chiefly in departments of political science, sociology, and history. By 1970 Canada's younger historians were increasingly reluctant to pursue descriptive-biographical studies. In history, as in sociology and political science, there was a reaching out toward the topics that were fashionable in the United States and Europe. The results are traced in other chapters of this volume. In the resulting ferment, Innis would not be forgotten: Canada could boast few original thinkers, and no nationalist could afford to neglect these few. The historical "new men" were not very interested in Innis, but they certainly expanded our knowledge of Canadian economic history. For instance, since working-class history has little point unless the workers are numerous and important, the new historians examined such non-Innisian topics as urbanization, industrialization, and living standards in central Canada during the years of industrialization.[10] Women's historians, interested as they were in the work-place experience of females, contributed in the same way.[11] Such work often seemed to put the "staple vision" in the place where K.A.H. Buckley had consigned it: an interesting idea, but of little significance after 1820, especially for the part of the country where most Canadians have always lived — the St. Lawrence basin.[12]

Innisian staples theorists dealt with such new work partly by ignoring it and partly by trying to incorporate it into a new and semi-Innisian synthesis of Marxism, dependency theory, "the national question," and the question of foreign ownership. By 1970 it was understood that in the course of the nineteenth century Canada acquired a sizeable industrial sector. Innis himself, and such disciples as Easterbrook, credited this to demand-propelled spinoff from staple development, and dated it much later, but the later Innisians allowed these Innisite confusions to vanish from sight unremarked. Folk had also noticed that much Canadian industry was foreign owned or foreign controlled. A link appeared in an early quasi-Innisian paper by Watkins,[13] where it was suggested that if the backward and forward linkages were "wrong," or went wrong, a staple-based region might be unable to industrialize because the regional capitalists would be too committed to "mercantile pursuits" — short-term lending and an avoidance of long-term fixed investment.

Watkins attracted doctoral students, one of whom, R.T. Naylor, produced a doctoral dissertation which was published as *The History of Canadian Business*.[14] In spite of detailed and devastating criticism from economists and historians,[15] Naylor's work has proved to be immensely influential, although more among sociologists and political scientists than among economic historians. Naylor argued that nineteenth-century Canada had indeed been caught in a "staple trap." Canada's business and financial system, he thought, was so committed to "commercial capitalism" that it avoided industrial capitalism, or invested in the wrong sort of manufacturing industry, thus leaving the way open for American direct investment, and for the characteristic Canadian economic structure of the later twentieth century.

Innis's staples thesis was thus deployed in the service not only of nationalism but of Marxism — two "isms" that many scholars believe Innis detested. Other scholars meanwhile were hard at work to radicalize the good grey Canadian conservative, and to link him with their own visions of a Canada united by anti-American cultural and economic nationalism, and marching toward socialism under an Innisite banner.[16]

Although rational discussion of these issues proved increasingly difficult, outside the camp of the "new political economy" few found Watkins-Naylorism satisfactory, while within the camp the sects warred over its meaning, and its relation to Marxist orthodoxy. Michael Bliss's work showed how badly capitalist reality fitted Naylor's categories:[17] there had been plenty of indigenous industry, plenty of Canadian ownership, plenty of commercial and financial capital at the disposal of those domestic industrial entrepreneurs. The general conclusion reached by Evans and Quigley — that in the nature of the case it is impossible to refute the Naylor thesis definitively, but that all the available evidence tells against it — is the one which most careful historians have reached.[18] The "Naylor thesis," in fact, did not fit the evidence. The conflict became ever clearer as industry studies accumulated.[19] Such studies revealed that there were more things in Canadian economic history than Innis had dreamt of.[20]

II

Meanwhile, talented young Canadians continued to travel abroad for doctoral work, to imbibe new ideas in foreign universities, and to write theses on Canadian historical topics. Returning to Canada, such scholars formed the main means by which the "new economic history" (often called cliometrics), which consciously and explicitly applies mainstream (as opposed to Marxist) analysis, was domesticated. They were never numerous,[21] although insofar as they themselves supervised doctoral candidates, by 1985 their influence had begun to spread. And just as there are favourite topics for American "cliometricians," so the Canadians have concentrated on a few problems: the timing of settlement on the Canadian prairies, the explanation of income and productivity disparities between Quebec and Ontario, and the tariff and the performance of the Canadian economy in comparison with the American.[22] Some have also worked on monetary topics and on particular problems in certain extractive industries. As yet they have shown little interest in manufacturing or mining,[23] and they have not been the only ones to work on monetary and banking topics.[24] As for quantitative work that is not inspired by the new economic history, there has been important work on real wage rates and earnings, on national income aggregates all the way back to the creation of the Dominion, and on retail price indices. Furthermore, a vast archival study of Atlantic ships and shipping — impossible before the age of the computer — has immensely expanded our knowledge of Canada's "eastern approaches" during the nineteenth century. A survey economic history of Quebec has been inspired by the spirit of the "new economic history," and a narrative of Ontario's economic history, though much less self-conscious in its use of formal theory, shows the same influence,[25] as do the Marr-Paterson and Pomfret economic histories of the country.[26]

The "new economic history" has not received unalloyed praise. Undergraduates and historians find the material hard going, if only because it assumes knowledge of economics and interest in that subject. Historians, in particular, are critical. One Québécois reviewer called Armstrong's survey *"le Québec du Pangloss,"*[27] and it is common to observe that Canada's "new economic historians" seem to share that conservative outlook which is often said to inspire mainstream economists everywhere. Much of this criticism rests upon a misunderstanding: other scholars have trouble recognizing that the economist's "preference for market solutions" is commonly not a matter of ideology, and that one can be radical, in several respects, while still emphasizing the decent long-run performance of the capitalist system and the mixed economy. Nonetheless, although the difference in ideology can be exaggerated, it does seem to exist. Much more important, there is also a difference of viewpoint. In Canada, as elsewhere, the new economic history has trouble dealing with fundamental structural and institutional change. Yet it is precisely these long-run dynamics of the economy that many people want to understand. In this respect some of the older works in applied macro-economics, such as the books of Viner, Safarian, and Buckley, retain their interest.[28] However, such works did not address the really deepseated changes — the emergence of industrial capitalism, the creation of an industrial proletariat,[29] the loss of artisan control at the work place, the emergence and perpetuation of regional disparities, the peculiarities of the Quebec and Maritime economies — that now attract so much attention.

Few mainstream economists or "new economic historians" find such questions interesting. Indeed, Marr and Paterson discuss the seigneurial system chiefly as a device for spreading risk through the intermingling of strips. Such emphases serve to increase the scepticism with which the generality of historians regard the "new economic history."

In discussions of such major structural change the influence of Marxism has been very great. But its sway has not been total. Ouellet's interpretation of Québécois wage-labour and technological change in the fur trade between the Conquest and the War of 1812 is anything but Marxist:[30] Ouellet shows that rapid agricultural development created an upward pressure on wage rates that compelled the fur traders to substitute boats for canoes, and large combines for small competitive firms. Pentland's work on the emergence of wage labour before 1850 is influenced by Marxism, but that influence is little more than terminological, so that Pentland has been criticized for that most heinous of Marxist sins: eclecticism.[31] For others the Marxist element is more systematic and self-conscious. Teeple argues that wage labour appeared in upper Canada before 1850 only because the speculators held land off the market, thus preventing the creation of a free peasantry.[32] Palmer believes that in upper Canada there was a wave of original accumulation in the 1840s, driving peasants off the land.[33] Greer asserts that the Maritime provinces and central Canada were once lands of "individual commodity producers," and that no explanation of Canadian economic development is satisfactory until or unless the transformation of such societies into capitalist ones has satisfactorily been explained. He and others also find elements of classical Marxist feudalism in the settlement system of Prince Edward Island and in the seignieurial system of Quebec — a regime that others believe to be no more than a system of land settlement.[34]

In studying Innis's great staple industries historians and economic geographers have also been at work both in the new ways[35] and in more traditional fashion. McCalla has been exploiting archives so as to clarify the history of agriculture and lumbering in nineteenth-century Ontario, and to delineate the activities of local merchants.[36] Van Kirk has examined "women and the fur trade." Rich has produced a magisterial and methodologically traditional history of the Hudson's Bay Company, drawing upon archival materials that were unavailable to Innis. Rotstein and Ray, completing the tale of the "three Rs of the fur trade," have embroiled themselves in a complicated controversy respecting price-flexibility in fur-trading. Were furs traded at flexible prices, or at rigid ones? If the latter, why? And did the Indians respond to market opportunities as rational economic actors? Or did they trade for non-economic reasons and in non-economic ways? On these topics the jury is still out.[37]

New France began as a "staple" fur trading colony. The trade dominated the colony's life and work until the British conquest and, indeed, for forty years thereafter. At the time of the conquest agriculture had begun to develop. Merchants were neither numerous nor wealthy, but they were energetic and active. Yet seventy years after the Conquest, there was little sign of commercial life among the francophones, most of whom seemed to live miserable lives as subsistence farmers. What had happened?

The economic development of Quebec cannot be understood until one has explained this structural change, with which Innis did not concern himself. Many years ago, Abbé Groulx argued that the Conquest had decapitated the nascent francophone commercial class, because most of the merchants went back to France, while a new mercantile group of anglophone furtraders arrived. More recently Igartua and Ouellet have shown that there were plenty of francophone Montreal merchants after the Conquest, and that, for at least twenty years, they shared in the fur trade with the new anglophone merchants.[38] What happened to them? Ouellet argues that they continued to operate small-scale, family firms, and to use the canoe, during a period when competitive pressures, rising labour costs, and the need to extend the trade ever further, were all tending to favour large firms and boats. Here we have an "entrepreneurial failure" explanation, the sort that is commonly deployed to explain the relative economic retardation of Britain in the late nineteenth century.

While the anglophones were gradually displacing the francophones from the management of the Canadian fur trade, the wage-labour continued to come largely from the francophone *habitants* of Quebec. Natural increase produced a rapid growth of the francophone population, a filling-up of arable land, and an intensification of agriculture, which was therefore able to absorb extra labour at rising wage rates — thus putting pressure on wage rates in the fur trade. Quebec became a regular exporter of wheat. These happy developments continued until some time in the nineteenth century, when it is now generally agreed that some sort of "agrarian crisis" took place, probably in the period 1820-1840. Yields fell, exports ceased, and according to Ouellet the *habitants* came to depend upon the potato. What did actually happen? when? and why?[39]

A whole panoply of methodologies, old-style and new, has been deployed to answer these questions. The agricultural crisis has also caused scholars to take a new look at the seigneurial system and at the revenues of the Catholic Church. During the long period of agrarian expansion that followed the Conquest, valueless land acquired rentable value, so that tithes and seigneurial exactions became important — easily borne at first, but a serious burden in the years of "crisis." The seigneuries became attractive investments, and many of them passed into the hands of astute anglophones, although francophone seigneurs, both clerical and lay, never vanished from the scene. Scholars therefore speculate, along lines that will be familiar to students of European economic history, about the economic effects of the seigneurial system. Though the tenurial system of Quebec did not reproduce all the distressing elements of the European, and though some local practices were logically separate from the seigneurial system, the seigneuries may not have been particularly helpful to agricultural progress, especially since the seigneurs themselves rarely acted as English-style "improving landlords."

There is a continuing debate about the performance of the Quebec economy. Deploying mathematics and many assumptions, Lewis and Mc-Innis have argued that at mid-century Quebec farmers were using capital and land as effectively as Ontario farmers who were certainly more prosperous and more obviously "modern." [40] Raynauld has shown [41] that, at least after 1870, Quebec industrialized and urbanized as rapidly as Ontario did, creating a working-class living standard for both anglophone and francophone Québécois that Copp has described in appropriately Dickensian terms. [42] Whether it would have been better to stay on the farms and eat potatoes, either in Quebec or in Ireland, is the usual open question. It has also been shown that, contrary to the assertions of another familiar myth, the Catholic Church did not oppose industrialization, and that the Quebec Government was eager to spend on transport and on development: in the late nineteenth century its per capita outlays were larger than those of "progressive," Protestant Ontario, even though in Quebec the Church provided many of the educational and social services that the Ontario government had to pay for. [43] Hydroelectric development, also, has been shown to be at least as precocious in Quebec as in her western neighbour. [44] There have also been general accounts of Quebec's economic history, concentrating on the pre-1867 years and attempting integrated synthetic treatments which have yet to be attempted for other provinces. [45]

III

What have Innis's "staple products" to do with the industrialization and urbanization of Quebec — or of Ontario? The more we learn about industrial development in central Canada, the less satisfactory do Innisian explanations appear. Innis saw the industrial development of central Canada as simply a spinoff from the various staple exports — square timber, wheat, cheese, metals. Few economic historians would now agree. Both the timing and the magnitudes are wrong.

The first blasts on this particular trumpet were sounded in the late 1950s by Dales, [46] Firestone, and Buckley. [47] By 1960 it was clear that the "long depression of the late nineteenth century", which staples-theorists attributed to the "absence of a staple," had not occurred.[48] Additional fuel was added to the fire by Raynauld and Bertram, when they provided the first convincing statistics on industrial development in Quebec and in Ontario.[49] These studies revealed just how rapid, and how broadly based, had been the late-nineteenth-century industrialization of central Canada. As industry studies accumulate, this impression becomes stronger still.[50]

The staple approach suffered another sort of blow in 1966 when Chambers and Gordon, asking a very non-Innisian question about living standards, reached a very anti-Innisian conclusion about the impact of the prairie wheat boom of 1900-1913. Employing a simple economic model of a kind that Innis would never have deployed, they concluded that the wheat boom had had an insignificantly small effect on Canadian per capita incomes, and therefore could not have affected anything very much. From Innis's university came a quick defence of the Master.[51] But Canadian historiography has not looked the same since Chambers-Gordon. Furthermore, scholars have become interested to discover just what did happen to living standards at various times and in various places.[52] This question did not interest Innis at all: he simply supposed that European settlers aspired to a certain standard of living, so that they would arrange their affairs — largely by exporting staple products — with an eye to attaining it.

Since Canada is a small open economy, the terms on which it trades are bound to affect the living standards of its people, and since it has been a protectionist nation at least since 1879 and in some senses since the late 1850s, the height and design of the tariff must have implications not only for industrial development but for living standards; a price-taker in world markets, Canada cannot hope to shift the burden of the tariff to its foreign suppliers. Orthodox "mainstream" economics can generate these conclusions with no historical research at all, and for the moment that is where the subject rests. We have an accumulation of somewhat elderly descriptive and institutional studies,[53] several more recent archivally-based works on the mechanics of international tariff-bargaining,[54] and some detailed studies of tariff-impacts.[55] But to see how the tariff actually affected industrial development and living standards we would need a much larger mass of industry studies, and a great deal more information about consumer prices and wages.

The tariff has long been a major inter-regional irritant, because manufacturing industry has concentrated itself in central Canada while the western provinces produce "staple products" for export, and the eastern provinces remain comparatively poor and backward. Before Confederation the three Maritime Provinces contained not only a certain amount of agriculture and small-scale industry but a great deal of prosperous "commercial capitalism" — a mercantile economy of lumbering, shipbuilding, shipping, and fishing. In the island Colony of Newfoundland a single "staple trade" — codfish — dominated the economy. Less prosperous than the mainland colonies in 1867, Newfoundland, like Iceland, might still have expected to enjoy a future of modest comfort; after Confederation, the Maritime Provinces might have expected to share in the boom-times of the new Dominion. Yet by the early 1930s all the expectations had been disappointed.

The recent economic historiography of Maritime Canada has concerned itself partly with the ocean-oriented mercantile capitalism of the period before 1900, but also with regional retardation and inter-regional inequality since Confederation. For Newfoundland, the "Canadian question" cannot take the same form: before 1949 Newfoundland's troubles cannot be blamed upon Canada's national government. For the Maritimes Saunders' Innisian and "centralist" study, which was authoritative for more than thirty years, noted that railway subsidies, tariffs, and bounties help to sustain what industrialization the Maritimes managed to achieve.[56] More recently Graham, writing in the same tradition, observed that the Maritimes were poor because they were not well-endowed with natural resources, and because they were remote from continental markets.[57] Other have noted that the region's iron and coal resources were always hard to refine and expensive to mine.[58] Such conclusions have not proved popular, and in recent years a great deal of revisionist work has been done along very different lines. Much of this is small-scale, local, and archivally based. It has expanded our knowledge of the regional economies, especially of shipbuilding, shipping, and the mercantile capitalists who controlled this industry.[59] Such work has cast new light upon the large regional question: why did commercial wooden-ship capitalism fail to become a capitalism of steel-built steam shipping? Beyond it, to explain the larger regional problem one finds familiar lines of argument — entrepreneurial failure, immobility of capital funds, pumping out of surplus, Ottawa's ineptitude with respect to tariff-fixing and railway rate-setting, foolish or treasonous behaviour by local capitalists and shipowners. Dependency theory in its many variants, and numerous sorts of Marxism-Leninism, are all on offer.[60] In quality and persuasiveness this work is uneven, nor is it innovative methodologically or conceptually.

Special interest has attached to the work of Roy George because he is believed to have shown that during the 1960s costs for Maritime manufacturers were no higher than in central Canada;[61] the manufacturers' problem, George concludes, must lie within themselves — "entrepreneurial failure" again. There is an obvious logical problem: any actual surviving Maritime manufacturers must, by definition, be capable of matching the costs in central Canada, but it does not follow that an expanded Maritime manufacturing sector, especially if it had ventured into such products as heavy electrical equipment and motor cars, could ever have done so. This logical difficulty has not bothered Maritime scholars. Few have accepted George's "entrepreneurial failure" hypothesis; more have used his work as a club with which to beat the national government, the capitalists of central Canada, or both. After all, if Maritime factories *are or were* cost-competitive, only malign external forces can explain the non-industrialization and de-industrialization of the region. Or so it is thought.[62]

The economic historiography of Newfoundland is much more intellectually impressive, but it is very largely the work of one man, David Alexander.[63] While at Memorial University Alexander worked with his colleagues to establish the immense, archivally-based Maritime History Project. This was no less than a reconstruction and re-interpretation of the ocean history of Atlantic Canada and Newfoundland in the nineteenth century.[64] He also published a few general interpretative papers on Newfoundland's modern economic history. These establish his reputation as Canada's most creative economic historian since Innis.

Although Alexander was adept at the marshalling of numerical data, he was not a "new economic historian." His special gift was to see his adopted province as a whole, and by so doing to interpret the essence of its modern economic history, not only on its own but in comparison with the economic histories of other regions. For Alexander the essence of the Newfoundland story was not exploitation by outsiders; it was failure among the local elites, both political and commercial. Fatally attracted by the rapidity of economic development in continental North America during the late nineteenth century, they tried to apply the same medicine in their own tiny state — railway building, import-replacing industrialization behind protective tariffs, even agricultural settlement and large externally-controlled blocks of direct investment. They neglected the fishery. The result was disaster —

bankruptcy, poverty, a derelict fishery, an externally dominated economy, the loss of self-government, and absorption by Canada. Another element of elite failure was the remarkably low level of literacy. This deficiency caused low labour productivity, "sluggish intellectual life," and "a political culture which was sunk in a mediocrity which the country and its people did not need." Pondering these interdependencies, Alexander wrote of the need for an "intellectual portrait of the country, for in such a work lies more of the answers to the problems of Newfoundland's economic history than its economic historians are ever likely to supply." [65]

At first sight no position could seem more remote from that of Innis. Yet there is, oddly enough, a common element that links the older scholar with the younger. Alexander regretted that Newfoundland had not opted for "economic...development indigenous to its location in respect to resources, entrepreneurship, labour, and, for the most part, capital.... To accept the model definition of development can be to accept perpetual backwardness along all dimensions; at best the periphery might achieve a shabby dignity or a shabby replica of what exists in the heartland."[66] For Innis, Canada comes into existence because settlers model themselves on the metropole; for Alexander, Newfoundland passes out of existence for the same reason. The shadow of Innis is found in unexpected corners. Whatever the economists may eventually do with Innis's staples thesis, the historians and geographers have been at work on an immense project that was largely inspired by Innis and, indeed, is dedicated to him: the *Historical Atlas of Canada*.[67] The *Atlas* contains a vast amount of indispensable information, much of it the product of imaginative new research, concerning Canada's economic past. It may well be Innis's most enduring memorial. So life after Innis, it seems, will be long.

Endnotes

1. The present essay derives from a paper first presented to the History of Economics Society at Boston in June 1987, and later to departmental economics seminars at Victoria University, Wellington, New Zealand, and the Universities of Glasgow and Stirling. Thanks are due to the members of these gatherings and to Craig Brown, Donald Moggridge, Neil Quigley, Donald Paterson, and Donald McCloskey for their helpful and stimulating comments. These endnotes are meant to illustrate or document tendencies in the recent literature, not to provide a complete bibliography of Canadian economic history. For this, consult the notes and bibliography in William Marr and Donald Paterson, *Canada: An Economic History* (Toronto: Macmillan, 1980), and the regular bibliographical summaries in the *Canadian Historical Review*.

2.   See, among other works, Harold Innis: *The Fur Trade in Canada* (New Haven: Yale University Press, 1930), and *The Cod Fisheries* (Toronto: Ryerson, 1940), as well as the essays collected after Innis' death in Mary Q. Innis, ed., *Essays in Canadian Economic History* (Toronto: University of Toronto Press, 1956).

3.   W.A. Mackintosh, *The Economic Background of Dominion-Provincial Relations* (Ottawa: King's Printer, 1939; reprinted Toronto: McClelland and Stewart, 1964). Mackintosh's study was done for the Royal Commission on Dominion-Provincial Relations.

4.   See in particular *The Fur Trade in Canada*.

5.   See Mary Quayle Innis, *An Economic History of Canada* (Toronto: Ryerson, 1935); and W.T. Easterbrook and Hugh H.G. Aitken, *Canadian Economic History* (Toronto: Macmillan, 1956).

6.   William L. Marr and Donald J. Paterson, *Canada: An Economic History* (Toronto: Macmillan, 1980); Richard Pomfret, *The Economic Development of Canada* (Toronto: Methuen, 1981).

7.   Many of the contributions of this school are noted and summarized in Paul Phillips' introduction to H. Clare Pentland, *Labour and Capital in Canada, 1650-1850* (Toronto: James Lorimer, 1981).

8.   V.C. Fowke: *The National Policy and the Wheat Economy* (Toronto: University of Toronto Press, 1957); *Canadian Agricultural Policy: The Historical Pattern* (Toronto: University of Toronto Press, 1946).

9.   Exceptions would be Kevin Burley, N.C. Quigley, and Alexander Dow.

10. See in particular Greg Kealey, *Toronto Workers Respond to Industrialism, 1867-1892* (Toronto: University of Toronto Press, 1980); Bryan Palmer, *A Culture in Conflict* (Montreal: McGill-Queen's University Press, 1979); Terry Copp, *The Anatomy of Poverty: The Condition of the Working Class in Montreal, 1897-1929* (Toronto: McClelland and Stewart, 1974); Michael Piva, *The Condition of the Working Class in Toronto, 1900-1921* (Ottawa: University of Ottawa Press, 1979).

11. For a summary and evaluation see David J. Bercuson, "Through the Looking-Glass of Culture: An Essay on the New Labour History and Working-Class Culture in Recent Canadian Historical Writing," *Labour/Le Travailleur* 7 (Spring 1981), 95-112.

12. K.A.H. Buckley, "The Role of Staple Industries in Canada's Economic Development," *Journal of Economic History* 18:4 (1958), 439-52.

13. M.H. Watkins, "A Staple Theory of Economic Growth," *Canadian Journal of Economics and Political Science* 29:2 (1963), 141 ff.

14. R.T. Naylor, *The History of Canadian Business* (Toronto: James Lorimer, 1975).

15. See L.R. Macdonald, "Merchants against Industry: An Idea and Its Origin," *Canadian Historical Review* 56:3 (1975), 263-81, for a criticism of Naylor's distinction between commercial and industrial capitalism. See also Michael Bliss, *Histoire sociale/Social History* 9: 18 (November 1976), 446-49, and 9: 19 (May 1977), 160-63, for an examination of the defects in Naylor's basic argument and in his use of evidence. Naylor's rejoinder to Bliss is in *ibid.*, 152.

16. A valuable cross-section of such papers appeared in the *Journal of Canadian Studies* 12:5 (1977), 6-45, 73-105. For an introduction to the "new political economy" see Daniel Drache and Wallace Clement, eds., *The New Practical Guide to Canadian Political Economy, Updated and Expanded* (Toronto: James Lorimer, 1985).

17. Michael Bliss: *A Canadian Millionaire: The Life and Business Times of Sir Joseph Flavelle, Bart., 1858-1939* (Toronto: Macmillan, 1978); and *Northern Enterprise* (Toronto: McClelland and Stewart, 1987).

18. L.T. Evans and N.C. Quigley, "Discrimination in Bank Lending: A Test Case Using Data from the Bank of Nova Scotia, 1900-37," *Canadian Journal of Economics* 23:1 (January 1990).

19. Among many works that might be quoted, see L.D. McCann, "The Mercantile-Industrial Transition in the Metal Towns of Pictou Country, 1857-1931," *Acadiensis* 10:2 (Spring 1981), 29-64; Gerald Tulchinsky, *The River Barons: Montreal Businessmen and the Growth of Industry and Transportation, 1837-53* (Toronto: University of Toronto Press, 1977); Tom Traves, "The Development of the Ontario Automobile Industry to 1939," and Peter George, "Ontario's Mining Industry," both in *Progress Without Planning: Ontario's Economic Development, 1867-1941*, ed. Ian M. Drummond (Toronto: University of Toronto Press, 1987); Kris Inwood, *The Canadian Charcoal Iron Industry, 1870-1914* (New York: Garland, 1986); Ron Rudin, *Banking en Français: The French Banks of Quebec, 1835-1935* (Toronto: University of Toronto Press, 1985); Lewis R. Fischer and Eric W. Sager, eds., *The Enterprising Canadians* (St. John's: Memorial University of Newfoundland, 1979), and *Mercantile Shipping and Economic Development in Eastern Canada*, (St. John's: Memorial University of Newfoundland, 1982); and T.W. Acheson, "The Great Merchant and Economic Development in St. John, 1820-1850," *Acadiensis* 8:2 (Spring 1979), 3-27.

20. Yet Innisism was not dead. For a latter-day application of his staple thesis see Rosemary E. Ommer, "What's Wrong with Canadian Fish?" *Journal of Canadian Studies* 20:3 (Fall 1985), 122-42.

21. The beginnings of penetration are recorded in Peter J. George and Ernest A. Oksanen, "Recent Developments in the Quantification of Canadian Economic History," *Histoire sociale/Social History* 4 (November 1969), 46-98

22. Among recent examples are Robert Armstrong, "The Efficiency of Quebec Farms in 1851," *Histoire sociale/Social History* 17: 33 (1984), 149-64; R. Marvin McInnis, "A Reconsideration of the State of Agriculture in Lower Canada in the First Half of the Nineteenth Century," *Canadian Papers in Rural History* 3 (1982), 9-49; Frank Lewis and Marvin McInnis, "The Efficiency of the French-Canadian Farmer in the Nineteenth Century, *Journal of Economic History* 40:3 (September 1980), 497-514.

23. But see George's paper on mining, in Drummond, *Progress without Planning*, cited above.

24. Besides the work cited above, see Peter Baskerville, "The Pet Bank, the Local State, and the Imperial Centre, 1850-1864," *Journal of Canadian Studies* 20:3 (Autumn 1985), 22-47; John F. Whiteside, "The Toronto Stock Exchange and the Development of the Share Market to 1885," *ibid.*, 64-82; Douglas O. Baldwin and Helen M. Gill,"The Savings Bank of Prince Edward Island: Philanthropy and Self-

Interest in the Nineteenth Century," *Journal of Canadian Studies* 20:4 (Winter 1985-6), 115-26.

25. The archival study of Atlantic ships and shipping is K.J. Rea, *The Prosperous Years* (Toronto: University of Toronto Press, 1983); the survey economic history of Quebec is Robert Armstrong, *Structure and Change: An Economic History of Quebec* (Toronto: Gage, 1984); the narrative of Ontario's economic history is Drummond, *Progress without Planning*. See also O.J. Firestone, *Canada's Economic Development, 1867-1953,* (Cambridge: Bowes and Bowes, 1958); M.C. Urquhart and K.A.H. Buckley, eds., *Historical Statistics of Canada,* (Toronto: Macmillan, 1965); and F.H. Leacy, ed., *Historical Statistics of Canada,* 2d ed. (Ottawa: Statistics Canada, 1983). Because the two *Historical Statistics* volumes are not cumulative, both must be consulted. Preliminary results of the new national-income estimates for 1870-1926 are in Stanley Engerman and Robert E. Gallman, eds., *Long-term Factors in American [sic] Economic Growth*, Vol. 51 of *Studies in Income and Wealth* (Chicago: University of Chicago Press, 1986).

26. Marr and Paterson, *Canada: An Economic History*; Pomfret, *The Economic Development of Canada*.

27. José Igartua in *Revue d'histoire de l'Amérique français*, 39:2 (*automne* 1985), 253-61.

28. K.A.H. Buckley, *Capital Formation in Canada, 1896-1930* (Toronto: University of Toronto Press, 1955); A.E. Safarian, *The Great Depression in Canada* (Toronto: University of Toronto Press, 1959; reprint Toronto: McClelland and Stewart, 1970); and Jacob Viner, *Canada's Balance of International Indebtedness, 1900-1913* (Cambridge: Harvard University Press, 1924; reprint Toronto: McClelland and Stewart, 1975).

29. For a strikingly doctrinaire paper on this topic by a young Marxist scholar see Allan Greer, "Wage Labour and the Transition to Capitalism: A Critique of Pentland," *Labour/Le Travail* 15 (1985), 7-25.

30. Fernand Ouellet, "Dualité économique et changement technologique au Québec (1760-1790)," in *Histoire sociale/Social History* 9:18 (November 1976), 256-96.

31. Greer, "Wage Labour," 7-25.

32. Gary Teeple "Land, Labour, and Capital in Pre-Confederation Canada" in *Capitalism and the National Question in Canada*, ed. Gary Teeple (Toronto: University of Toronto Press, 1972).

33. Bryan Palmer, *A Culture in Conflict*, Ch. 1.

34. Allan Greer, *Peasant, Lord, and Merchant: Rural Society in Three Quebec Parishes, 1740-1840* (Toronto: University of Toronto Press, 1985); R. Cole Harris, *The Seigneurial System in Early Canada: A Geographical Survey* (Madison and Quebec: University of Wisconsin Press and Presses de l'université Laval, 1966); John Mc-Callum, *Unequal Beginnings: Agriculture and Economic Development in Quebec and Ontario until 1870* (Toronto: University of Toronto Press, 1980). Fernand Ouellet: "Libèré ou exploité: le paysan québécois d'avant 1850," *Histoire sociale/Social History* 13: 26 (November 1980), 339-68; "L'agriculture bas-canadienne vue a travèrs les dîmes et la rente de nature," *Histoire sociale/Social History* 8:16 (Novem-

ber 1971), 5-44; and *Le Bas-Canada, 1791-1840. Changements structureaux et crise* (Ottawa: Éditions de l'université d'Ottawa, 1976); Claude Baribeau, *La seigneurie de la Petite-Nation, 1801-1854): le role économique et sociale du seigneur* (Hull: Asticon, 1983).

35. The new approach, combined with common-property theory, has been extended to the study of the oldest Canadian "staple industry," in McManus's "economic analysis of the fur trade." See J. McManus, "An Economic Analysis of Indian Behaviour in the North American Fur Trade," *Journal of Economic History* 32:1 (1972), 36-53.

36. Douglas McCalla, *The Upper Canada Trade, 1834-1872: A Study of the Buchanans' Business* (Toronto: University of Toronto Press, 1979).

37. Sylvia Van Kirk, *Many Tender Ties: Women in Fur Trade Society in Western Canada, 1670-1870* (Winnipeg: Watson and Dwyer, 1980); Abraham Rotstein, "Fur Trade and Empire: An Institutional Analysis" (Ph.D. diss., University of Toronto, 1967); E.E. Rich, *The Hudson's Bay Company*, 2 vols. (London: Hudson's Bay Record Society, 1958-9); Arthur J. Ray and Donald Freeman, *"Give Us Good Measure": An Economic Analysis of the Relations between the Indians and the Hudson's Bay Company before 1763* (Toronto: University of Toronto Press, 1978).

38. F.X. Garneau, *Histoire du Canada* (Paris: Alcad, 1928). José Igartua, "The Merchants of Montreal at the Conquest: Socio-Economic Profile," *Histoire sociale/Social History* 8:16 (November 1975), 275-93; Ouellet, "Dualité."

39. For a summary statement see T.J.A. LeGoff, "The Agricultural Crisis in Lower Canada, 1802-1812: A Review of a Controversy," reprinted in *Perspectives on Canadian Economic History*, ed. Douglas McCalla (Toronto: Copp Clark Pitman, 1987). See also Gilles Paquet and Jean-Pierre Wallot: *Patronage et pouvoir dans le Bas-Canada (1794-1814): un essai d'économie historique* (Montréal: PUQ, 1973); and "Stratégie foncière de l'habitant: Québec (1790-1835)," *Revue d'histoire de l'Amérique français* 39:4 (printemps 1986), 551-82. Certain older views are reported in M. Seguin, *La "nation canadienne" et l'agriculture (1760-1850): essai d'histoire économique* (Trois Rivières: Editions du Boréal Express, 1970).

40. Lewis and McInnis, "The Efficiency of the French Canadian Farmer."

41. André Raynauld, *Croissance et structure économiques de la province de Québec* (Québec: Ministère de l'industrie et du commerce, Province de Québec, 1961).

42. Copp, *Anatomy of Poverty*.

43. William F. Ryan, *The Clergy and Economic Growth in Quebec, 1896-1914* (Quebec: Presses de l'université Laval, 1966); Ruth Dupre, "Public Expenditure in Quebec, 1867-1971" (Ph.D. diss., University of Toronto, 1987). Municipal institutions were admittedly better-developed in Ontario, so that a simple comparison of provincial-government expenditures may be less revealing than it seems.

44. J.H. Dales, *Hydroelectricity and Economic Development: Quebec, 1898-1940* (Cambridge: Harvard University Press, 1957).

45. Jean Hamélin and Yves Roby, *Histoire économique du Québec, 1851-1896* (Montreal: Fides, 1971); Jean Hamélin, *Économie et societé en nouvelle France* (Québec: Presses de l'université Laval, 1960); Albert Faucher, *Québec en Amérique*

au XIXe siecle: essai sur les charactères économiques de la Laurentie (Montreal: Fides, 1973); *Économie québécois, 1525-1965* (Cahiers de l'université du Québec, 1969). Fernand Ouellet: *Economic and Social History of Quebec, 1761-1850* (Toronto: Macmillan, 1980; translation of French edition, Montreal: Fides, 1966); and *Lower Canada, 1791-1840: Social Change and Nationalism* (Toronto: McClelland and Stewart, 1980).

46.   Dales, *Hydroelectricity.*

47.   Buckley, "Role of Staple Industries"; and O.J. Firestone, *Canada's Economic Development, 1867-1953* (London: Bowes and Bowes, 1958).

48.   It was also incorrect to argue that there had been "no staple": these were the great years for the Ontario export trades in cheese and bacon. But that is another story. See Bliss, *Flavelle*; and H.A. Innis, ed., *The Dairy Industry in Canada* (Toronto and New Haven: Ryerson and Yale University Press, 1937).

49.   Raynauld, *Croissance*; Gordon W. Bertram, "Historical Statistics on Growth and Structure of Manufacturing in Canada, 1870-1957," in *Papers of the Canadian Political Science Association Conference on Statistics, 1962 and 1963*, eds. J.Henripin and A. Asimakoupulos (Toronto: University of Toronto Press, 1964), 93-146.

50.   See above, note 19, for some important studies. See also Patricia Roy, "Direct Management from Abroad: The Formative Years of the British Columbia Electric Railway," *Business History Review* 47:2 (1973), 239-59; H.V. Nelles, *The Politics of Development*, (Toronto: Macmillan, 1972); and H.V. Nelles and Christopher Armstrong, *Monopoly's Moment*, (Philadelphia: Temple University Press, 1987), for revealing vignettes of the development of Canadian utilities firms.

51.   E.J. Chambers and D.F. Gordon, "Primary Products and Economic Growth: An Empirical Assessment," *Journal of Political Economy* 74:4 (1966), 315-32; J.H. Dales, J.C. McManus, and M.H. Watkins, "Primary Products and Economic Growth: A Comment," *Journal of Political Economy* 75:6 (1967), 876-79.

52.   J.H. Dales, *The Protective Tariff in Canada's Development* (Toronto: University of Toronto Press, 1966); Piva, *The Condition of the Working Class*; and Copp, *The Anatomy of Poverty.*

53.   Douglas Annett, *British Preference in Canadian Commercial Policy* (Toronto: Ryerson, 1948); O.J. McDairmid, *Commercial Policy in the Canadian Economy* (Cambridge: Harvard University Press, 1946); John Young, *Canadian Commercial Policy* (Ottawa: Queen's Printer, 1957).

54.   Among others, Ian M. Drummond, *British Economic Policy and the Empire, 1919-1939* (London: Allan and Unwin, 1972); Ian M. Drummond and Norman Hillmer, *Negotiating Freer Trade* (Waterloo: Wilfred Laurier University Press, 1988); J.L. Granatstein and Robert Cuff, *American Dollars and Canadian Prosperity* (Toronto: Samuel and Stevens, 1978).

55.   H.S. Eastman and S. Stykolt, *The Tariff and Competition in Canada* (Toronto: Macmillan, 1967); Tom Traves, *The State and Enterprise: Manufacturers and the Federal Government, 1917-1931* (Toronto: University of Toronto Press, 1979).

56. S.A. Saunders, *Economic History of the Maritime Provinces* (Ottawa: King's Printer, 1940). T.W. Acheson's introduction to the new edition (Fredericton: Acadiensis Press, 1982) puts Saunders' work in historiographical context, although Acheson is probably too uncritically kind to some of the more recent scholarly work in the Atlantic Provinces.

57. John Graham, "Why Nova Scotia is a Low-Income Province," in *Fiscal Adjustment and Economic Development: A Case Study of Nova Scotia* (Toronto: University of Toronto Press, 1963), 93-142.

58. Inwood, *Charcoal.*

59. Fischer and Sager, *Enterprising Canadians: Shipping and Economic Development.*

60. T.W. Acheson, "The National Policy and the Industrialization of the Maritimes, 1880-1910," *Acadiensis* 1:2 (1972), 3-28; Robert Brym and R. James Sacouman, eds., *Underdevelopment and Social Movements in Atlantic Canada* (Toronto: New Hogtown Press, 1979); Michael Clow, "Politics and Uneven Capitalist Development: The Maritime Challenge to the Study of Canadian Political Economy," *Studies in Political Economy* 14 (Summer 1984), 117-40; David Frank, "The Cape Breton Coal Industry and the Rise and Fall of the British Empire Steel Corporation," *Acadiensis* 7:1 (1977), 3-34; Bruce Archibald, "Atlantic Regional Underdevelopment and Socialism," in *Essays on the Left*, ed. Laurier Lapierre (Toronto: McClelland and Stewart, 1971), 103-120; Douglas O. Baldwin, "The Growth and Decline of the Charlottetown Banks, 1854-1906," *Acadiensis* 15:2 (1986), 28-53; Ernest R. Forbes, "Consolidating Disparity: The Maritimes and the Industrialization of Canada during the Second World War," *Acadiensis* 15:2 (1986), 3-27.

61. Roy E. George, *A Leader and a Laggard: Manufacturing Industry in Nova Scotia, Quebec, and Ontario* (Toronto: University of Toronto Press, 1970).

62. The belief that the financial structure "pumped out surplus" or otherwise contrived to discourage industry is widespread among Maritime historians.

63. David Alexander's most important papers, together with some ephemera, are to be found in *Atlantic Canada and Confederation: Essays in Canadian Political Economy*, compiled after his death by Eric W. Sager, Lewis R. Fischer, and Stuart O. Pierson (Toronto: University of Toronto Press, 1983).

64. See David Alexander and Keith Matthews, *A Computer Index to the Crew Lists and Agreements of the British Empire* (St. John's: Maritime History Group, 1974); David Alexander and Rosemary Ommer, eds., *Volumes not Values: Canadian Sailing Ships and World Trades* (St. John's: Maritime History Group, 1979); and several short papers by Alexander listed in *Atlantic Canada and Confederation*, 150-51.

65. *Atlantic Canada and Confederation*, 136-37.

66. *Ibid.*, 19-23.

67. R. Cole Harris, editor, and Geoffrey J. Mathews, cartographer/designer, *Historical Atlas of Canada, Volume 1, From the Beginnings to 1800* (Toronto: University of Toronto Press, 1987). Work on Volumes 2 and 3, which will cover later periods, is well advanced.

3

Writing About Ideas

Doug Owram

It is perhaps an appropriate time to look at the evolution and state of Canadian intellectual history. For a little over the past quarter-century this field has been a distinct subdiscipline with its own enthusiasms, supporters, and courses. It now has formed a caucus within the Canadian Historical Association complete with newsletter, membership list, and enthusiastic plans.

The field is also well enough established now that its biases become apparent. For, as the following pages will argue, Canadian intellectual history has particular quirks and prejudices resulting from the timing and nature of its development. It also reflects the all-pervasive problems of Canadian history — including a gulf between French and English writing, an obsession with Canadian nationalism, and a fear that we may be nothing more than a branch plant of the United States. The field is also far from unified. Not only is there the expected and commendable diversity that comes from differences in chronology and topic but there is also some uncertainty as to the appropriate boundaries of the field, the proper methodologies to be used, or the best future direction to be taken. Like Canadian historical writing as a whole, intellectual history has not yet reached the stage where it can easily achieve a common position or approach. These doubts also make it worthwhile to investigate just what the past quarter-century has brought to bear.

I

The essence of intellectual history is fairly easy to define. But in the details and at the margin things become complex. Intellectual history is that sub-discipline of history which gives a central place to the role of the mind in the historical process. The mind in question may be a great one — that of an Augustine, a Darwin, an Adam Smith, or an Edmund Burke — and the idea a momumental one. It does not have to be, however. The mind in question might be the mass mind and its pastimes, fears, and hopes. As American intellectual historian John Higham put it, intellectual history "includes Little Orphan Annie as well as Adam Smith."[1]

As with most sub-disciplines of history, intellectual history has affinities with other areas of study. It draws inspiration from, and sometimes overlaps with, literary studies, philosophy, pyschology, and, within its own discipline, social history, and it is often identified with cultural history. Yet it is a distinct field because of the particular approach it takes toward ideas. It is, as one historian has noted, distinct because it accepts an apparent contradiction about ideas, that they "are false but important."[2] They are "false" in the sense that intellectual history stresses the degree to which ideas are the product of a particular era and social milieu rather than universal. Yet they are "important" because intellectual history considers ideas to be a major force in the shaping of historical events as a whole.

Of course historians have used ideas as long as there has been history. Nevertheless, even internationally, intellectual history as a distinct sub-discipline is of comparatively recent origin.[3] Only as an increasing number of professionally-trained historians appeared in the years after 1900 did the concept develop that ideas in themselves were important in understanding the past. Dissatisfied with the easy descriptive-narrative and patriotic traditions of their predecessors or with the restrictive fact-grinding of the German historicist school, historians in Europe, Great Britain, and the United States began to examine the deeper undercurrents to understand the nature of their society and their nation. Borrowing from other disciplines, the analysis of historical circumstance became increasingly subtle and complex.

Intellectual history did not emerge overnight, but only gradually distinguished itself as a separate field. The way in which it emerged had a profound effect on the sub-discipline and still shapes much of the debate about it. As one main branch there developed a study of the history of significant ideas that have influenced the past. These ideas might be those of a single important thinker such as the eighteenth-century *philosophe*, Jean Jacques Rousseau. Alternatively the study might be of a major ideal in a society's life, such as democracy, liberty, or religious piety. Such studies evolved naturally from philosophy's interest in ideas and from earlier historical writings, especially in theological history. Intellectual history broadened as an increasingly secular age departed from the earlier emphasis on religious themes. It has also tended to include in a loose way the study of intellectual and cultural institutions — educational ideas and figures, schools of philosophy, historiography, art, and other themes tied in one way or another to the life of intellect or creativity.

This approach, normally characterized as the history of ideas, had several implications. First, though historians of ideas were distinct from many philosophers in that they had an interest in both the historical context and the impact of the idea, they tended, as did the philosophers, to emphasize the internal analysis and continuity of thought. The implications of that thought for society were tangential or presumed. Second, the approach of the field was elitist as it studied for the most part the great and articulate thoughts of the past. Such an approach implied that articulate thought shaped the intellectual forces of history. Finally, such elitism discouraged the development of intellectual history in Canada. Since Canada was a small, colonial society with few intellects of world renown, Canadian historians presumed that the history of ideas had little relevance to their own past. Even today a common response among those unfamiliar with intellectual history is to comment that a study of the Canadian field must be one of the shortest courses on record.[4]

The other main branch of intellectual history evolved in quite a different way. Social, political, and economic historians, seeking to reinforce their understanding of their own areas, drew increasingly upon concepts of ideology, belief, and prejudice to explain the actions of their groups and individuals. This approach borrowed as much from the social sciences as from philosophy or literature and sought to explain not so much the great ideas as the "mood" which would encourage or allow certain actions to occur.

As with the history of ideas this approach had certain implications. First, what made an idea worth studying was not its intrinsic worth, but its impact upon society. The idea might be important and articulate, of course, but conversely it might be illogical or even base. The psychology and rhetoric of Nazi anti-semitism or the biases and prejudices of other forms of racism provide obvious examples of ideas that are important due to their impact rather than their logic. Second, even as this side of the field became more autonomous it retained an emphasis on the external relationship between ideas and society. The impact of those ideas was often emphasized while the internal analysis of their evolution or their relationship to other ideas was treated casually, if at all. And if the "history of ideas" became difficult to distinguish from philosophy at the margin, many practitioners of this external approach to intellectual history would have considered themselves as social or even economic historians. Ultimately, this "externalist" approach to intellectual history proved especially important to the early development of the Canadian field.

These two approaches to intellectual history have never been completely merged and the internal emphasis on the causal relationship between ideas and the external emphasis on the relationship between ideas and events continues to provide the most fundamental tension within the discipline. At its best this tension is a mutually healthy relationship which acts, as we will see later, to reinforce scholarship. It does indicate a degree of uncertainty within the profession, however, as to the proper parameters and most appropriate topics of discussion.

American precedent proved most important to the Canadian field. South of the border intellectual history was well-established by the 1940s. Works like Vernon Parrington's sweeping literary study *Main Currents in American Thought* (1927), Merle Curti's synthesis *The Growth of American Thought* (1943), Joseph Haroutunian's *Piety versus Moralism: The Passing of New England Theology* (1932), and Perry Miller's massive *The New England Mind: The Seventeeth Century* (1939) all signalled the firm establishment of that field in the United States.[5] The founding in 1940 of the *Journal of the History of Ideas* gave the field the ultimate claim to respectability — its own journal.

For all these early developments, the great era of American intellectual history really took place only after the Second World War. During those post-war years, memories of the depression, contemporary conflicts over the Cold War, and the disturbing feeling that ideology was becoming unimportant in American life made the search for guiding principles and prejudices in the history of the American republic a subject of fascination for historians. Intellectual history both asserted its autonomy from other areas of history and claimed for its proper jurisdiction not only the traditional history of ideas but the broader scope of the "American mind" in all its phases.[6] Many of the great classics of the field were written in the next fifteen years, including the second volume of Perry Miller's massive study of *The New England Mind* (1953), and Henry Nash Smith's study of the American frontier, *Virgin Land: The American West as Symbol and Myth* (New York, 1950).[7]

The greatest enthusiasm, even obsession, of many of these American intellectual historians was nationalism. In work after work they sought a greater understanding of the American national psyche, of the nation's evolution toward twentieth-century democracy or related topics. Sometimes this made for a truly "political intellectual history" focused on the various myths and ideals of American politics — the essence of Jacksonian democracy, the nature of the Jeffersonian concept of the yeoman farmer, or, in the most daring example of politics as intellectual history, Louis Hartz's attempt to define the range of all American ideology in his 1955 *Liberal Tradition in America.*[8]

The most common approach to this interest in the national character was what became known as the "myth and symbol" school. Adherents of this school investigated different forms of communication (literature, papers, or speeches) to see what rhetoric and imagery had been used to evoke particular values or beliefs. Thus Henry Nash Smith's study of the frontier as a place of democratic renewal looked at generations of writers to try to understand this basic theme of American history. Later works would look at the rhetoric of patriotism and at the symbolism of various political and military leaders.

In the longer term all this affected Canadian historical writing. The American field helped give succour and legitimacy to those who sought to overcome resistance to the idea that Canada had any intellectual history. After all, the United States was a democracy that had not, at least since the early days of the republic, boasted a dominant intellectual class. Nor, in this nation where the pursuit of material gain seemed all-important, was there any strong tradition of formal philosophic or theological thought. However, as Curti, Smith, and others demonstrated, this lack in no way lessened the vitality or importance of thought in American history.

Yet, for a long time, the exciting material produced in the United States seemed to have little parallel in Canada. There were some individual efforts, especially among Maritime historians, in the realm of intellectual history.[9] In general, however, Canadian historians shied away from the whole field. While American historians were actively developing this new and distinct field, Canadians seemed content to watch from afar. Perhaps because they were mesmerized by economic history through the 1930s or perhaps because they felt Canadians had no intellectuals or intellectual traditions, historians here concentrated on other things.

At least one enthusiast advocated the need for Canadian intellectual history. Born in Ontario in 1889, academic and journalist Frank Underhill was educated at the University of Toronto and Oxford before becoming an historian at the young University of Saskatchewan in 1914. In the mid-1920s he moved to the University of Toronto where he remained for the rest of his career. Throughout his life Underhill was, for an academic, an unusually public figure. A political activist, he helped found the social democratic League For Social Reconstruction in the 1930s. He also contributed frequently to journals like the *Canadian Forum* and got himself into trouble more than once for his outspoken speeches.[10]

The role of ideas in history, at least in political history, soon caught Underhill's interest. As early as 1927 he gave a paper to the Canadian Historical Association on radical thought in pre-Confederation Canada.[11] A few years later he published a commentary emphasizing the failure of ideas in the face of interest politics in the years after Confederation.[12] But not until 1946, did Underhill, as incoming President of the Canadian Historical Association, use his inaugural address to set out more fully his views on the importance of ideas in Canadian history.

Underhill began with the sort of acerbic jab at Canadian culture typical of his style. "In the world of ideas we do not yet play a full part. We are still colonial." In both the United States and Great Britain, he continued, political debate had been carried on, at least in part, in a highly articulate way. Basic principles and symbols had been at stake as the forces of party contended for the hearts and minds of the people. In Canada, however, parties were nothing more than "mere confused interest groups" that had neither the capacity for nor the interest in a high level of principled discussion. History writing, he felt, mirrored this past lack of interest in ideas. For the prior decades economic history had dominated in Canada. He remained hopeful however. "I have the feeling that Canadian historiography has come to the end of an epoch." The "abstract history without names or real flesh or blood individuals..., the ghostless ballet of bloodless economic categories" was about to end. "The time seems about due for a new history-writing which will attempt to explain the ideas in the heads of Canadians that caused them to act as they did, their philosophy...."[13]

Underhill's 1946 address is symbolic: a point after which it is possible to discuss the evolution of intellectual history in English Canada. His prediction that historical writing in Canada had reached the end of an epoch proved correct. Economic history would fade as new approaches took over. Those approaches, however, were centred not on ideas but on political biography. Canadians did indeed turn their back on the bloodless categories of economic history in favour of significant and presumably thoughtful historical figures.[14] However, the burgeoning number of biographers of the next fifteen years or so mostly saw their heroes as pragmatic nationalists. Ideology, myths, symbols, (and hence ideas), played at best at minor role in the fact of the pragmatic tasks of national unity, brokerage parties, and the daily life of politics.

Part of the reason for the apparent failure of Underhill's appeal becomes clear when one looks closely at the personal perceptions which animated it. Underhill's own experience, as well as his romantic vision of an intellectually-engaged society, supported the ideal of the educated as being involved in articulate and principled debate. The League for Social Reconstruction, of which he had been a founding member, was just such an academically-inclined body. The League had become linked with the new socialist Cooperative Commonwealth Federation party and Underhill had helped write that party's initial platform. For Underhill the need to study ideas was intensely personal, inseparable from and occasionally confused with his strong desire to participate in the politics of reason. Much of his rhetoric about how the past should be approached, therefore, was really an appeal to the present. Intellectuals should become engaged in debating the high principles of a civilization and a nation. Very often his call for intellectual history seemed to be nothing more than a call for political debate on the part of historians.

The trouble was that his negative image of earlier Canadian political debate did much to nullify his call for historical study of the mind of the past. For if there was, indeed, no intellect of note, no principle, no sense of mission at work in the past, then the application of intellectual history to the study of that past was, of necessity, irrelevant. If you thought John A. Macdonald was an opportunist whose philosophy of politics was expediency, then to spend any great amount of time looking into Macdonald's values was pointless. Even if any values could be discerned they were unlikely to have shaped his actions.

Whatever such inconsistencies, however, Underhill powerfully influenced the coming of Canadian intellectual history. At the time the University of Toronto was the only significant centre for doctoral study in history within English Canada; hence Underhill was ideally situated to carry his ideas to the next generation of Canadian historical scholars. Moreover, by all accounts he was an enthusiastic and engaging teacher who could capture the spirit of those in his classroom. Thus his energetic call for attention to the role of ideas gradually hammered away at the existing presumptions that there was something quixotic about investigating the life of the mind in Canada.

Underhill's call was one of the earliest and most forceful expressions of interest in intellectual history in Canada, but in the post-war years several others recognized how important the study of ideas was for historical understanding. Donald Creighton, the biographer of John A. Macdonald, saw an intimate connection between the Liberalism of Canadian historians and the failure to treat Macdonald with due justice.[15] J.M.S. Careless's doctoral thesis from Harvard on George Brown and the Toronto Globe led him to investigate the character of mid-Victorian liberalism.[16] Elizabeth Wallace's biography of the nineteenth-century Canadian, Goldwin Smith, published in 1957, probably came the closest to Underhill's vision of what the historian should be doing to resurrect ideas.[17] As early as 1950 there was a conference on Canadian ideas at Kingston. None of these publications or activities was revolutionary, but cumulatively they did serve to remind the larger community of Canadian historians that ideas did exist — even if only occasionally and even if the place accorded these ideas was often secondary.

Still, what was not looked at in the generation after World War Two is interesting. Canadian historians generally ignored Canadian culture, perhaps taking to heart the lament made by many, including Underhill, that there was none. There were, if Canadian historians were to be believed, practically no literary figures worth discussing: no philosophers, no art movements, no economic theorists, no journalists or demagogues whose rhetoric contained within it a philosophy of meaningful pedigree.[18] Only in the occasional article on the historical discipline itself was there any exception to this lack of interest in Canadian culture but, of course, a discipline is always fascinated by its own development.[19] Hence, when other disciplines did receive historical treatment, it was usually by people from those disciplines rather than by historians.[20]

The lack of attention paid to cultural history is very revealing. Though this generation of Canadian intellectuals thought of themselves as nationalists they still had about them certain remnants of a colonial mentality. Few of those teaching Canadian history in the decade or decade and a half after the war had received their graduate training in Canada. Oxford, Cambridge, Harvard had provided their historical education. Higher learning and higher culture was something that one received abroad. To write about the small Canadian university scene and to write about "Canadian traditions" of philosophy, psychology, economics, or literature seemed parochial, even pretentious. Political nationalists they might be, but, with few exceptions, they felt as Underhill himself did, that "for our intellectual capital we are still dependent upon a continuous flow of imports from London, New York, and Paris, not to mention Moscow and Rome."[21]

Canadian intellectual history thus had a distinct genesis. People traditionally think of the history of ideas as preceding the more general and encompassing field of intellectual history, but in Canada the "externalist" concern for the relationship between ideas and society, rather than the history of ideas with its emphasis on internal causation, formed the basis of the field. Even more specifically, as with so much other historical writing, intellectual historians concentrated on the relationship between political thought in Canada and that elusive search for the Canadian national identity.[22] As intellectual history developed and grew, it would continue to emphasize both the external relationships and the national character.

II

In the 1960s several circumstances coincided to encourage the development of intellectual history (as well as other fields) in Canada. First, given that intellectual history rested on nationalist concerns, the 1960s was an ideal period for it to flourish. Obsession with the elusive Canadian identity reached new heights. In Quebec the onset of the Quiet Revolution raised disturbing questions about what common characteristics, if any, held the nation together. On a more optimistic note, the approach of the Canadian centennial created a wave of curiosity and even enthusiasm about things national. Governments handed out money to academics to talk about things Canadian and publishers looked with hopeful eyes on the potential markets that some patriotic Canadianism might conjure up.

Second, since World War Two the university population had been expanding. From the beginning of the 1950s to the late 1960s university enrolment in Canada more than quadrupled.[23] In response the number of academics grew rapidly. Departments multiplied in size and, given the new enthusiasm for things Canadian, Canadian history grew even more rapidly. There were now sufficient people teaching in the discipline to allow the luxury of specialization both in research and in courses.

Finally, all of this happened at a time when, as discussed earlier, American intellectual history was at its height. Canadian historians who looked south of the border for possible models for research and speculation were bound to be affected by the excellent works of intellectual history that existed. In particular, the flourishing "myth and symbol" school fit nicely with the predeliction in Canada to look at historical problems through the prism of national questions. Thus, whatever inspiration Underhill may have provided and whatever exceptions might be found in articles by people like Careless, only in the 1960s was Canadian intellectual history born.

Once born, the field developed rapidly. By the mid-1960s a number of historians were undertaking research aimed at theses or publication. Perhaps one historian, however, deserves credit for being the first to emerge as a distinct defender of intellectual history's importance, especially because his work showed sufficient imagination and deftness to encourage others to follow. In 1965 S.F. Wise published "Sermon Literature and Canadian Intellectual History," in the little known *Bulletin* of the Committee of Archives of the United Church of Canada. Two years later he published an article "Upper Canada and the Conservative Tradition" and in the same year published, with R.C. Brown, a brief study of Canadian perceptions of the nineteenth-century United States.[24] All three works were explicitly intellectual history and all were to have a profound effect on Canadian historical writing.

Wise was very conscious that he was moving into new terrain and in his 1965 piece on sermon literature he set out the argument in favour of the new field. "No connected history of formal thought in Canada is possible," he argued, but that did not rule out the study of intellectual history. The absence of a body of formal thought, he felt, limited the type of intellectual history that could be done. "The Canadian intellectual historian must be concerned primarily with the interrelationship between ideas and actions, and therefore the intellectual commonplaces of an age, its root notions, assumptions, and images, will be of more significance to him than the study of coherent bodies of abstract thought." He continued by arguing that of all such commonplaces and root assumptions, the place at least to start was with "political rhetoric".[25] Drawing on the "myth and symbol" school of the United States as well as on the inspiration of Underhill's teaching, Wise noted that various commonplace historical terms like "loyalty," "liberty," and "authority" all had a special meaning to contemporaries that served as shorthand for a whole set of social values. Political rhetoric based on such terms (and the ideas they represented) sufficiently justified the study of intellectual history, Wise concluded.[26]

Wise's approach thus reinforced the political and external orientation of intellectual history in Canada. His subsequent works, in one degree or another, retained the basic assumptions set out in this first piece. There is thus a continuity in the evolution of Canadian intellectual history. From Underhill, through the biographers of the 1950s to Wise's early intellectual history of the mid-1960s, the centre of history was politics. Politics might be approached through biography, or perhaps through ideology and the mind, but politics and its application to the evolution of the Canadian nation dominated.

Aside from reinforcing the emphasis on the external, Wise had another major influence on Canadian intellectual history. His works set out a clear, if controversial, argument about the nature of Anglo-Protestant political thought before Confederation. The roots of English Canada were not, as some of his predecessors had casually assumed, liberal and democratic in tone, but conservative, monarchial, and profoundly hostile to the American experiment south of the border. Wise's intriguing depiction challenged existing pre-Confederation historiography and has made the early nineteenth century the heart of some of the most lively and interesting intellectual history done in Canada.[27] The challenges presented by Wise and by other pre-Confederation historians meant that much of the best pre-Confederation history in English Canada during the 1960s and 1970s was intellectual history.

Even as Wise was beginning to publish in the area, others began to move into the new field. A young student just finishing his doctorate at the

University of Toronto, Carl Berger, presented a paper (at the 1965 annual meeting of the Canadian Historical Association) on the historical ideas of John George Bourinot and the next year published a classic example of the myth and symbol approach to intellectual history in his "True North Strong and Free: The Myth of the North in Canadian History." Non-historians also began writing intellectual history. Thus, for example, in 1965 English professor Norman Shrive published an excellent biography of the nineteenth-century poet and expansionist Charles Mair.[28]

By the early 1970s the field had moved beyond its early experimental stages and had become firmly established in Canadian historical writing. Several universities established courses in intellectual history and even existing general survey courses began incorporating the ideas of people like Wise and Berger. Two particular books, however, mark the end of this developmental stage in the field. The first, Carl Berger's *Sense of Power*, a revised version of his doctoral study of the ideas of Canadian imperialism, appeared in 1970.[29] One of the most influential pieces of academic history written in the 1970s, this work reinforced some of Wise's earlier arguments concerning the conservative pro-British emphasis in nineteenth-century Canadian thought. What Berger did was to show that this viewpoint, suitably modified, did not exist just in the early nineteenth century, but survived to the First War. Moreover, and most importantly, he demonstrated that, at least for the imperialist mind, the essence of Canadian nationalism was complementary rather than hostile to the imperialist outlook.

The second important work was a collection of essays entitled the *Maple Leaf Forever* published by Ramsay Cook in 1971. Cook's interest in ideas had been longstanding and derived both from his undergraduate philosophy minor and from an interest in the political debates of seventeenth-century British history.[30] These interests were channelled in Canadian directions by his exposure to Queen's historian Arthur Lower's interest in the problems of French and English duality in Canada. Yet Canadian historians simply did not think in terms of intellectual history as such and thus Cook's first book had been a political biography, albiet of an intellectual figure.[31]

Yet Cook remained intrigued both by ideas and by the problems of Canadian nationalism. His interest led to a series of historical and political essays on French Canada which combined historical perspective with commentary on contemporary issues — exactly the sort of high level discussion that Underhill would have admired. The *Maple Leaf Forever* confirmed Cook's new orientation toward intellectual history and expanded his work to include English as well as French aspects of nationalism. These reflections on the evolution of the Canadian condition also gave further impetus to those historians who wanted to treat the ideas and thoughts of the past seriously.

The work of Berger and Cook did much to attract the next generation of historians into intellectual history. The field continued to grow with new courses being established and new works being published on a regular basis in spite of the generally static size (by the early 1970s) of the historical profession as a whole. By the end of the decade all the major universities in Canada possessed a specialist in intellectual history with ancillary courses and fields of graduate study. These years also saw the development of a specialized regional intellectual history as historians sought to understand their particular part of the nation. There were even, by the 1970s, reflective articles on the state of the discipline, a sure sign of — if not maturity — at least introspective adolescence.[32]

It would be impossible and tedious in a brief essay like this to chronicle the individual works that have buttressed the field since the early 1970s. Two additional points, however, must be mentioned. First, in Francophone writings the genesis and the resultant tradition of intellectual history was quite different from that in English Canada. French Canadian historiography had always been dominated by the issue of national survival. Further, in the nineteenth and first part of the twentieth centuries that nationalism had been defined in terms of conservatism and Catholicism. "La survivance" was, accordingly, tied to a set of intellectual values. Ideas and principles, the absence of which in English Canadian history Underhill so lamented, were present in abundance in French Canada.

This emphasis on ideas was clear in the work of most of the well-known historians up to the Second World War. The background and work of perhaps French Canada's most influential historian of the first half of the twentieth century, Abbé Lionel Groulx of the University of Montreal typified this emphasis. Trained in theology, Groulx saw the persistence of French Canadian society as inseparable from its conservative and Catholic character. His works thus gave central importance to the force of such ideas as faith, race, and destiny. "Perhaps we should not over-emphasize material well-being which counted for little in this small society of Frenchmen," wrote Groulx on one occasion. "The ascendancy of their faith and of their race led them to a more nearly perfect social state, where a hierarchy of values would of itself be established. The ascendancy would begin by keeping alive in a kindred of lumberjacks the persistent tradition of intellectual culture."[33] Such traditions meant that the history of ideas in French Canada long preceded the establishment of intellectual history as a distinct field.

This strong emphasis on the theological and the conservative bred a reaction that profoundly altered the direction of French Canadian historiography and the history of ideas. In the period after World War Two a new generation of French Canadian historians turned against the older clerical schools and promoted instead a new "scientific" approach to history. Out of this emerged a new dominant approach based on the *Annales* school of French historical writing. This view of history emphasized structure rather than events and tended towards the use of mass data and microstudies. It also very consciously turned away from studies of the elite and sought to look at the lives of ordinary people. Thus, in many ways, the approach of the *Annales* school seemed antithetical to that of the intellectual historian.

In the face of this onslaught traditional intellectual history — the history of ideas — had a difficult time. It was associated with a different era and with a different set of values. Intellectual history has persisted and has developed, but what is interesting is the degree to which the *Annales* school has penetrated it as well. Intellectual historians writing in French in Canada are much more conscious of methods and models than are their English Canadian counterparts. The search for a scientific history has led to the widespread use of models such as the Marxism of D. Monière's, *Le développement des idéologies au Québec* (1977) resting on the *Annales* fascination with quantification.[34] The dominant works in intellectual history in French have thus become focused on the rather formal studies of ideology or on the quantifiable aspects of mass cultural phenomena.[35] Intellectual history in Quebec is, for better or worse, shaped, directed, even dominated by, the seemingly all-powerful influence of the social sciences in general and the *Annales* school in particular.[36]

Yet this has its benefits. By the 1960s social historians in Quebec were much more aware of the importance of the intellectual climate to their own studies than were social historians in English Canada. Thus one of the finest pieces of intellectual history written in French comes from an historian who would not think of himself as an intellectual historian at all. Fernand Ouellet's *Histoire économique et sociale du Québec, 1760-1850* (1966) undertook a massive quantification of wheat yield and prices while maintaining an emphasis on the *mentalité* of the peasant farmer of Quebec.[37] For

Ouellet the intellectual climate was inseparable from the hard realities of economics. Both determined the shape of the past. His study demonstrated the integrated nature of our past and serves as a valuable lesson to both intellectual and social historians today.

The other change of importance has been the rise of cultural history in English Canada. Indeed, the flourishing of cultural history has been the vehicle for the introduction of the history of ideas into the writing of Canadian intellectual history. Cultural history and the history of ideas were bound to develop once intellectual history got underway. As historians began to take seriously the notion that Canadians did have ideas, it made sense to try to understand what institutions and what formal principles transmitted those ideas from generation to generation. This questioning was reinforced by the fact that many of those who appeared central to Carl Berger's study of Canadian imperialism were educators like George Munro Grant, principal of Queen's from 1877 to 1901, or George Parkin, administrator of the Rhodes trust. Before long the educational system, the text books, and especially the leading figures within the universities began to come under scrutiny.

The results have been rewarding. Generally, though much work has yet to be done, research to date has demonstrated how important it is to comprehend the history of ideas and their transmission in Canada if we are to comprehend fully the relationship between ideas and the external world. People like Wise and Berger had demonstrated how Canadians had created a unique view of the world, drawing upon Anglo-Scottish values but twisting them to colonial perspectives and a North American environment. Those who followed Wise and Berger have shown just how these ideas were derived and how they were altered in crossing the Atlantic. Such conclusions, in turn, have opened the way for new approaches to the external relationships between ideas and events in society.

Perhaps the best example of this sort of mutual interchange between the history of ideas and the view of intellectual history as external relationships can be shown in the study of the force and nature of religion in the late nineteenth and early twentieth centuries. In a general sense religion and its importance had been downplayed by historians from World War Two until the 1960s. Perhaps because they were so often self-consciously secular themselves they tended to regard formal religion as suspect. Those studies of religion that were done looked not at ideas, but at institutions and their transmutation. Indeed, it was a sociologist, not an historian who was most noted for his study of religion in Canadian history.[38]

For intellectual historians, of course, it was impossible to ignore for long the role of religion in Canadian history. It had been a powerful force not just as an institution but as a system of belief. To ignore it because of modern secularism made about as much sense as ignoring feudalism because there were no longer powerful feudal baronies. Thus both Berger and Wise noted the importance of religion in their writings. Indeed, as will be remembered, Wise's first piece of intellectual history was on sermon literature. Their concern was matched by others like Gordon Stewart and George Rawlyk who investigated religious fervour in eighteenth-century Nova Scotia.[39]

In the study of religion one of the most intriguing areas of potential investigation involved the period from the late nineteenth century through the first third of the twentieth. During this period a vast secularization took place in English Canadian life. Laws, church attendance, writings, educational, and social institutions all saw a marked decrease in religious influence. Questions of how the process occurred, what shifts in thought underlay the change, and what impact the change had on subsequent developments posed major problems to historians in Canada. The search for solutions, moreover, presented a task for which the intellectual historian was especially well-adapted.

The first major work to look at this period in specific terms was Richard Allen's *The Social Passion* published in 1971.[40] This work, which was in many ways a political history (except that it was organized around an idea rather than an organization or policy), argued that religion did not fade in Canada in the early twentieth century, but was transformed from a question of dogma and salvation to a question of social reform. In the latter guise it was rejuvenated and continued well into the twentieth century. The emphasis was on the impact of the ideas on society. Indeed Allen was not as interested in the fine points of theology as in the way in which the debate shaped or prevented social reform in Canada. The main point was clear, nevertheless. Religion was an important social and moral force in Canada even after the period of so-called secularization.

Over the next few years articles and monographs added to the concept of the social gospel. Indeed, the term threatened to become so all-encompassing that it would become meaningless. Then in 1979 A.B. McKillop added greatly to the debate with his investigation of the impact of Darwinism and other modern forces on religion and philosophy. In effect, McKillop investigated the complex set of ideas that Allen took as given. McKillop also modified the Allen argument somewhat. Religion had to cede much, he argued, to science and to the modern belief in "critical enquiry." By the time the social gospel emerged, traditional religion had really given way to a form of philosophic idealism.

McKillop's book was also important because it was very much a study in the history of ideas. Only at the end is the external world of reformism and the social gospel brought in and then only briefly. It was thus one of the first works in Canada to investigate the causal relationship between ideas and yet it did so in such a way that it both complemented and advanced the discussion of an issue that had tremendous external implications.[41]

Although sympathetic to the social gospel McKillop's work brought to the fore the question of whether the social gospel wasn't the final gasp of religion rather than its renewal. Did modernism, as critics argued, open the way to secularization? Subsequently various works have concentrated on the issue. In order to further investigate the problem, some works have continued to consider the later nineteenth century, the way in which religion shaped other aspects of Canadian thought, and how interdependent all those beliefs were. Carl Berger, for instance, looked at the connection, in the last decades of the century, between the enthusiasm for nature and the form of religion that was being increasingly challenged during that time. Ramsay Cook's *The Regenerators* has approached the central question most directly and focuses specifically on the relationships between modernism and secularization by looking at various types of social reformers and their relationship to religion. Doug Owram moved forward in time to look at the transformation of religiously and morally based social reformism in the more secular world of social scientific planning. Marlene Shore, in another work that indicates the growing importance of the history of ideas in Canada, has carefully traced the complex interaction between religious motivation and secular training in the shaping of one of Canada's more important interwar intellectuals, Carl Dawson of McGill.[42]

Out of all this, certain conclusions have been reached. First, Allen's optimistic emphasis on the continuity of religion in new form in the twentieth century has been considerably modified. Religion had a continuing influence on reformers and that influence was often all-important even as late as the 1930s and 1940s.[43] In spite of this, however, the fact remains that religion ceased to be at the centre of Canadian thought or action sometime after the First War. As Cook has demonstrated, it was not possible to yield to modernist criticisms without at the same time making religion a rather hollow shell for the average person.[44] Thus the very forces which unleashed the social gospel also helped bring about the end of religion as a major force in Canadian society. Religion continued to influence important individuals and important causes but it ceased to pervade the nature of Canadian society, and religious presumptions no longer shaped Canadian social policy.

This debate on religion, reform, and secularization is probably the most extensive one yet conducted in Canadian intellectual history. There are many other interesting areas and important works, just as there are some subjects that have barely been investigated and many areas that remain untouched. Yet the debate is illustrative both of the evolving nature of the field in Canada and of its importance. First, it has fundamentally revised basic assumptions and ways of looking both at our past and at our own contemporary society. Second, works like McKillop's and Shore's demonstrate the growing strength of both the history of ideas and the cultural institutions in which they are fostered and transmitted. The interaction between such approaches and the more traditional emphasis on external relationships is what has made the debate so constructive.

In sum then, Canadian intellectual history in the past decade has achieved a new dimension. The addition of the history of ideas and cultural history means that Canadian ideas are now seen as serious in their own right and Canadian intellectuals are not glibly dismissed as irrelevant. The result is that whole new areas of research become available and, as with the studies in religious history, the interaction between the two sides of intellectual history will be crucial in resolving the controversies that arise.

III

This brief history and description of an intellectual field leaves the impression of a fairly self-satisfied subdiscipline. Yet intellectual history is not without its problems. In the United States, which has been such an important model for Canadian academics in this area, there has been a sense of crisis in recent years. The great glorious years of the 1950s and 1960s have passed and the behaviourist mode of current social history has increasingly challenged the significance of ideas.[45] Can those ideas drawn from newspapers, pamphlets, speechs or wherever truly be said to represent the population? Even if a sufficiently wide range of sources could be found, is there anything to say that the rhetoric of the day meant anything in terms of social action? Did people not operate on more basic levels of material need and self-interest? Is it true, as Donald Akenson recently charged, that intellectual historians tend to create formal ideologies and systems of thought unperceived even to the contemporaries who were supposed to possess them?[46]

Canadian intellectual history is especially vulnerable to such challenges: from Frank Underhill on, intellectual historians in Canada have urged their discipline on the profession as a way of understanding social and political change and, ultimately, the Canadian character. The formal history of ideas, which might otherwise provide a refuge, is weakly developed in Canada and even recent work done in the history of institutions and ideas included in their rationale the understanding of such externalist themes as social reform and political action.

Nor is the charge by Akenson and others completely without foundation. Intellectual historians, drawing upon the literary and elitist traditions existing within the field, have often made gross generalizations based on too few sources or on inappropriate ones. All too often, a few rhetorical flourishes by a few individuals have been taken as proof of a whole generation's way of thought. The reality of an historical circumstance can fade into irrelevance in the face of the search for the metaphor, for the formal ideologies, for the single moving force of an age.

Yet Akenson's comment about intellectual history is really one that applies no more to this sub-field than to any other, including social history. All historians have been capable of building castles in the air and the reality of history can just as easily fade away behind numerical tables as behind symbols and myths. His message is really one that applies equally to the profession as a whole and which has a lesson for social historians like himself. History isn't just a game. It is an attempt to accurately recreate actual occurrences. Therefore, the historian must try as much as possible to comprehend the whole set of forces which were arrayed in the shaping of a society at any given time. Akenson's comment is really about bad history, wherever it might occur.

There will always be bad history, of course, but the dominant trends of recent years show some cause for optimism rather than despair. Recent theses, books, and articles indicate that both intellectual and social historians are learning from each other. Intellectual historians are taking into account, with increasing frequency, the hard and fast institutional and social context in which ideas developed. In other words, the emphasis on external relationships continues but with greater attention to the linkages between idea and action. In all areas there is, at least in the better work, a care not to overgeneralize or to detach rhetoric from reality.

For its part, social history seems to be taking more and more account of ideas. The concept of the *mentalité*, as has been mentioned, has always existed among certain social historians, but most recent works have been less willing to make glib generalizations about the state of mind and have actually gone out and investigated what that state of mind was. Thus, a study of labour relations provides us with the most accomplished analysis of Mackenzie King's ideology.[47] A study of World War One gives us one of the best accounts of the transformation of the idea of nationality that occurred in the minds of Members of Parliament.[48] In a micro-study of the Canadian frontier there exists one of the best accounts of the outlook of the capitalist farmer.[49]

In all cases these works remove social and political history at least one step from behaviouralist roots. The mind, as even many Marxist historians now admit, is a powerful and autonomous force rather than just a reflex responding to material conditions. The intellectual historian, on the other hand, has for the most part long been willing to see ideas as determined by the physical and social environment of the time. The points of contact thus already exist and there is more common ground than many on either side might admit. Tensions will continue to exist, of course, but these are no more a reason for crisis now than they were a generation ago.

So what are the challenges? Where is intellectual history likely to go in the next generation? First, it is very possible that the sort of cultural-historicist studies of higher education will spread, not only to other institutions and individuals, but downward to the ideas and ideologies embodied in the school system and related institutions. Recently educational historians like Allison Prentice have written of important themes in this area that raise all sorts of possibilities for intellectual historians.[50]

The serious study of ideas intermixed with close examination of the specific institutions in which those ideas emerged is already a well-established tradition in Canadian intellectual history. It is also the intellectual historians' version of the sort of behaviouralist-idealist mix that has been displayed in recent social history. The trend, in other words, may be away from the sweeping myth and symbol school of the 1960s — though that field will continue, for its very generalizations are often what make intellectual history so exciting — and towards a sort of historicism, smaller in its focus, but containing within it implications of importance for the larger canvas of history. Nearly two decades ago J.M.S. Careless argued that Canadian history had to focus on the concept of "limited identities" rather than on a single national experience.[51] It may be that this is what is occurring in intellectual history.

Some will argue that this cedes too much to social history and that intellectual history will cease to have a separate existence. On a serious level one could note that the perspectives will always remain different as will the balance between the study of the ideas and the institutions. On a more frivolous note one might say, as a final friendly rejoinder to the critics of intellectual history, that, on the contrary, this may represent the final triumph of intellectual history as it absorbs the remnants of social history into its own web. What is more important than the conceit of any sub-discipline, however, is the accurate and lively re-creation of the past. The ways that can contribute to this should and will thrive. Those that cannot will wither. Otherwise historians are not doing their job.

Endnotes

1. John Higham, "Intellectual History and Its Neighbours," *Journal of the History of Ideas* 15 (June 1954), 340.

2. Laurence Veysey, "Intellectual History and the New Social History," in *New Directions in American Intellectual History*, eds. John Higham and Paul Conklin (Baltimore, 1979), 4.

3. Leonard Krieger, "The Autonomy of Intellectual History," *Journal of the History of Ideas* 32 (Dec. 1973), 501.

4. Clarence Karr noted this sneering phenomenon. See his article "What is Canadian Intellectual History?" *Dalhousie Review* 55 (1975), 431.

5. Vernon Parrington, *Main Currents in American Thought* (New York, 1927); Merle Curti, *The Growth of American Thought* (New York, 1943); Joseph Haroutunian, *Piety Versus Moralism: The Passing of New England Theology* (Hamden, Connecticut, 1964); Perry Miller, *The New England Mind: The Seventeenth Century* (New York, 1939).

6. Franklin Baumer, "Intellectual History and Its Problems," *Journal of Modern History* 21 (September 1949), 191-203, provides a good example of the early assertion of intellectual history as a distinct field in the United States and of its appropriate parameters.

7. Perry Miller, *The New England Mind: From Colony to Province* (New York, 1953); Henry Nash Smith, *Virgin Land: The American West as Symbol and Myth* (New York, 1950).

8. Louis Hartz, *The Liberal Tradition in America: An Interpretation of American Political Thought Since the Revolution* (New York, 1955).

9. See, as two early examples, Margaret Ellis, "Loyalist Attitudes," *Dalhousie Review* 15 (October 1935), 320-34; and D.C. Harvey, "The Intellectual Awakening of Nova Scotia," *Dalhousie Review* 13 (April 1933), 1-22.

10. There is considerable material on Underhill. See Carl Berger, *The Writing of Canadian History*, 2d ed. (Toronto, 1986), Ch. 3; Douglas Francis, *Frank Underhill: Intellectual Provocateur* (Toronto, 1986).

11. Frank Underhill, "Some Aspects of Upper Canadian Radical Opinion in the Decade Before Confederation," in Canadian Historical Association, *Annual Report*, 1927, 46-61.

12. Frank Underhill, "The Development of National Political Parties in Canada," *Canadian Historical Review* 16 (December 1935), 367-87.

13. F.H. Underhill, "Some Reflections on the Liberal Tradition in Canada, " Canadian Historical Association Presidential Address, 1946; reprinted in his *In Search of Canadian Liberalism* (Toronto, 1960), 5-7, 11, 20-21.

14. Carl Berger, *The Writing of Canadian History, 221.*

15. Donald Creighton, "Sir John A. Macdonald and Canadian Historians," *Canadian Historical Review* 29:3 (March 1948), 1-13.

16. J.M.S. Careless, "Mid-Victorian Liberalism in Canadian Newspapers, 1850-1867," *Canadian Historical Review* 31 (1950), 221-36.

17. Elizabeth Wallace, *Goldwin Smith: Victorian Liberal* (Toronto, 1957).

18. See also Clarence Karr, "What is Canadian Intellectual History," *Dalhousie Review* 55 (1975).

19. W.S. Wallace, "The Life and Work of G.M. Wrong," *Canadian Historical Review* 29 (1948), 229-39; J.K. McConica, "Kingsford and Whiggery in Canada," *Canadian Historical Review* 40 (1959).

20. See, as an example, John Irving, "The Development of Philosophy in Central Canada, from 1850 to 1900," *Canadian Historical Review* 31 (1950), 252-87.

21. Frank Underhill, "Some Reflections on the Liberal Tradition in Canada," 6.

22. On Canadian historical writing generally and nationalism see Ramsay Cook, "La Survivance English Canadian Style" in his *Maple Leaf Forever* (Toronto, 1971). On intellectual history and nationalism see A.B. McKillop, "Nationalism, Identity, and Canadian Intellectual History," *Queen's Quarterly* 81 (Winter, 1974), 533-50.

23. M.C. Urquhart and K.H. Buckley, *Historical Statistics of Canada* 2d ed. (Ottawa, 1983), W1-9.

24. S.F. Wise: "Sermon Literature and Canadian Intellectual History," in *Canadian History Before Confederation: Essays and Interpretations*, ed. J.M. Bumsted

(Georgetown, 1979), 248-62; "Upper Canada and the Conservative Tradition," in *Profiles of a Province*, ed. Edith Firth (Toronto, 1967), 19-33; and S.F. Wise and R.C. Brown, *Canada Views the United States: Nineteenth Century Political Attitudes (Toronto, 1967)*.

25. S.F. Wise, "Sermon Literature," 250.

26. *Ibid.*, 249-50.

27. For two recent examples of work that continues the Wise debate see Jane Errington, *The Lion and the Eagle and Upper Canada: A Developing Colonial Ideology* (Montreal, 1987); David Mills, *The Idea of Loyalty in Upper Canada* (Montreal, 1988).

28. Carl Berger: "Race and Liberty: The Historical Ideas of Sir John George Bourinot," Canadian Historical Association, *Report*, 1965; "The True North Strong and Free. The Myth of the North in Canadian History," in *Nationalism in Canada*, ed. P. Russell (Toronto, 1966); Norman Shrive, *Charles Mair, Literary Nationalist* (Toronto, 1965).

29. Carl Berger, *Sense of Power: Studies in the Ideas of Canadian Imperialism*, 1867-1914 (Toronto, 1970).

30. My thanks to Ramsay Cook for this information.

31. Ramsay Cook, *The Politics of John W. Dafoe of the Free Press* (Toronto, 1963).

32. Karr, "What is Canadian Intellectual History,"; McKillop, "Nationalism, Identity and Canadian Intellectual History"; J.M. Bumsted, "Canadian Intellectual History and the Buzzing Factuality," *Acadiensis* 7:1 (Autumn 1977), 115-21.

33. Cited in Serge Gagnon, *Quebec and Its Historians 1840 to 1920* (Montreal, 1982), 116. On Grouix see S.M. Trofimenkoff, ed., *Abbé Groulx: Variations on a Nationalist Theme* (Toronto, 1973).

34. D. Monière, *Le développement des idéologies au Québec* (Montreal, 1977).

35. Along this line see Yvan Lamonde, "Les biblioteques de collectivites à Montréal, (XVII-XIX siècles)" (Montreal, 1979). Of course interest in important institutions like the church did not die because of the reaction against earlier historical viewpoints. See Fernand Porter, *L'instruction catechistique du Canada: deux siècles de formation religieuse*, 1633-1833 (Montreal, 1949).

36. Serge Gagnon, *Quebec and Its Historians: The Twentieth Century* (Montreal, 1988), 164.

37. Fernand Ouellet, *Histoire économique et sociale du Québec, 1760-1850: structures et conjecture* (Montreal, 1966).

38. S.D. Clark, "Religious Organization in the Development of the Canadian Community," Part 2 of his *The Developing Canadian Community* (Toronto, 1962).

39. G. Stewart and G. Rawlyk, *A People High Favoured of God: The Nova Scotia Yankee and the American Revolution* (Toronto, 1972).

40. Richard Allen, *The Social Passion: Religion and Social Reform in Canada, 1914-28* (Toronto, 1971).

41. A.B. McKillop, *A Disciplined Intelligence: Critical Inquiry and Canadian Thought in the Victorian Era* (Montreal, 1979). Another example of the growing emphasis on ideas comes in S.E.D. Shortt's, *Search for an Ideal: Six Intellectuals and Their Convictions in an Age of Transition* (Toronto, 1976).

42. Carl Berger, *Science, God and Nature in Victorian Canada* (Toronto, 1983); Ramsay Cook, *The Regenerators: Social Criticism in Late Victorian English Canada* (Toronto, 1985); Doug Owram, *The Government Generation: Canadian Intellectuals and the State, 1900-1945* (Toronto, 1986); Marlene Shore, *The Science of Social Redemption: McGill, The Chicago School, and the Origins of Social Reform in Canada* (Toronto, 1987).

43. Thomas P. Socknat, *Witness Against War: Pacifism in Canada, 1900-1945* (Toronto, 1987); Frank Milligan, "Eugene Forsey: An Intellectual Biography" (Ph.D. diss., University of Alberta, 1987).

44. See in this area, David Marshall, "The Clerical Response to Secularization" (Ph.D. diss., University of Toronto, 1987).

45. For a good discussion of this from the American perspective see Laurence Veysey, "Intellectual History and the New Social History," in *New Directions in American Intellectual History,* eds. John Higham and Paul K. Conkin, (Baltimore, 1979), 3-26.

46. Donald Harmon Akenson, *The Irish in Ontario. A Study in Rural History* (Toronto, 1984), 353.

47. Paul Craven, *"An Impartial Umpire": Industrial Relations and the Canadian State* (Toronto, 1980).

48. John English, *The Decline of Politics: The Conservatives and the Party System* (Toronto, 1977).

49. Paul Voisey, *Vulcan: The Making of a Prairie Community* (Toronto, 1988).

50. Allison Prentice, *The School Promoters: Education and Social Class in Mid-Nineteenth Century Upper Canada* (Toronto, 1977).

51. J.M.S. Careless, "Limited Identities in Canada," *Canadian Historical Review* 50 (March 1969), 1-10.

4

Writing About Regions

John G. Reid

A t the University of Sherbrooke, Quebec, on June 9, 1966, Canadian historians gathered to hear the presidential address to that year's meeting of the Canadian Historical Association. Margaret A. Ormsby of the University of British Columbia began her remarks by declaring that "tonight I speak as a Westerner...."[1] Ormsby, whose many studies of the history of her native province had been synthesized eight years before in her *British Columbia: A History*, was by no means the first Westerner to be president of the association.[2] Nor was she the only one of its members to have recently written a major provincial history. William L. Morton's *Manitoba: A History* had appeared in 1957, and W. Stewart MacNutt's *New Brunswick: A History, 1784-1867* in 1963.[3] What made Ormsby's address significant, however, was not just her opening assertion of a regional identity but also the subtlety of her interweaving of regional and national themes. Despite the idealistic pronouncements of the federalists who spurred Canada's westward expansion between 1869 and 1871, she argued, the lasting reality was that "it would be desperately difficult to secure the articulation of regional economies and of disparate cultural traditions." The process would be, in some important respects, destructive rather than creative. The historically multi-racial character of

71

Manitoba, for example, would be overrun by "the society of Upper Canada."[4] Nevertheless, the west had remained distinct from other regions, and any historical understanding of Canada as a whole would have to take account of the diversity so evident to the generation of Ormsby's pioneer grandparents: "that this is a country where there is such a succession of landscapes that only a few hold intimacy for any one individual."[5]

I

Margaret Ormsby's reflections in 1966 indicated an important shift that was taking place among Canadian historians of the mid-1960s, in their approaches to the relationships between regional and national history. Regional history was not new at that time. Studies of local communities, of provinces, and of regions that might embrace more than one province, had been produced in large numbers by both amateur and professional historians since the nineteenth century. In Quebec and in the west, such works were commonly regarded as essential to a correct understanding of Canadian, and North American, history. Quebec's pre-eminent historian of the second quarter of the twentieth century, the Abbé Lionel-Adolphe Groulx, wrote from the standpoint of a religious and cultural nationalism which urged Quebecers to nurture their own historically-developed character and values, with the rest of Canada seen as an important but outside influence. Groulx, and those of his more secular-minded students — such as Michel Brunet and Guy Frégault — who as professional historians in later years would adopt a "neonationalist" approach attuned more to analysis of social class than to Groulx's conservative values, would have rejected any suggestion that they were regional historians of Canada. They were, rather, national historians of Quebec. Nevertheless, in a Canadian context, the existence of distinct traditions of historical writing in Quebec served to underline the complexity of the Canadian past.[6] In the west, historians such as Walter N. Sage and W.L. Morton argued explicitly that regionalism was an essential fact of the Canadian experience. Sage, whose explorations of British Columbian and Canadian history were strongly influenced by the "frontier thesis" of United States history, suggested in 1937 that Canada consisted of five regions — the Maritimes, Quebec, Ontario, the Prairies, and British Columbia — each of which had more in common with neighbouring areas of the United States than with the other parts of Canada.[7] Morton, nine years later, vigorously denounced the centralist bias of most English-Canadian historical writing. That Canadian history should ignore the historical experience of other regions, he argued, confirmed that Confederation had operated as "an instrument of injustice."[8]

Regional interpretations, however, continued until the 1960s to exert only a limited influence on Canadian historiography as such. The "Laurentian thesis" had emerged in the 1930s as the main tool by which English-language historians attempted to fashion a coherent interpretation of Canada's economic and social development. Closely related to the 1930 study of *The Fur Trade in Canada* by the University of Toronto political economist Harold Innis, the Laurentian theory found its clearest exponent in Donald Creighton, a historian at the same university. According to Creighton in his *The Commercial Empire of the St. Lawrence* (1937), the building of Canada as a nation had depended on the trading networks, overland and overseas, developed by the merchants of the St. Lawrence valley.[9] Their commercial success had provided the economic basis for national development, and they provided leadership in extending the influence of central Canada east and west.

The thesis proved attractive for a number of reasons. It provided a readily understandable explanation of Canada's past, and one that could be applied to a host of specific problems of interpretation. It also rang true in the experience of the first half of the twentieth century, a time during which central Canada had emerged as the dominant commercial and manufacturing area of a maturing national economy, especially after the industrial capacity of the Maritime provinces had been devastated by the regional economic crisis of the 1920s. Creighton extended the Laurentian emphasis in political history with his biography of John A. Macdonald. The two volumes of this study, published in 1951 and 1955, contributed powerfully to the tenor and focus of history written in the 1950s and early 1960s. English language historians of Canada increasingly considered nation-building to be the proper subject for study, and favoured Creighton's approach: the political biography based on the centralist principles of the Laurentian thesis.[10]

By the late 1960s regionalists and other historians had begun to criticize these assumptions. Political biography focused on the activities of a wealthy, male, Anglo-Celtic elite, and the advocates of more trenchant social analysis called for studies of the experience and the creative influence of the working class, of women, and of disempowered ethnic groups. These were the years of student insurgency in the universities, and younger historians — as well as some who were not so young — rebelled against what they saw as the complacency of the historical establishment. Meanwhile, unprecedented nationalist activity in Quebec heightened the political significance of the work of historians. In Quebec, the writings of Brunet, Frégault, and their University of Montreal colleague Maurice Séguin, suggested that Quebec's historical development could lead readily to political sovereignty. In English Canada the fear of Canadian disunity led to agonized attempts to define the elusive identity of the country. In 1967 Ramsay Cook, a University of Toronto historian, reflected on the problem and offered a novel approach. "Perhaps," he argued, "instead of constantly deploring our lack of identity, we should attempt to understand and explain the regional, ethnic, and class identities that we do have. It might just be that it is in these limited identities that 'Canadianism' is found...."[11]

Historians sceptical of centralist bias quickly embraced Cook's striking phrase, "limited identities." It was elaborated in an influential article in 1969 by J.M.S. Careless. Careless connected regionalism with his own earlier work on metropolitanism — the suggestion that all across Canada there were cities that functioned as the centres of regional economies. He pointed also to the geographical size and ethnic diversity of the country. "The union of 1867," Careless declared, "was in large degree a coming together of regions and so has remained: regions articulated or integrated under a central régime, but surely not reduced or unified thereby."[12]

The indications of a new interest in regional history continued to mount. Also in 1969 came the publication of the proceedings of a series of seminars held in 1967 as the Canadian Historical Association's contribution to Canada's centennial celebrations. The seminars in Victoria, Saskatoon, Sudbury, Quebec, and St. John's, had focused on the theme, "Regionalism and the Canadian Community, 1867-1967." The resulting book did not, admittedly, go so far as to applaud Canada's regional character. Among the purposes of the project, wrote the editor, Mason Wade, was "to break down a still persistent regionalism by bringing together participants from all parts of the country and from both basic cultures to consider jointly their common national problems."[13] Nevertheless, the sixteen articles offered a formidable array of regional scholarship, and some among the authors were fully prepared to celebrate regionalism. G.A. Rawlyk of Queen's University, for example, published another article that year in *Queen's Quarterly*, in which he predicted the beginning of "a new golden age of Maritime historiography." A new generation of scholars with interests in social history, and especially in the post-Confederation era, would transform historical understanding of that region.[14]

Rawlyk was correct. Nowhere was the new emphasis on regional study more enthusiastically welcomed than in the Maritime provinces and Newfoundland. Although it is difficult to isolate particularly influential works from what became a flood of high-quality scholarly writing on Atlantic Canadian history, the studies of T.W. Acheson, E.R. Forbes, and David Alexander can serve as major examples. Acheson's seminal article of 1972, "The National Policy and the Industrialization of the Maritimes, 1880-1910," exploded the myth that the Maritimes had always been an industrially backward part of Canada. The region *had* industrialized in the late nineteenth century, Acheson insisted, but had then seen its economy reduced to branch-plant status by the imperialistic interventions of central Canadian financial centres. Forbes documented the decline of the Maritimes' political influence in Ottawa, the series of damaging federal policies in the early twentieth century which the region was powerless to resist, and the all-too-brief Maritime Rights movement in the 1920s. Alexander, meanwhile, used detailed analytical techniques in economic history to make what was not only an academic but also a political and ethical argument: small societies such as Newfoundland (and by extension Atlantic Canada as a whole) could be economically healthy if they were not obstructed by the self-serving policies of more populous areas even within the same Confederation.[15] The determination of these and other historians to right past wrongs gave emotional as well as intellectual energy to the cause of regional scholarship. The new journal *Acadiensis*, begun in 1971, provided an important forum for such viewpoints. P.A. Buckner declared in his opening editorial that the Fredericton-based journal was intended "to encourage scholarship in an area badly neglected by historians and only infrequently dealt with in established journals."[16]

As Buckner pointed out, Atlantic Canada, unlike all other parts of Canada, lacked an established journal of its regional history. Even so, *Acadiensis* was not the only new initiative. In 1968, *B.C. Studies* had begun publication in Vancouver, as an interdisciplinary journal of which one of the two founding editors, Margaret Prang, was a historian. *Prairie Forum*, the journal of the Regina-based Canadian Plains Research Center, was inaugurated in 1976; interdisciplinary in scope and edited by a geographer,

Alexander Paul, it published a substantial proportion of historical articles.[17] The approach of western historians was also changing. In British Columbia, ethnic complexity received unprecedented attention in works such as Robin Fisher's *Contact and Conflict: Indian-European Relations in British Columbia, 1774-1890*, and the studies of the origins of the prejudice encountered by British Columbians of Chinese and Japanese origin written by Patricia Roy and W. Peter Ward.[18] Prairie historiography, meanwhile, also saw a flowering of native and ethnic studies, along with works in urban history and political history seen in relation to society and economy. By the mid-1980s, works of synthesis by authors such as J. Arthur Lower and Gerald Friesen had made modern interpretations of Prairie history more accessible than ever before.[19]

In the west as well as in Atlantic Canada, there was a strong undercurrent of scepticism of the historiographical *and* the political pretensions of central Canada. Regionalists tried in the late 1970s to come together in parts of Canada that had all too often been regarded as outlying hinterlands. Joint sessions of the Atlantic Canada and Western Canada Studies Conferences were held in Fredericton and Calgary in the spring of 1978. Meanwhile, David Jay Bercuson's introduction to a collection of essays in western and Maritime history entitled *Canada and the Burden of Unity* summed up the discontent. "What emerges from this book," Bercuson declared, "is a picture of the power of Central Canada, manifest through the federal government and other 'national' institutions, which has created regional disparity and imposed its own version of national character and ambitions on Westerners and Maritimers."[20]

Such charges, at a time when the approach of the Quebec referendum on sovereignty-association seemed to put the entire future of Canada in jeopardy, pushed regionalism's claims too far for some. University of Manitoba historian Lovell Clark attacked the "irrationalism" of the contributors to Bercuson's book and of all riders on "the bandwagon of regionalism."[21] By now such early advocates of the regional approach as Cook and Careless — while not writing in the same acerbic vein as Clark — were beginning to reconsider, as articles in the early 1980s revealed. Careless, writing in *Manitoba History* in 1980, noted the "strenuous chorus of dissatisfactions voiced from Newfoundland to British Columbia," and complained that regional historians had drawn an "over-simple dichotomy" between "the poor but honest good guys of 'the hinterland'... [and] the scheming, greedy autocrats of 'the metropolis'...." Cook, writing three years later in *Acadiensis*, suggested that "as a tool of analysis, 'regionalism' is a concept whose time has gone."[22] Such comments did not dismay the advocates of the regional approach. William G. Godfrey, for example, reflecting in *Queen's Quarterly* in 1984 on the fifteen years that had passed since Rawlyk's "Golden Age" article in that journal, identified "the new sense of confidence, creativity, and accomplishment found today in Maritime studies."[23] But regionalists also recognized that much less impressive progress had been made in inducing historians of national subjects to incorporate diverse regional experiences.[24] Regionalism as an approach to Canadian history was alive and well. But it had its detractors. Their criticisms deserved — and still deserve — serious consideration by the proponents of the regional approach.

II

So why take a regional approach to Canadian history? The first answer to the question is almost a cliché. Nevertheless, it bears repeating. A vast and diverse country, Canada has had an accordingly varied historical experience. The physical environment of the Maritime provinces differs from that of the Canadian Shield. Both are different from the Arctic islands, from the coast of Labrador or the coast of British Columbia. And so on. Partly in response to these environmental variations, and also because of differing cultural traditions, the social characteristics of aboriginal peoples have developed an immense diversity. Apart from the fundamental distinctness of Inuit and Indian peoples, it is clear enough that, say, the Haida and the Mississauga, the Iroquoian peoples and the Dene can be sharply distinguished not only by language but also by social and cultural character. There is an authentic native experience in Canada, cutting across these divisions, an experience that can be defined by the original common elements of native societies and by the need to respond to the colonial attempts of non-native people. Nevertheless, the native experience in Canada can never be defined by a crude lumping together of distinct cultures.

Furthermore, over the past five centuries, the historical experience of both native and non-native peoples had proceeded according to quite different time scales, varying according to region. In Newfoundland, the Maritimes, and Quebec, European contact began in the early sixteenth century — perhaps even earlier along parts of the Atlantic coast — and colonization got under way seriously early in the seventeenth century. Through the fur trade, contact was then extended quickly to parts of the west and the north. Actual settlement by non-native colonists, however, was a phenomenon of the eighteenth century in Ontario, and of the nineteenth in the territories further west. In the meantime, the original settlers in both Acadia and Quebec had undergone a colonizing experience of their own, with conquests by Great Britain in 1710 (Acadia) and 1759-60 (Quebec). In Acadia, the conquest was followed forty-five years later by the expulsion of the majority of the Acadian people and by resettlement of the Maritime region by successive waves of British and British-sponsored settlers, while in Quebec British immigrations created a situation where an English-speaking minority long exercised a disproportionate share of economic and political power. By the time the western prairies were colonized in the nineteenth century, the immigrants included large numbers of eastern Europeans as well as British and French. British Columbia also received these immigrant groups, as well as substantial Asian immigration. In the North, meanwhile, the colonization experience of native people came later yet. Even in the late twentieth century there are many areas where the non-native presence is evident more in technological and cultural change than in the presence of any substantial non-native population.

The political economy of Canada also evidences regional variations. Confederation in 1867 brought together two quite different economies: that of New Brunswick and Nova Scotia, based mainly on seaborne trade, and the more diverse and continentally-oriented economy of Quebec and Ontario. The National Policy introduced by the federal government in 1879 attempted through industrial development and new transportation links to integrate these original economies and those of Prince Edward Island, Manitoba, and British Columbia, which entered Confederation during the 1870s. The creation of the provinces of Saskatchewan and Alberta in 1905 underlined the extent to which the prairie wheat-belt had emerged — albeit on the basis of unrealistically optimistic expectations — as another major component of the national economy.[25] Newfoundland's entry in 1949 added a much longer-established, sea-based economy. During the decades following the Second World War, mineral exploitation and economic development in the north continued the series of changes in Canada's post-Confederation political economy. These had proceeded conspicuously along regional lines even though dominated consistently – brief florescences of energy-led prosperity in Alberta and Newfoundland during the late

1970s and early 1980s notwithstanding – by the populous and heavily industrialized areas of central Canada and, to a lesser extent, southern British Columbia.

It is tempting simply to stop at this point. Surely the profound environmental, cultural, social, economic, and political variations within Canada, not to mention the different chronological patterns that have affected their interactions, make the case for regional history? The question is not so much why a regional approach is needed, but rather what other kind of approach could possibly be valid. In general terms, that kind of certainty seems well-justified. I have argued elsewhere that the most convincing general histories of Canada written in recent years are those that have been sensitive to regional variation.[26] Nevertheless, although one may sketch broadly the regional outlines of Canadian history, history is – or should be – a precise discipline, and at some point even the advocate of a regional approach has to confront the problem of how to define a "region". Given that Canada itself is a politically defined entity, one obvious way of recognizing a region is to use political criteria. A region would be an area politically identifiable as less than the nation itself, but more than a locality. When expressed in such a simplistic way, however, this definition is unsatisfactory: it could apply just as well to a province as to a region. Some scholars have even argued that the entire concept of a region is an unnecessary complication of what is really a straight-forward principle, namely, that Canada is a country composed of provinces. "Why not call a region what it really is," asked Ramsay Cook in 1983: "a province."[27]

Yet this problem becomes acute only if it is assumed that the terms "province" and "region" are in competition with one another. Cook's comment was made in a review of a multi-authored study of Canadian geography published in 1982: *Heartland and Hinterland*, edited by L.D. McCann. The book divided the country into "heartland regions" — the industrialized areas of Quebec and Ontario — and the other, "hinterland" regions. In the preface, McCann defined a region as "a homogeneous segment of the earth's surface with physical and human characteristics distinct from those of neighbouring areas." Regional identity, he continued, was shaped by "the interplay of land, economy, and society," by "a group consciousness that voices regional grievances and demands," and by "the behaviour of society as expressed most commonly through political actions."[28] McCann, therefore, chose to define region in terms that gave a prominent place to political culture. Cook was right to point out that a province could fulfil the criteria. Nevertheless, by incorporating economic and environmental factors, and the existence of a group consciousness, McCann had fashioned a definition that could also be applied to wider areas made up of more than one province or territory.

Thus defined, the notions of region and province are not mutually exclusive. To portray the essential truth that the Canadian historical experience has been diverse, the historian might use a province as an essential tool of analysis. British Columbia, for example, can readily be seen as a distinct region. So, with qualifications, can Quebec and Ontario. Quebec, as a national society in itself, obviously cannot be seen simply as a region, but in a pan-Canadian context a clear case can be made for treating it as such. Until the 1970s, Ontario was rarely perceived as a region, as the intellectual historian Carl Berger remarked in 1986: "possessing no tradition of regional grievance, having confidently accepted its dominant role within Confederation, Ontario had simply been confused by historians with the country as a whole."[29] Given the new historiographical interests that had arisen from the late 1960s on, that kind of confusion is no longer possible, or at least no longer excusable.

More complex, however, are questions of regionalism in the north, on the prairies, and in Atlantic Canada. As Bruce Hodgins and Shelagh Grant commented in a 1986 review article on the historiography of the north, "by any recognizable descriptive definition, Canada's North is certainly more than one region."[30] There is no merit in forcing together disparate, though neighbouring, parts of Canada for the sake of an apparently tidy regional division. The same objections can be raised for ill-considered efforts to make of the Maritimes and Newfoundland a homogeneous region of Atlantic Canada, or to assume a similar homogeneity for the prairie provinces. The political scientist Roger Gibbins, for example, identified in 1980 elements of "mythology and even romance" in portrayals of regionalism in western political culture.[31]

Used crudely or uncritically, therefore, the concept of regions that transcend provincial and territorial boundaries does not help to advance the cause of understanding Canadian history. Used carefully, it can be a powerful tool for doing so. Gibbins' study argued that since the Second World War "a new prairie society" had emerged in which provincial self-interest, rather than any sense of regional identity, increasingly dominated political culture. Nevertheless, Gibbins based his conclusions on a thorough analysis of "the ascent of regionalism" from 1905 to 1939.

During these years, he maintained, the grain economy combined with ethnic and social characteristics to create "a relatively distinct and homogeneous socio-economic region within Canada."[32] That regional identity may not be permanent or immutable does not mean that it has not existed; the mutability simply imposes on the historian a responsibility to define the concept properly and use it with care.

Morris Zaslow, publishing in 1971 a pioneer study of *The Opening of the Canadian North, 1870-1914*, opted for a wide definition based on the recognition that " 'North-West' and 'North' are more than geographical expressions. They also constitute a process: the advance of frontiers and frontier experience from the rear of the Province of Canada to the prairie northwest, then gradually northward along several fronts to the northern coasts of Canada and the islands beyond." For a later period, this definition would not have been defensible, but for Zaslow's purposes it was precise and workable.[33] David Alexander published in 1978 an essay entitled "Economic Growth in the Atlantic Region, 1880 to 1940." In a political sense, of course, no Atlantic region existed during those years, since Newfoundland joined Canada only in 1949. Nevertheless Alexander, who declared his intention to "encourage historians of the Atlantic region to make more efforts to bridge the Cabot Strait," delivered a convincing analysis in which "economic and social similarities" made it worthwhile to consider the Maritimes and Newfoundland together, and concluded by assessing the consequences for each of their respective decisions of the 1860s for and against confederation.[34] Ernest R. Forbes, in his 1979 study of the Maritime Rights movement of the 1920s — subtitled "A Study in Canadian Regionalism" — dealt with the concept of region in a similarly painstaking way. Rather than assuming the existence of a Maritime region, Forbes traced early developments in a chapter on "the birth of a region" within Confederation. His detailed consideration of Maritime Rights proceeded from his demonstration that the movement "had its roots firmly grounded among the deepest concerns and aspirations of the people — aspirations of a political, social, and cultural nature which were seriously threatened by the relative decline of the Maritime provinces in the Canadian dominion."[35]

One of the major reasons, therefore, for writing about the history of regions in Canada is that the country's experience has been so diverse that the only way to understand it fully is to start from an accurate awareness of regional variation. In part, this can be supplied through the history of provinces and territories. But these political divisions do not always adequately express the complex realities produced by the interaction of environment, economy, and society. Larger regions have existed. Given careful definitions in space and time, their exploration by historians yields insights important to all of Canadian history.

III

The development of regional study as a branch of historical enquiry is not confined to Canada. Regional micro-studies have assumed importance in historical fields studied internationally: rural history, migration history, the history of various ethnic groups, and aspects of North American colonial history, are examples. In these areas, Canadian regional historians have been influenced by colleagues in France, the British Isles, the United States, and elsewhere, and have contributed in turn. The growth of regional history in Quebec — involving, that is, regions *within* Quebec — is one major example. During the 1960s Quebec historiography underwent a profound transition, as social and economic approaches were used to revise the nationalistic interpretations of scholars such as Brunet, Frégault, and Maurice Séguin. The publication of Fernand Ouellet's *Economic and Social History of Quebec, 1760-1850* in 1966 was especially influential.[36] Ouellet directly challenged the "neo-nationalists" of the University of Montreal, who had blamed the British conquest for distorting Quebec's social and economic development in the eighteenth and nineteenth centuries. Instead, Ouellet argued, the conquest had had little socio-economic effect. Rather, a profound agricultural crisis in the early nineteenth century had led to a "hardening of mentalities" and thus to an unprecedented degree of traditionalism in rural areas.[37]

Ouellet's book was not primarily a study of regions. The author was concerned with structural change in the Quebec economy as a whole. Indeed, he acknowledged an intellectual debt to, among others, Innis and Creighton for their earlier economic interpretations of the significance of the St. Lawrence Valley. The debates immediately stimulated by the appearance of the *Economic and Social History* likewise concentrated on the general question of the socio-economic development of Quebec.[38] Nevertheless, Ouellet's methodology contributed to setting the historiography of Quebec in a new direction. Influenced by the French *Annales* school of historians, Ouellet sought to write a "quantitative and comprehensive history."[39] Detailed analysis of every aspect of economy and society — *histoire totale*, in the phrase most closely associated with the *Annales* school — would lead to an understanding of underlying social structures, of cycles of economic change, and of the changes in society and mentality that result from the impact of one on the other. Although some of the *Annales* historians pursued their studies on a grand scale — Fernand Braudel's *The Mediterranean and the Mediterranean World in the Age of Philip II* is the prime example — others recognized that the ideal of *histoire totale* could also be approached by taking a more limited subject. As the French historian Emmanuel LeRoy Ladurie showed in his 1966 study of *The Peasants of Languedoc*, the sharp focus of regional study could produce a more precise version of *histoire totale* than could works with a wide scope and an unmanageably large body of source materials.[40]

Accordingly, regional studies began in the 1970s to assume a prominent place in Quebec historiography. Louise Dechêne's 1974 study of both urban and rural life in Montreal and its vicinity in the seventeenth century was directly influenced by the *Annales* methodology.[41] Later in the decade, Normand Séguin published the results of minutely-detailed research on the history of a single parish in the Saguenay-Lac Saint-Jean region, Notre Dame d'Hébertville. Séguin showed that the harsh realities of life in this new community in the second half of the nineteenth century were far from the idealized view of agriculture that historians had associated with the efforts of the Quebec clergy at that time to promote rural life by "colonizing" new areas of land. On the contrary, the Hébertville pioneers experienced hard individual struggle, regional underdevelopment, and the oppressive influence of large outside-owned timber companies.[42] Gérard Bouchard, also writing on the Saguenay-Lac Saint-Jean region, was less severe on the role of the timber companies but suggested other reasons for underdevelopment, connected especially with remoteness from the metropolitan influence of Quebec City. Bouchard's studies formed part of a major group research project in historical demography, which sought to trace settlement and migration patterns in Saguenay-Lac Saint-Jean.[43]

Thus, as Quebec regional studies developed, new themes and approaches appeared. While still influenced by the *Annales* school, historians such as Séguin and Bouchard also drew upon development theories — such as Andre Gunder Frank's *Capitalism and Underdevelopment* — and thus linked Quebec regional history with studies of uneven development elsewhere.[44] The work of Bouchard and his colleagues also set the Saguenay-Lac Saint-Jean case in the context of settlement and migration studies in other parts of North America. While they found that the religious and linguistic homogeneity of the Saguenayan population contrasted with the diversity of migrant populations in Ontario and in the United States, there were other respects — reproduction patterns and the extreme mobility of the inhabitants — in which similar patterns could be identified. Saguenay-Lac Saint-Jean, therefore, could be considered within a North American-wide comparative framework designated "frontier studies."[45]

Migration studies have also been central to the development of regional history in Ontario. Of all Canada's provinces, Ontario has been least associated with regional history. Yet, studies of the region have produced a long-established journal of provincial history in *Ontario History*, and a large collection of scholarly books, published since 1971 in the Ontario Historical Studies Series. Ontario has also contributed regional micro-studies that, like those in Quebec, are significant far beyond the boundaries of the province. The works of David Gagan on Peel County, for example, again portrayed a society in which people moved around so frequently that in any ten-year period the majority of the families traced in the county at the beginning would have left by the end of the decade. By the 1850s and 1860s, Gagan argued, Peel County was facing a crisis of declining availability of land for a growing population: a situation which may well have had an effect on the stimulation of Ontario's interest in the prairie west. Gagan's work thus had clear affinities with that of Bouchard and of migration historians elsewhere in North America, as well as contributing to Canadian history as such.[46]

In a different context, the 1987 study by Chad Gaffield of the origins of the controversy over French-language schooling in Ontario also showed the wide significance which regional studies may have. Focusing on Prescott County, in the Ottawa Valley, Gaffield set the politics of language in the context of family economies and demographic change. Thus, the book's conclusions related not only to the history of Franco-Ontarians and of French-English relations in Canada, but also gave a vivid sense of the creation of ethnic identity as "part of the history of family strategies, of children and parents coming to grips with the world they face."[47] The work of Donald Akenson on Irish migration to rural central Ontario explored another manifestation of ethnic identity. In *The Irish in Ontario*, Akenson concentrated on Leeds and Lansdowne townships and challenged the accepted wisdom of many previous historians of Irish migrants, who had assumed that the Irish, incapable of settling successfully into rural and small-town life, instead congregated only in large urban areas. In Leeds and Lansdowne, by contrast, Irish-Catholic farmers formed a local elite, and Akenson concluded that Irish migrants were "much less circumscribed by putative cultural limits inherited from the Old Country than is usually believed."[48]

A further example of regional ethnic research that has wider historiographical implications can be found in the work of J.M. Bumsted on Scottish emigration to the Maritime colonies. In an *Acadiensis* article which argued in 1981 that "Scottish — mainly Highlander — immigrants to the Maritimes constituted one of the powerful components of the exodus which departed from Britain [before 1815] in defiance of public attitudes," Bumsted concluded that "these were not demoralized refugees, but a people who saw British North America as a positive alternative to their situation at home." This article was followed the next year by a study of Scottish emigration from 1770 to 1815 in which the above conclusion emerged as the theme.[49] Bumsted's subsequent work on the early development of the land question and of political culture on Prince Edward Island did not focus so closely on the Scots, but also had both regional and transatlantic significance. Prince Edward Island's early history, Bumsted insisted, was not that of a colony condemned to inconsequentiality by its small size: "comparisons with heavily populated West Indian islands were common among those who saw [for it] a great future...." Thus, the struggles to find solutions to the Island's problems over the politics of land ownership represented an issue that was important in the larger history of the British Empire as well as in the history of the Island itself.[50]

The field of seventeenth- and eighteenth-century colonial history in the Maritime region offers additional evidence of the combination of regional study with an international historiography. French Acadia functioned in the context of close economic links with New England, and after the conquest of 1710 these were supplemented in British Nova Scotia by political contacts and eventually linkage by means of north-eastward migration. The end of the American Revolution brought renewed migration, with the Loyalist influx to British North America. Thus, studies that have explored the subtle implications of Acadian-New England contacts have had both a regional and a North American historiographical significance.[51] Similarly, work on the Great Awakenings in Nova Scotia in the late eighteenth century has dealt with communities populated by migrants from New England and their descendants, and with a movement that had a significant effect on New England itself, and so belonged to the religious history of the United States as well as that of the Maritime region.[52] Studies of the Loyalist refugees are likewise necessarily to be understood in a North American context. Loyalist ambitions to create a model colonial community in New Brunswick, for example, reflect the earlier experiences of the New Brunswick Loyalist leaders, while the rapid loss of a Loyalist sense of identity had some of the refugees slipping quietly back to resume their lives in the very United States they had once so much despised.[53]

The study of regional Canada thus contributes to fields of historical analysis that have significance beyond Canada itself. Regional historians in Canada have responded to international historiographical movements and, consequently, their works have found readerships outside of Canada. If regional study has sometimes been regarded as parochial, and unduly narrow in scope, the international historiographical affinities of so much current regional scholarship go far towards refuting such charges.

IV

Writing the history of Canada's regions is an integral part of the writing of Canadian history, and lends itself readily to comparative and transnational approaches. But regional history can also be self-sustained. The history of a region belongs to the community just as much as to historians. Amateur local historians — people who do not make a living from practising history — have rarely overlooked this truth. Professional historians, to their own ultimate loss, have all too often done so. Traditionally, a wide gulf has been assumed to exist between the aims of the "local historian" and the professional: the local historian tells a story for the benefit of a purely local readership, the professional historian deals with broader, more analytical issues, and writes for a widespread but largely academic audience. While, as with most stereotypes, there is a certain amount of truth in these characterizations, the distinction is by no means absolute. Donald Akenson, for example, specifically described his book on the Irish in central Ontario as a "local study," primarily based as it was on the townships of Leeds and Lansdowne; yet the book was the work of a professional historian, published by an academic press.[54] By comparison, Marion Robertson, author of a 1983 history of the early years of Shelburne, Nova Scotia, would be described by personal interests and background as a local historian; yet nobody, professional or otherwise, could dispute the insight provided by her thoroughly-researched book into the early Loyalist experience.[55] Both books, in short, have much to offer to academic and non-academic readerships alike.

To be sure, distinctions can be made. The main goal of a work of non-academic local history may well be to inform community members of their own past, of the traditions that are important to the community itself. The main goal of the professional, academic historian writing about local or regional subjects may well be to further an analysis relating to the national experience, to *histoire totale*, or whatever larger subject may be at hand. In this context, incidentally, the difference between "local" and "regional" is not a sharp one: a "local" study such as that of Akenson can be seen as a contribution to the regional history of central Ontario as well as to the history of Canada and of the Irish. Similarly, the influential New England community studies completed in the 1970s by a number of academic historians could be seen as contributions to the regional history of New England as well as to the history of North American colonization and of the United States.[56] The term "region" generally implies an area larger than a locality, but the difference is — within the limits imposed by McCann's definition cited above — one to be expressed on a continuum rather than sharply drawn. The important point is that for the academic historian a local or regional subject may often be studied as part of the process of answering a larger question.

Larger question or not, one of the developments that has accompanied the rise of regional history since the late 1960s has been an increasing acceptance by professional historians of responsibilities towards the communities they study. One such responsibility is to take seriously the contributions made by non-academic historians who, as David Sutherland has recently commented, "repeatedly call attention to vital aspects of our past which, till now, have suffered serious neglect."[57] Another is the responsibility to reclaim the past from neglect and distortion. Regional history is valid for regions of all sorts. Nevertheless, it is noticeable that the deepest commitment to the regional approach has been in so-called "hinterland" regions — those neglected and politically alienated regions whose historians have had to grapple with the question of how neglect and alienation originated. All too often, the causes are interrelated: regional economic and social underdevelopment has led to a conventional wisdom that the important events of history must have happened elsewhere. As Carl Berger has remarked, the new regional historians of the 1960s and 1970s responded that "history was not something that happened somewhere else — it happened in *this* place and was therefore worthy of attention and study."[58]

Therefore, regional historians can and should set out to rescue the regional past from damaging myths and stereotypes, some of which have been created or perpetuated by other historians. The notion that the Maritime provinces have been mired in a continuous economic depression since the 1870s, with the implied canard that the region has always been the poor cousin of Confederation, surfaces too often even in recent general histories of Canada. This idea deserves all the scorn that Maritime regional historians can heap on it.[59] Other mythologies have begun as romantic ideas and evolved into something more sinister. Another Maritime example provides an illustration: the invention during the 1920s and 1930s of Peggy's Cove, Nova Scotia, as a supposedly quaint Maritime fishing village in a traditional mould. As the historian Ian McKay has shown, this "pastoral vision" has, in recent years, grown from a pure romance into an assiduously cultivated tourist promotion which bears scant resemblance to the historical reality of Peggy's Cove or of coastal Nova Scotia.[60] Sometimes myths are created by governments for political reasons. When the government of Prince Edward Island chose to celebrate the hundredth anniversary of the province's entry into Confederation by eulogizing the benefits that had followed for the Island, it did so at a time when it had recently signed a controversial economic agreement with Ottawa. Two historians — Harry Baglole and David Weale — led a public counter-campaign. Arguing that "the Centennial Commission is, in fact, trivializing Island history," they went on to maintain, in the introduction to a book on *The Island and Confederation*, that the province was, by 1973, in the throes of "the second major installment of the Confederation crisis."[61]

The regional historian provides accessibility to the past as well as reclaiming it by attacking myths and stereotypes. Scholars need to be open to the insights of non-academic historians and they must be willing to put their own work at the disposal of the communities they study. Academic historians, regionally or nationally, have not traditionally done well at meeting this challenge.[62] However, Gerald Friesen's *The Canadian Prairies: A History* suggested what could be achieved by an author who set out to use the "most recent scholarly research" in a book intended for the general reader. Friesen succeeded in giving due weight to both the native — Indian and Métis — and the non-native experience of the region over a period of four centuries.[63] Conferences can also, occasionally, fulfil the same purpose. The joint Atlantic Canada and Western Canada Studies Conferences of 1978, with their sessions in Fredericton and Calgary, were promoted as "the Great Chautauqua" and managed to attract a total attendance of over six hundred.[64] The same year an international convention on Acadia and the Acadians held at the University of Moncton attracted an audience of both academic and non-academic historians. The convention in turn inspired a demand for "a wide-scope study...of the whole Acadian reality" which was published in 1980 by an interdisciplinary group of specialists in Acadian studies.[65] A further example of a conference which successfully brought together participants from academic and non-academic backgrounds was the twenty-third congress of the Quebec federation of historical societies, which met in Chicoutimi in May 1988. Devoted to celebrating the one hundred and fiftieth anniversary of colonization efforts in Saguenay-Lac Saint-Jean, it included a keynote address by Gérard Bouchard and a variety of presentations on other topics concerning the region.[66] Anniversaries, although sometimes distorting history, have at times occasioned significant studies, such as the book edited by John Norris in 1971 on the history of ethnic groups in British Columbia.[67]

Regional history does not exist in isolation from the community. Although the academic regional historian does not write solely for a community readership, the tasks of reclaiming the past and making it accessible are important responsibilities, especially for those who write about hitherto neglected regions. In this respect, regional historians have much in common with, say, the women's historians who declare that "the first task of the feminist historian...is the simple retrieval of women from obscurity," or with the editors of a collection of lectures in labour and working-class history who define their purpose as being "to make more accessible to Canadian workers their own history."[68] In Canadian regional history there are balances to be restored, and historiographical inequities to be put right. The fulfilment of that task may even contribute to the righting of political and socio-economic inequities in the future.

V

In a lecture delivered in 1981 and published a year later, R. Cole Harris spoke of "the Canadian Archipelago." Although a political map might give the misleading impression that Canada contained a vast area populated from east to west and from north to south, Harris argued that, in reality, the country had been settled as a series of "islands" and that settlement had remained "disjointed and discontinuous."[69] It was significant that this statement was made by an historical geographer, since the regional approach implies a spatial preoccupation that gives it clear affinities with the discipline of geography. Historical geographers have often provided fuller analyses of the Canadian past in regional terms — in McCann's *Heartland and Hinterland*, in the earlier *Canada Before Confederation* by Harris and Warkentin, and most recently in the *Historical Atlas of Canada* — than have historians.[70] Nevertheless, during the years since 1966, when Margaret Ormsby illustrated Canada's regional character by evoking – as did Harris in describing the "archipelago" – the lights flickering upwards amidst stretches of darkness that could be seen on a night flight across Canada, historians have also explored the phenomenon of regional variation.[71]

They have done so in diverse ways and with diverse aims. Carl Berger was right enough in observing in 1986 that regional studies had "displayed no unanimity about the basic unit of analysis, the region...."[72] Yet, as long as careful definitions of region were maintained in particular studies, there were compelling reasons for adopting the regional approach — reasons which could command wide acceptance even among historians of widely varying approaches and methodologies. The Canadian historical experience has been complex, and only if its regional variations are understood can it be properly interpreted. Regional analysis also links Canadian history with the wider international world of historical interpretation. The process brings comparative insights to Canadian history and allows the Canadian experience to contribute in turn to international historiographical developments. Finally, regional history can serve regional and local communities by contributing to the reclamation of the past from mythologies that, notably in areas that have suffered from economic underdevelopment, have often been as false as they are demeaning.

The future agenda of regional historians in Canada will undoubtedly continue to be influenced by these considerations. The 1990s should see the persistence of efforts to synthesize regional perspectives with those of other revisionist fields, and the steady reinterpretation of Canadian history accordingly. Region, until the late 1960s, was as much a neglected aspect of Canadian history as were class, gender, and ethnicity. Now that all of these have had two decades of specialized study, with the accumulation of large bodies of scholarly writing, it is time that the results were embodied in a redrawing of historical contours. There is scope, as Barry Ferguson has pointed out in a recent review of regional, class, and ethnic studies in Prairie historiography, for "vigorous debate about the interrelations of these factors": regionalism can never be a static or an isolated concept.[73] Nevertheless, regional diversity is a crucial element of Canada's historical experience, as some general histories have recognized.[74] Regional historians must press for more recognition until, in the words of Phillip Buckner and David Frank, "our national historiography really does incorporate the insights contained in journals like *Acadiensis....*"[75] Insofar as all of this involves the righting of historiographical inequities, one hopes that it will prove to be a task that will not go on forever. In the longer term, though, Canadian historians will be — or at least should be — writing about regions as long as Canadian history is written.

Endnotes

1. Margaret A. Ormsby, "Presidential Address," in Canadian Historical Association, *Historical Papers Presented at the Annual Meeting Held at Sherbrooke, June 8-11, 1966*, eds. John P. Heisler and Fernand Ouellet, 1. I thank Professor M. Brook Taylor for helpful comments on the first draft of this chapter.

2. Margaret A. Ormsby, *British Columbia: A History* (Toronto: Macmillan, 1958).

3. W.L. Morton, *Manitoba: A History* (Toronto: University of Toronto Press, 1957); W.S. MacNutt, *New Brunswick: A History, 1784-1867* (Toronto: Macmillan, 1963).

4. Ormsby, "Presidential Address," 8-9.

5. *Ibid.,* 1.

6. Susan Mann Trofimenkoff: *Action française: French Canadian Nationalism in the Twenties* (Toronto: University of Toronto Press, 1975), 90-91; *The Dream of a Nation: A Social and Intellectual History of Quebec* (Toronto: Gage, 1983), 218-32; Yves F. Zoltvany, *The Government of New France: Royal, Clerical, or Class Rule?* (Scarborough, Ont.: Prentice-Hall, 1971), 90-92.

7. W.N. Sage, "Geographical and Cultural Aspects of the Five Canadas," in Canadian Historical Association, *Annual Report*, 1937, 28-34. Because Sage was writing before 1949, Newfoundland did not appear in his analysis, either as a region in itself or as part of a larger Atlantic region.

8. W.L. Morton, "Clio in Canada: The Interpretation of Canadian History," *University of Toronto Quarterly* 15 (1945-6), 232.

9. Harold Adams Innis, *The Fur Trade in Canada: An Introduction to Canadian Economic History* (New Haven: Yale University Press, 1930); D.G. Creighton, *The Commercial Empire of the St. Lawrence, 1760-1850* (Toronto: Ryerson Press, 1937). See also Carl Berger, *The Writing of Canadian History: Aspects of English-Canadian Historical Writing Since 1900,* 2d ed. (Toronto: University of Toronto Press, 1986), Ch. 4,9.

10. D.G. Creighton: *John A. Macdonald: The Young Politician* (Toronto: Macmillan, 1951); *John A. Macdonald: The Old Chieftain* (Toronto: Macmillan, 1955). See also Berger, *The Writing of Canadian History*, 221-22.

11. Ramsay Cook, "Canadian Centennial Cerebrations," *International Journal* 22 (1967), 663.

12. J.M.S. Careless: " 'Limited Identities' in Canada," *Canadian Historical Review* 50 (1969), 4; "Frontierism, Metropolitanism, and Canadian History," *Canadian Historical Review* 35 (1954), 1-21.

13. Mason Wade, ed., *Regionalism in the Canadian Community, 1867-1967: Canadian Historical Association Centennial Seminars* (Toronto: University of Toronto Press, 1969), vi.

14. G.A. Rawlyk, "A New Golden Age of Maritime Historiography?" *Queen's Quarterly* 76 (1969), 55-65.

15. T.W. Acheson, "The National Policy and the Industrialization of the Maritimes, 1880-1910," *Acadiensis* 1 (Spring 1972), 3-28; Acheson, "The Maritimes and 'Empire Canada'," in *Canada and the Burden of Unity*, ed. David Jay Bercuson (Toronto: Macmillan, 1977), 87-114; Ernest R. Forbes, "Misguided Symmetry: The Destruction of Regional Transportation Policy for the Maritimes," in *ibid.*, 60-86; Forbes, *The Maritime Rights Movement, 1919-1927: A Study in Canadian Regionalism* (Montreal: McGill-Queen's University Press, 1979); David G. Alexander, *Atlantic Canada and Confederation: Essays in Canadian Political Economy*, compiled by Eric W. Sager, Lewis R. Fischer, and Stuart O. Pierson (Toronto: University of Toronto Press, 1983).

16. P.A. Buckner, "Acadiensis II," *Acadiensis* 1 (Autumn 1971), 9.

17. *B.C. Studies* 1 (1968-9); *Prairie Forum*, 1 (1976).

18. Robin Fisher, *Contact and Conflict: Indian-European Relations in British Columbia, 1774-1890* (Vancouver: University of British Columbia Press, 1977); Patricia E. Roy, "The Soldiers Canada Didn't Want: Her Chinese and Japanese Citizens," *Canadian Historical Review* 59 (1978), 341-57; W. Peter Ward, *White Canada Forever: Popular Attitudes and Public Policy Toward Orientals in British Columbia* (Montreal: McGill-Queen's University Press, 1978). See also Allan Smith, "The Writing of British Columbia History," *B.C. Studies* 45 (Spring 1980), 73-102.

19. J. Arthur Lower, *Western Canada: An Outline History*, (Vancouver and Toronto: Douglas and McIntyre, 1983); Gerald Friesen, *The Canadian Prairies: A History* (Toronto: University of Toronto Press, 1984). See also Gerald Friesen, "Recent

Historical Writing on the Prairie West," in *The Prairie West: Historical Readings*, eds. R. Douglas Francis and Howard Palmer (Edmonton: Pica Pica Press, 1985), 5-18; and Barry Ferguson, "Limited Identities Without Pain: Some Recent Books on Prairie Regional, Class and Ethnic History," *Journal of Canadian Studies* 23:1 and 2 (Spring/Summer 1988), 219-34.

20. David Jay Bercuson, "Canada's Burden of Unity: An Introduction," in Bercuson, *Canada and the Burden of Unity*, 14. See also David Jay Bercuson and Phillip A. Buckner, eds., *Eastern and Western Perspectives: Papers from the Joint Atlantic Canada/Western Canada Studies Conference* (Toronto: University of Toronto Press, 1981).

21. Lovell Clark, "Regionalism? or Irrationalism?" *Journal of Canadian Studies* 13:2 (1978-9), 119-28.

22. J.M.S. Careless, "Limited Identities — Ten Years Later," *Manitoba History* 1 (1980), 3,6; Ramsay Cook, "Regionalism Unmasked," *Acadiensis* 13 (Autumn 1983), 141.

23. W.G. Godfrey, "'A New Golden Age' Recent Historical Writing on the Maritimes," *Queens Quarterly* 91 (1984), 372.

24. W.G. Godfrey, "Canadian History Textbooks and the Maritimes," *Acadiensis* 10 (Autumn 1980), 131-35; P.A. Buckner and David Frank, "Preface," *The Acadiensis Reader*, 2 vols. (Fredericton: Acadiensis Press, 1985), Vol. 1, 7-10; P.A. Buckner, "'Limited Identities' and Canadian National Scholarship: An Atlantic Provinces Perspective," *Journal of Canadian Studies* 23:1 and 2 (Spring/Summer 1988), 177-98.

25. See Doug Owram, *Promise of Eden: The Canadian Expansionist Movement and the Idea of the West, 1856-1900* (Toronto: University of Toronto Press, 1980), esp. 218-20; David C. Jones, *Empire of Dust: Settling and Abandoning the Prairie Dry Belt* (Edmonton: University of Alberta Press, 1987), 5-19; David H. Breen, *The Canadian Prairie West and the Ranching Frontier, 1874-1924* (Toronto: University of Toronto Press, 1983), 167-70; John Herd Thompson, *The Harvests of War: The Prairie West, 1914-1918* (Toronto: McClelland and Stewart, 1978), 45-72.

26. John G. Reid, "Towards the Elusive Synthesis: The Atlantic Provinces in Recent General Treatments of Canadian History," *Acadiensis* 16 (Spring 1987), 107-21.

27. Cook, "Regionalism Unmasked," 140.

28. L.D. McCann, ed., *Heartland and Hinterland: A Geography of Canada* (Scarborough, Ont.: Prentice-Hall, 1982), vii.

29. Berger, *The Writing of Canadian History*, 284.

30. Bruce W. Hodgins and Shelagh Grant, "The Canadian North: Trends in Recent Historiography," *Acadiensis* 16 (Autumn 1986), 175.

31. Roger Gibbins, *Prairie Politics and Society: Regionalism in Decline* (Toronto: Butterworth, 1980), 12.

32. *Ibid.*, 58-9, 195-214; see also the discussion of western regionalism and the First World War in Thompson, *Harvests of War*, esp. 168-72.

33. Morris Zaslow, *The Opening of the Canadian North, 1870-1914* (Toronto: Mc-Clelland and Stewart, 1971), xi.

34. David Alexander, "Economic Growth in the Atlantic Region, 1880 to 1940," *Acadiensis* 8 (Autumn 1978), 47-76.

35. Forbes, *Maritime Rights*, 37. Forbes has written further on the regional theme in *Aspects of Maritime Regionalism, 1867-1927* (Ottawa: Canadian Historical Association, 1983); see also the discussion of Maritime regionalism over an even larger timespan in G.A. Rawlyk, ed., *The Atlantic Provinces and the Problems of Confederation* (St. John's: Breakwater, 1979), 1-47.

36. Fernand Ouellet, *Histoire économique et sociale du Queébec, 1760-1850* (Montréal: Fides, 1966); translated as *Economic and Social History of Quebec, 1760-1850* (Ottawa: Carleton Library, 1980).

37. Ouellet, *Economic and Social History*, 592.

38. *Ibid.*, xxiii; see also Gilles Paquet and Jean-Pierre Wallot, "Crise agricole et tensions socio-ethniques dans le Bas-Canada, 1802-1812: éléments pour une réinterprétation," *Revue d'histoire de l'Amérique française* 26 (1972-3), 185-237.

39. Ouellet, *Economic and Social History* xii, xxiii.

40. Fernand Braudel, *The Mediterranean and the Mediterranean World in the Age of Philip II*, 2 vols. (New York: Harper and Row, 1972-3; first published Paris, 1949); Emmanuel Le Roy Ladurie, *The Peasants of Languedoc* (Urbana: University of Illinois Press, 1974; first published Paris, 1966).

41. Louise Dechêne, *Habitants et marchands de Montréal au XVIIe siècle* (Paris and Montréal: Plon, 1976).

42. Normand Séguin, *La conquête du sol au 19e siècle* (Sillery: Boréal Express, 1977); see also Séguin, ed., *Agriculture et colonisation au Québec: aspects historiques* (Montréal: Boréal Express, 1980).

43. Gérard Bouchard, "Initiation a l'étude de la société saguenayenne aux XIXe et XXe siècles," *Revue d'histoire de l'Amérique française* 31 (1977-78), 3-27; Bouchard and Jeannette Larouche, "Dynamique des populations locales: la formation des paroisses rurales au Saguenay (1840-1911)," *Revue d'histoire de l'Amérique française* 41 (1987-88), 363-88.

44. Séguin, *La conquête du sol*, 29-37; Andre Gunder Frank, *Capitalism and Underdevelopment in Latin America: Historical Studies of Chile and Brazil* (New York: Monthly Review Press, 1967); Eric Sager, "Dependency, Underdevelopment, and the Economic History of the Atlantic Provinces," *Acadiensis* 17 (Autumn 1987), 117-37.

45. Bouchard and Larouche, "Dynamique des populations locales," 364-65. For a fuller discussion of the regional approach in Quebec history, see Camil Girard, "Développement et régions périphériques au Québec," *Acadiensis* 16 (Autumn 1986), 165-73.

46. David Gagan: "Land, Population, and Social Change: The 'Critical Years' in Rural Canada West," *Canadian Historical Review* 59 (1978), 293-318; *Hopeful Travellers: Families, Land, and Social Change in Mid-Victorian Peel County, Canada West*

(Toronto: University of Toronto Press, 1981). Gagan's works also had a considerable combined effect with the urban analysis of Michael B. Katz, *The People of Hamilton, Canada West: Family and Class in a Mid-Nineteenth Century Canadian City* (Cambridge, Mass.: Harvard University Press, 1976).

47. Chad Gaffield, *Language, Schooling, and Cultural Conflict: The Origins of the French-Language Controversy in Ontario* (Kingston and Montreal: McGill-Queens University Press, 1987), 189.

48. Donald Akenson, *The Irish in Ontario: A Study in Rural History* (Kingston and Montreal: McGill-Queens University Press, 1984), 353. Also including numerous regional studies from all parts of Canada are the essays contained in Donald Akenson, ed., *Canadian Papers in Rural History*, 6 vols. to date (Gananoque, Ont.: Longdale Press, 1978-88).

49. J.M. Bumsted, "Scottish Emigration to the Maritimes, 1770-1815: A New Look at an Old Theme," *Acadiensis* 10 (Spring 1981), 65, 85; Bumsted, *The People's Clearance, 1770-1815*, (Edinburgh and Winnipeg; Edinburgh University Press and University of Manitoba Press, 1982).

50. J.M. Bumsted, *Land, Settlement, and Politics on Eighteenth-Century Prince Edward Island* (Kingston and Montreal: McGill-Queens University Press, 1987), ix-x.

51. Jean Daigle, "Les relations commerciales de l'Acadie avec le Massachusetts: le cas de Charles-Amador de Saint-Etienne de La Tour, 1695-1697," *Revue de l' Université de Moncton* 9 (1976), 53-61; W.G. Godfrey, *Pursuit of Profit and Preferment in Colonial British America: John Bradstreet's Quest* (Waterloo, Ont.: Wilfrid Laurier University Press, 1982), 1.

52. Gordon Stewart and George Rawlyk: *A People Highly Favoured of God: The Nova Scotia Yankees and the American Revolution* (Toronto: Macmillan, 1972); Rawlyk, *Ravished by the Spirit: Religious Revivals, Baptists, and Henry Alline* (Kingston and Montreal: McGill-Queens University Press, 1984).

53. Ann Gorman Condon, *The Envy of the American States: The Loyalist Dream for New Brunswick* (Fredericton: New Ireland Press, 1984); Neil MacKinnon, *This Unfriendly Soil: The Loyalist Experience in Nova Scotia, 1783-1791* (Kingston and Montreal: McGill-Queens University Press, 1986).

54. Akenson, *The Irish in Ontario*, 333.

55. Marion Robertson, *King's Bounty: A History of Early Shelburne, Nova Scotia* (Halifax: Nova Scotia Museum, 1983).

56. Examples would be Philip J. Greven, Jr., *Four Generations: Population, Land, and Family in Colonial Andover, Massachusetts* (Ithaca, N.Y.: Cornell University Press, 1970); and Kenneth A. Lockridge, *A New England Town, the First Hundred Years: Dedham, Massachusetts, 1636-1736* (New York: Norton, 1970).

57. David Sutherland, "Parish Perspectives: Recent Work in Community History Within Atlantic Canada," *Acadiensis* 17 (Autumn 1987), 150.

58. Berger, *The Writing of Canadian History*, 282-83.

59. For further discussion, see Reid, "Towards the Elusive Synthesis," 113, 121.

60. Ian McKay, "Among the Fisherfolk: J.F.B. Livesay and the Invention of Peggy's Cove," *Journal of Canadian Studies* 23:1 and 2 (Spring/Summer 1988), 23-45.

61. David Weale and Harry Baglole, eds., *Cornelius Howatt: Superstar!* ([Summerside]: Williams and Crue, 1974), 81; Weale and Baglole, *The Island and Confederation: The End of an Era* ([Summerside]: Williams and Crue, 1973), 12.

62. See J.M. Bumsted, "Canadian Popular History in the 1980s," *Acadiensis* 16 (Autumn 1986), 188-97.

63. Friesen, *The Canadian Prairies*, xiii.

64. Bercuson and Buckner, *Eastern and Western Perspectives*, x.

65. Jean Daigle, ed., *Les acadiens des maritimes: études thématiques* (Moncton: Centre d'études acadiennes, 1980), 11; the work was translated as *The Acadians of the Maritimes: Thematic Studies* (Moncton: Centre d'études acadiennes, 1982).

66. *Nouvelles: bulletin de la fédération des sociétés d'histoire du Québec* 3:6 (February 1988), 1.

67. John Norris, ed., *Strangers Entertained: A History of the Ethnic Groups of British Columbia* (Vancouver: British Columbia Centennial '71 Committee, 1971). See also Smith, "The Writing of British Columbia History," 95.

68. Ruth Pierson and Allison Prentice, "Feminism and the Writing and Teaching of History," *Atlantis* 7 (Spring 1982), 41; W.J.C. Cherwinski and Gregory S. Kealey, eds., *Lectures in Canadian Labour and Working-Class History* (St. John's and Toronto: Committee on Canadian Labour History and New Hogtown Press, 1985), 7.

69. R. Cole Harris, "Regionalism and the Canadian Archipelago," in McCann, *Heartland and Hinterland*, 466.

70. McCann, *Heartland and Hinterland*; R. Cole Harris and John Warkentin, *Canada Before Confederation: A Study in Historical Geography* (Toronto: Oxford University Press, 1974); R. Cole Harris, editor, and Geoffrey J. Matthews, cartographer/designer, *Historical Atlas of Canada, Volume I: From the Beginning to 1800* (Toronto: University of Toronto Press, 1987).

71. Ormsby, "Presidential Address," 12.

72. Berger, *The Writing of Canadian History*, 289.

73. Ferguson, "Limited Identities Without Pain," 232.

74. An example is John Herd Thompson and Allan Seager, *Canada 1922-1939: Decades of Discord* (Toronto: McClelland and Stewart, 1985).

75. P.A. Buckner and David Frank, "Preface," in Buckner and Frank, eds., *The Acadiensis Reader, Volume One: Atlantic Canada Before Confederation* (Fredericton: Acadiensis Press, 1984), 9.

5

Writing About Rural Life and Agriculture[1]

John Herd Thompson

Canada was born in the country and moved to the city.[2] Today less than one-quarter of the population resides in rural areas, but in 1871 over eighty percent did so; the population of cities and towns did not outnumber that of the countryside until 1931. Only four percent of Canadians now live on farms, but in the first census after Confederation more than half of Canadian men reported their occupations as farmers or farm labourers. Until 1941 "workers in agricultural pursuits" (as the census-takers called farmers, farmers' sons, and hired hands) remained the largest category in the male labour force; if the uncounted hours of labour put in by farm wives had been formally recognized by the statisticians, agricultural workers would have been the largest single category within the female labour force as well.[3]

Until very recently, however, historians of Canada have had little to say about Canada's rural past. "The most striking characteristic of monograph material on Canadian agriculture," concluded V.C. Fowke in 1941, was "its scarceness"; forty years later the dean of American agricultural historians could echo Fowke's lament.[4] Few university history departments offer specialized courses in rural history, and few survey courses deal with it seriously. J.L. Finlay and D.N. Sprague's *The Structure of Canadian*

History (third edition, 1988), the most widely-used college and university text, has thirty-six index references for "Trudeau, Pierre" but not a single entry for "agriculture," "farm," or "rural." If historians of agriculture and rural life dared to brave the wrath of those who write women's history, they could argue with considerable justice that it is farm families who have been Canadian history's true "neglected majority."[5]

I

The historiographical neglect of this now-vanished rural majority was a symptom of the general indifference of historians of Canada to social history, the category to which the history of agriculture and rural life belongs. The methodological pioneers of rural history were the school of French historians whose name derives from that of the journal in which they published much of their work: *Annales d'histoire économique et sociale,* founded in 1929.[6] Rejecting political and diplomatic history, the *Annalistes* added the insights of the social sciences to the traditional tools of history and looked to the study of everyday life as a way to understand the totality of the past. "Agrarian history" as defined by Marc Bloch's *Les caractères originaux de l'histoire rurale française* (1931), became an important (although by no means the only) focus of their research.[7] But until the 1950s the *Annalistes* had little influence on French-Canadian historians and none at all on their English-Canadian counterparts. Political history and economic history of a very different sort remained the dominant genres within which the history of Canada was written.

Canadian economic history had no connection to the "economic and social" history in the title of *Annales.* Instead, it was written by political economists who worked within the analytical framework of the staple theory most closely identified with Harold Adams Innis (see Chapter 2, "Writing about Economics"). Obsessed with commodities exported to overseas markets, staple theorists discussed farming only as the provisioner of those who traded for furs or cut timber. Agriculture in and of itself became a subject worthy of study only when wheat became an export staple, as it did in Ontario between 1830 and 1860 and again during the western "wheat boom" of the first three decades of the twentieth century. In Easterbrook and Aitken's *Canadian Economic History* (1956), which remained the standard university text into the 1970s, two of the twenty-three chapters deal with the Ontario and western staple wheat economies; otherwise agriculture is resolutely ignored.[8]

Three political economists wrote most of the staple-theory agricultural history cited in *Canadian Economic History*: W.A. Mackintosh from Queen's and the University of Saskatchewan's George E. Britnell and Vernon C. Fowke. Individually or jointly, they contributed several books and dozens of articles: Mackintosh's *Economic Problems of the Prairie Provinces* (1935); Britnell's *The Wheat Economy* (1939); Fowke's *Canadian Agricultural Policy: The Historical Pattern* (1946) and *The National Policy and the Wheat Economy* (1957); and *Canadian Agriculture in War and Peace, 1935-1950* (1962) jointly authored by Britnell and Fowke.[9] Although the newest of them is a quarter-century old, they are very important books; they are, however, very much products of the staple theory. The authors emphasized the macro-economic problems of the wheat economy and were more concerned with its relationship to the national and international economy than with the internal structure of rural communities.

Constitutional and political history preoccupied Canada's academic historians, both French- and English-Canadian. Ramsay Cook suggests that this was an expression of their "overriding concern with survival, with nationalism," but whatever the cause, the result was that social history was "practically ignored in Canada." In 1970 there was so little of it that Cook could pronounce social history as "hardly even begun."[10] To historians whose mission was to define a nation, important events took place in parliament or at imperial conferences, not in farmhouses or at country markets. A handful of historians looked at agriculture and rural life from the perspective of immigration and settlement policy, but political history left no room for broader studies of agriculture and rural life.[11]

The one interpretive framework which might have connected these themes to political history was Frederick Jackson Turner's frontier thesis, which postulated that the frontier had been the crucible of democracy and egalitarianism. Whatever the merits of Turner's arguments (and recent scholarship suggests there are few) it became one of the major analytical frameworks for American political history, an interpretive framework which could accommodate rural history and which provided the farmer with a special place in the mythology of American nation-building.[12] Most historians of Canada, however, rejected frontierism as irrelevant to the Canadian experience. *The Canadian Frontiers of Settlement Series* (1932 to 1940),[13] the most extensive investigation ever undertaken of Canadian rural society, is sometimes mistakenly assumed to represent the triumph of Turner's ideas in Canada, but none of its nine volumes could be considered an endorsement of the frontier thesis. The general editor, W.A. Mackintosh, was a staple theorist, and the author of *Settlement and the Mining Frontier* (1936) was Harold Adams Innis himself.[14]

Instead of frontierism, historians of Canada embraced its obverse. As J.M.S. Careless argued in 1954, Canada "had far less fertile acreage for agricultural settlement than has the United States. Hence the agrarian frontier has played proportionately less part in our history."[15] Careless turned the frontier thesis on its head: instead of the frontier shaping Canadian development, it was "the metropolis" — London, Montreal, Toronto — which "had a determining influence over the hinterlands."[16] "Metropolitanism" made the rural majority even more peripheral to Canadian history. Explained in metropolitan terms, the "agrarian radicalism" of the Ontario Clear Grits drew its ideology more from "prominent business or professional men" of Toronto than it did from back-concession farmers, while the prairie progressive revolt of the 1920s found "a good deal of its intellectual leadership" in Winnipeg rather than among western wheat growers.[17] The dominance of two genres, economic and political history, and of two paradigms, the staple theory and metropolitanism, stunted and shaped the limited historiography of Canadian agriculture and rural life written before the mid-1960s.

This is not to say that nothing was written about agriculture and rural life outside these patterns. Non-historical work by social scientists deserves mention because of its usefulness to those writing rural history today: economist George V. Haythorne's *Land and Labour: A Social Survey of Agriculture and the Farm Labour Market in Central Canada* (1941), sociologist Jean Burnet's *Next-Year Country: A Study of Rural Social Organization in Alberta* (1951), and economist Charles Lemelin's work on "The Social Impact of Industrialization on Agriculture in the Province of Quebec."[18] Twenty articles on Canadian topics appeared in the American journal, *Agricultural History*, in the first thirty-five years after its establishment in 1927; these articles dealt with such diverse topics as Acadian grain banks, rural *caisses populaires* in Quebec, Ontario farm newspapers, Marquis wheat, and Okanagan apple marketing.[19]

But these articles were marginal to the mainstream of Canadian historiography. A glance through the first fifty years of *The Canadian Historical Review*, from 1920 to 1970, shows that fewer than thirty of the more than one thousand articles published could be considered to be rural or agricultural history by even the most generous definition of the term. As further evidence of the marginality of the rural majority, some of the most important contributions to its history were made by scholars who taught in American universities: Louis A. Wood's *History of Farmers' Movements in Canada* (1924); Robert L. Jones' *History of Agriculture in Ontario, 1613-1880* (1946); Paul F. Sharp's *The Agrarian Revolt in Western Canada* (1948); E.K. Francis's series of articles on Manitoba Mennonite rural communities;[20] and geographer Andrew Hill Clark's *Three Centuries and the Island: A Historical Geography of Settlement and Agriculture in Prince Edward Island, Canada* (1959).[21]

Social history matured as a genre in the 1960s and 1970s, as historians of Canada responded to Eric Hobsbawm's challenge to make social history "the history of society." But, in English Canada especially, these new social historians at first remained oblivious to rural history. Instead, their effort went into filling in other blanks (almost always in an urban setting) on the historiographical canvas — working class history, ethnic history, women's history, and histories of social reform.[22] Urban history quickly acquired sub-genre status, with its own journal and a multitude of practitioners who proudly defined their work as "the new urban history."

Why did these historians who wanted to uncover the lives of ordinary people and to "write history from the bottom up" resist the urge to look at the bottom of the manure pile? The generation of the 1960s was too open-minded to absorb the prejudices of an earlier generation; instead they evolved an anti-rural bias all of their own. As an American rural historian has suggested, rural/agricultural history, like rural-dwellers themselves, had an image problem. Rural people were seen as rustic reactionaries, the "Okie from Muskokie" in Merle Haggard's country and western song; therefore rural/agricultural history was also regarded as an anachronism.[23]

II

Almost imperceptibly, however, the forgotten rural majority began to find a more appropriate place in Canadian history. Canadian agricultural history acquired its first historiographical controversy when Fernand Ouellet's *Histoire économique et sociale du Québec, 1760-1850* touched off a heated and wide-ranging debate about Quebec agriculture during the first half of the nineteenth century.[24] Ouellet contended that Quebec had suffered a long-term "agricultural crisis" of declining yields brought about by the unwillingness or inability of French-Canadian *habitants* to modernize their farming practices. The same argument had been made by R.L. Jones twenty years earlier without anybody taking notice, but in the mid-1960s the question had new political significance. Canadian politics had been turned upside down by Quebec's demand for "equality or independence": Ouellet's "agricultural crisis" uncovered the roots of French-Canadian nationalism in the cultural despair which accompanied this alleged economic disaster a century and a half earlier. Almost immediately, Gilles Paquet and J.P. Wallot denounced Ouellet's explanation (with its demeaning view of the French-Canadian farmer) by denying that any such agricultural crisis had occurred.[25] Polemics flew and academic battle-lines formed; twenty years later the issue remains unresolved, but its political undertones at last won agriculture a niche within the historiographical mainstream. In addition to Ouellet and Paquet and Wallot, the quarrel has inspired articles by R.M. McInnis, Robert Armstrong, and Serge Courville, and formed a major theme of John McCallum's *Unequal Beginnings: Agriculture and Economic Development in Ontario and Quebec until 1870* (1980).[26]

Several of the articles appeared in the bi-annual journal *Histoire sociale/Social History*, launched in 1968 by an inter-disciplinary team at l'Université d'Ottawa and Carleton University. In its first years of publication, there were few articles specifically in rural history; what was important was that *Hs/SH* plugged Canada into an international milieu. The introductory statement to the first issue declared social history to be "the mother of all history," and dropped the names of Marc Bloch and a half-dozen of his colleagues;[27] subsequent issues featured articles and reviews by *Annaliste* Robert Mandrou and by British social history enthusiast Harold Perkin. Articles about techniques of quantification, research notes about methods of using sources like manuscript census questionnaires or probate court records, and lengthy reviews of important books in French and British rural history, all helped to create a context within which the history of rural Canada could grow. A young Canadian working in Paris summed up the importance of this new and broader context: "No European rural history will furnish us with models," concluded Louise Dechêne, but historians of Canada would find them invaluable for methodological guidance.[28] To use an obvious metaphor, the seeds sowed during the first ten years of *Hs/SH* yielded a heavy crop of excellent articles on rural topics in the journal's second decade.[29]

The inspirations for serious study of the countryside have not all been trans-Atlantic, however. Studies of rural communities in New England suggested other approaches,[30] as did the enthusiastic appeals of American Robert P. Swierenga for a "new rural history" which "would provide a necessary complement to the 'new urban history.'" His definition of rural history went beyond the histories of farming, agricultural marketing, and agrarian politics which had been done in the United States under the rubric of "agricultural history"; in Swierenga's vision the "new rural history" had to be "in the holistic tradition of Marc Bloch" and encompass "the systematic study of human behaviour over time in rural environments."[31]

Canadian rural history found its evangelist in Donald Harman Akenson, who founded and single-handedly edits the almost-annual journal *Canadian Papers in Rural History*. A Harvard-trained historian of rural Ireland, Akenson set out a bold manifesto for a "new rural history" of Canada in the foreword to his first issue:

> If we are to be true to the reality of the past, we must realize that until recently Canada was a rural nation...our history prior to World War II can only truly be understood if this fact is recognized. Further, as important as politicians and civil servants have been in shaping agricultural and rural social policy, the people themselves — literally the people working the ground — had more to do with shaping the country in its formative years than did their political superiors.... It was the people themselves who created the country, section by section, township by township.[32]

CPRH has grown steadily from the 109 pages which made up Volume I (1978) to the more than 350 pages of Volumes V (1986) and VI (1988). The fifty articles in the six volumes do not always live up to Akenson's manifesto, and vary widely in quality and significance; reviewers complain that they "range from the challenging, to the useful, to the puzzling and occasionally disappointing."[33] *CPRH*'s definition of "rural history" is never made explicit; some essays seem to be rural history only because their authors and the editor say they are. There are no unifying themes to individual volumes: Volume II, for example, includes an essay on the adoption of tractors in the prairie provinces, a methodological note on tracing property ownership in Ontario, a descriptive account of using "shell-mud" for fertilizer in Prince Edward Island, a study of an Ontario agricultural community, a paper on Scottish shipping, and a discussion of rural dialect in an Irish county. Whatever *CPRH*'s limitations, however, it is, in Ramsay Cook's words, "a major development in recent Canadian historiography" and required reading for students of the rural past.[34]

Akenson rejects any suggestion that his journal lacks a focus. He argues instead that the papers he publishes simply mirror the "diversity of scholarly viewpoints" from which Canadian scholars have begun to approach the rural past.[35] As the eclecticism of *CPRH* suggests, it is impossible to speak of a "school" of Canadian rural/agricultural history. It is still much easier to categorize historians by the regions that they write about than by their methodological approaches, which within each specific subject area are many and various, and which overlap and intersect.

Studies of individual communities are the backbone of rural history, but until very recently, "local" history has been a term of contempt among professional historians; they have left the field to amateurs, whose work they regard (sometimes with unwarranted snobbery) with disdain. There are literally thousands of these histories — one historian claims to have counted five thousand about communities in the prairie provinces alone.[36] Some local histories are worth attention,[37] but given the general level of these studies, even those that rise well above it are still not very important books. Paul Voisey has suggested ways in which they could be used as the basis for serious academic projects, but as he points out, virtually none of them have "significance that transcends the boundaries of the study area itself."[38]

Louise Dechêne's massive *Habitants et marchands de Montréal au XVIIe siècle* (1974) was the first scholarly study to meet this requirement. The importance of *Habitants et marchands* cannot be exaggerated: Dechêne was until that time "the only Canadian historian who ha[d] fully applied the best of the French [*Annaliste*] methodology."[39] Through a systematic examination of colonial censuses, notarial archives and parish registers, she painstakingly crafted a powerful portrait of population, commerce, agriculture, and their social setting during the first seventy years of French settlement of the Island of Montreal. As important as the example she set with her methods was the liberating effect of her conclusions. Dechêne lifted the dead hand of the staple theory by proving that the fur trade and agriculture had been largely unconnected, and swept aside the North American exceptionalism of the frontier thesis by demonstrating that the self-sufficient peasant agriculture of the countryside around Montreal shared many similarities with the peasantry of rural France. Dechêne's approach spread much faster among French-Canadian historians than their English-Canadian counter-parts, and by the mid-1970s, the influence of *l'École des Annales* dominated social historians in Quebec.[40]

It was not the only influence; other historians followed quantitative social historians in the United States in producing "microstudies" using evidence from "routinely-generated" records — the manuscript census[41] of population and agriculture, church registers, land records, tax assessments, wills — to reveal "the essential patterns and rhythms of life characteristic of an evolving...rural Canadian community." There is an astounding amount of such information — over two hundred individual pieces of information exist for each mid-nineteenth-century Ontario farm household, for example — and the records from each farm family had to be "linked" from census to census and through the different sources so that a dossier of information could be compiled.[42] Historians used computers to probe this mountain of data, and the enormity of the task meant that they worked in teams: the Peel County Historical Project, led by David P. Gagan, examined an Ontario county just west of Toronto from 1851-1871, while the Saguenay Project, directed by Gérard Bouchard, studied ten rural parishes around Chicoutimi, Quebec. The Peel County Project's results appeared as scholarly articles,[43] and in Gagan's *Hopeful Travellers: Families Land and Social Change in Mid-Victorian Peel County, Canada West* (1981). The Saguenay project remains active: Christian Pouyez *et al.*, *Les saguenayens: introduction à l'histoire des populations du Saguenay XVI-XXe siècles* was published in 1983 and articles by Bouchard and his colleagues continue to appear regularly. The notes of their most recent work provide the best bibliography of what has gone before.[44] Both teams have advanced important conclusions about rural demography. For example, they have found much greater geographical mobility than historians formerly imagined characterized rural life, and have challenged accepted notions of the way in which family farms were passed from generation to generation.

Individual historians have completed excellent local studies without the resources or the fanfare which accompanied the mega-projects: Normand Séguin on Notre-Dame-de-Hébertville, Quebec; J.I. Little on Compton County, Quebec; Darrell A. Norris on Euphrasia Township, Ontario; Lyle Dick on Abernethy and Neudorf, Saskatchewan; and Rusty Bitterman on Middle River, Nova Scotia.[45] When Allen Greer's *Peasant, Lord and Merchant: Rural Society in Three Quebec Parishes, 1740-1840* (1985) won the Sir John A. Macdonald prize, the Canadian Historical Association's most prestigious award, rural local history received symbolic recognition.[46] Rural historians make extensive use of quantitative evidence, but it is possible to do excellent work without using complicated techniques of statistical analysis, as Paul Voisey has shown in *Vulcan: The Making of a Prairie Community* (1988) a sensitive study of the development of a wheat-growing district in Southern Alberta.[47]

The social historians who write rural microstudies should not be confused with the "new economic historians" who write "econometric" history, however similar their mathematical methods might seem. These "cliometricians," as they are sometimes called, are almost all economists by discipline. They eschew the descriptive narrative which forms part of every historian's work, and instead explore specific hypotheses with models drawn from neo-classical economic theory. On occasion they employ a "counterfactual hypothesis" to ask what might have been if one of the variables in their model had been different. In the United States, "new economic historians" have taken on many agricultural history topics; in Canada they have largely confined themselves to two general questions. Kenneth Norrie, Robert Ankli, Trevor J.O. Dick, Frank D. Lewis, William Marr, and Michael Percy have assessed the significance of such variables as agricultural technique and technology, railway construction, and homestead and tariff policies in bringing about the settlement of the prairies;[48] their work has been useful in suggesting the limitations of the staple theory and dispelling the hardy myth that the "National Policy" created the prairie agricultural economy. R.M. McInnis, Frank Lewis, John Isbister, and Robert Armstrong have entered the Quebec "agricultural crisis" debate by comparing the efficiency of English- and French-Canadian farmers.[49] No one who wishes to study agriculture and rural life can ignore this work, particularly that of McInnis, but students should also be aware of its limitations. There are technical difficulties with econometric history,[50] but there is also a broader philosophical problem: many of the actions and emotions of the people who are the real subjects of history are impossible to explain through the calculus of the market.

Discussions of the agriculture of different ethnic groups, for example, have been better done by historians who push beyond "number-crunching," as Donald Harman Akenson does in *The Irish in Ontario: A Study in Rural History* (1984).[51] He sweeps aside the venerable stereotype of Irish immigrants as an urban proletariat and locates three-quarters of them in the countryside, where he finds them to be as good or better farmers than their non-Irish neighbours. But few ethnic historians in Canada have adopted Akenson's rural perspective. It is ironic that in the United States, supposedly the land of the "melting pot," studies of rural communities of European immigrants are the cutting edge of the "new rural history,"[52] while in Canada, which celebrates its pluralistic ethnic "mosaic," such studies are scarce. The ethnic groups most written about to date have been the Anabaptist religious sects, the Hutterites and the Mennonites;[53] Ukrainians, more numerous in the countryside, receive modern scholarly treatment only in the articles of geographer John C. Lehr.[54] Other groups await their historians. It's time to start asking some basic questions: What effects did ethnic differences have on rural settlement patterns and on agricultural practices? How many of the observable differences were the result of "cultural heritage" and how many had to do with such things as the physical environment in which groups settled and the capital available to them? Akenson's conclusion that the Irish in Ontario were "much less circumscribed by putative cultural limits inherited from the old country than is generally believed" deserves to be tested in studies of other ethnic agricultural communities. For this we need two kinds of comparative studies: comparisons among different ethnic groups within Canada and comparisons between the rural context of the migrant's homelands and that of Canada, as Dechêne does so effectively in *Habitants et marchands*.

Given the dynamism of feminist historians, it is surprising that there have been as yet few studies of rural women. Most of what has been published is based on (or is an edited version of) memoirs of individual women, on interviews, or, in one case, on women as portrayed in fiction.[55] The limitations of research dependent on unsystematic surveys of literary sources is obvious: how reliable and how representative can they be? There is much more to be said about farm women, and the most fruitful line of enquiry would seem to be an examination of women's economic role in the production process on the farm. In "The Decline of Women in Canadian Dairying," for example, Marjorie Griffin Cohen argues that the "great transformation" from self-sufficient to commercial production and the shift to factory production of butter and cheese undermined the economic importance of farm women.[56]

Unlike rural women who toil in obscurity, male farmhands are emerging from the no man's land between rural and labour history. Ten years ago a bibliography on farmworkers would have had exactly one item, a paper by David McGinnis; but articles by Joy Parr, John Herd Thompson, Allen

Seager, J.W.C. Cherwinski, and Cecilia Danysk have since joined the list.[57] It was once assumed that being a hired man was a stage a young man passed through on his way toward acquiring a farm of his own, but these historians describe farmworkers as more closely resembling a rural proletariat than apprentice farmers working their way up an "agricultural ladder" toward independence.

What dashed the hopes of many would-be proprietors was the ever-increasing cost of equipping a farm as agriculture underwent the "great transformation" from relative self-sufficiency to commercialism. Rural historians cannot study farm families without a better understanding of the evolving techniques and technology of farming, and the careful explanations in Paul Voisey's *Vulcan* have been equalled by few other historians. The discussions of the relationship of agricultural change to demographic change have, for example, been the weakest part of both the Peel County and Saguenay projects. There are as yet no Canadian monographs on the "great transformation" of agriculture to match Clarence Danhof's *Change in Agriculture: The Northern United States, 1820-1870* (1969), but David Spector, Claude Blouin, Alan E. Skeoch, and Ernest B. Ingles deserve credit for their research on the nuts-and-bolts aspects of agricultural history.[58] It is all very well to know the year a particular machine was invented; however, the history of its diffusion is more significant. Richard Pomfret, Robert Ankli, and R. Bruce Shepard have explored the pace at which new equipment has been adopted, but most innovative in this regard are Thomas D. Isern's investigations of "folk technology" — the ways in which farmers themselves adapted implements to unique local or regional conditions.[59]

The glaring failure in the modern social historians' attempts at "total history" has been the inability to integrate traditional political themes into their work. The standard books by W.L. Morton and Paul F. Sharp on the prairie agrarian insurgency which followed World War I, for example, are dated and do a poor job of relating politics to their socio-economic contexts.[60] With the partial exceptions of articles by Carl Betke, W.R. Young, David Monod, and Ian MacPherson,[61] most of the handful of modern studies don't do a much better job. Recent studies of the Saskatchewan Wheat Pool by Garry Fairbairn and of Quebec farmers unions by J.P. Kesteman not only lack a context in rural history but are both relentlessly favourable to their subjects.[62] Ramsay Cook and Russell Hann have explored the late-nineteenth century agrarian critique of industrial capitalism in the same terms that Lawrence Goodwyn does for the American populists in his

Democratic Promise: The Populist Moment in America (1976).[63] Beyond these studies, historians have abdicated the field to political scientists and sociologists, who repeat the same questions about the CCF in Saskatchewan and Social Credit in Alberta before reaching the unhelpful answer that farmers behaved as they did because they were a homogeneous class of "petit bourgeois independent commodity producers."

An *Annaliste* writing about early modern France can perhaps dismiss political history as peripheral to her work, but as a United States historian has argued, "In the modern era public events are not ephemera; they are often the central realities of everyday life. No individual, no community in modern America can live an isolated, unbroken life, insulated from the behaviour of the state."[64] Rural historians writing about post-Confederation Canada must deal with politics because government policies for colonization, land distribution, and marketing have been of critical importance to rural people. What we must do is relate the two; we must look at the way government policies affected the lives of rural communities. Wheat-marketing policy, for example, has been well-covered from an administrative perspective.[65] But the effects of the marketing system imposed by the Canada Wheat Board on individual farms and communities wait to be examined, as do the effects of most federal and provincial programs. Government actions (or failures to act) are not neutral. In the "great disjuncture" after World War II, they helped determine which farm families would survive and which would become statistics of rural depopulation. The dramatic restructuring of the Annapolis Valley apple industry and "the loss of local control which accompanied it," as Margaret Conrad has explained, "were deliberate policy decisions on the part of government."[66]

Some special resources for rural/agricultural history deserve mention. "Geography [went a tired old saw] is about maps and history is about chaps." Maps, however, are critical to historians of agriculture and rural life. The pathetic treatment of agriculture in D.G.G. Kerr's *An Historical Atlas of Canada* (1966) is partially compensated for by provincial atlases like John Warkentin and Richard I. Ruggles's *Historical Atlas of Manitoba* (1970). The encyclopedic *Historical Atlas of Canada*, of which Volume I, *From the Beginnings to 1800* (1987), has appeared, is indispensable. Volume II, *The Nineteenth Century* and Volume III, *Addressing the Twentieth Century*, will be of still greater utility when they appear.[67]

Statistical evidence is also vital to the study of agriculture and rural life. The two editions of *Historical Statistics of Canada* (1965 and 1982) provide aggregate data in abundance on the national and regional levels. The volumes of the *Census of Population and Agriculture*, taken in the first year of every decade since 1871, provide aggregate data for individual census districts within each province and territory.

Published collections of primary sources, often prepared by provincial historical societies, have long been a "staple" of Canadian historiography, but unfortunately there have been few on agriculture. Three recent volumes, each with an informative introductory essay, offer hope that this may be changing. James M. Nyce's annotated version of *The Gordon C. Eby Diaries, 1913-13: Chronicle of a Mennonite Farmer* (1982) gently reveals the seasonal rhythms of rural life; Wendy Owen's *The Wheat King: Selected Letters and Papers of A.J. Cotton, 1888-1913* (1985) opens up the commercial world of a spectacularly successful Manitoba grain grower; and David C. Jones's *We'll All Be Buried Down Here: The Prairie Dryland Disaster, 1917-1926* (1986) documents the spectacular failure of thousands of would-be "wheat kings" in the Alberta Dry Belt.[68]

III

What should be the agenda for writing the history of agriculture and rural life in the 1990s? As the historical gaps mentioned above suggest, there are many topics which deserve consideration — the problem is how to get them considered. Mass conversions to "the new rural history" seem unlikely. The approach that offers the most hope is to awaken historians working within other sub-genres to the existence of a rural majority. If, for example, ethnic historians examined agricultural block settlements, political historians looked at agrarian insurgencies, labour historians studied farm workers, and women's historians turned their attention to farm wives, rural history would be immensely better served. But for our forgotten rural past to be recreated, each of these studies must be carried out with an appropriate sensitivity to the rural context in which their subjects functioned. Rural history, after all, "is not simply the urban and industrial experience dressed in gingham and overalls."[69]

Rural histories of some regions are more desperately needed than of others. There is as much literature on Quebec as on the other regions combined: recent issues of the *Revue d'histoire de l'Amérique française*, the journal in which many historians of Quebec publish, might almost be titled

French-Canadian Papers in Rural History![70] Ontario is reasonably well-covered, but the literature about prairie agriculture is uneven and limited, considering the importance of agriculture historically to the region.[71] There are signs of stirring in the Maritimes, where there is a strong tradition of regional history and the excellent journal *Acadiensis*,[72] but a rural history bibliography of British Columbia would be very, very short.[73]

Must such histories always be regional? In their admirable summary "Agriculture, History of" in *The New Canadian Encyclopedia* (1988) Lyle Dick and Jeff Taylor divide their subject into regional sketches of the Maritimes, Quebec, Ontario, the Prairies, British Columbia, and the North. But some have been so bold as to hint that regional variations are not so great as to defy completely the possibility of using local and regional pieces as building blocks for a national synthesis, heretical as this may seem in the Canada of "limited identities." To cite two examples, Ian Winchester observes of the Peel County and Saguenay projects that "the similarity of their results and their conclusions" is "remarkable...given the wedge we tend to drive between the two founding cultures," and Peter Sinclair has compared the settlement of the clay-belts of Ontario and Quebec and found "many basic similarities between the two regions — both in government policy and settler behaviour."[74]

A synthesis would require studies on the twentieth century to extend the excellent work done on the nineteenth; instead of looking at the longue durée, historians of the twentieth century have been too preoccupied by short-term crises caused by war or depression.[75] A synthesis also requires a unifying conceptual framework. The concept of "modernization" seems the most useful. Rural communities underwent a "great transformation" from relative self-sufficiency to a stage at which self-sufficiency and commercial production were complementary, and then to the ever-greater commercialization which ended with the "great disjuncture" after 1940: the massive exodus from rural Canada and the reshaping of those who remained into a society which has become in many ways a rural echo of urban mass culture.[76] In the process, agriculture, which had once been a way of life, became a business. The notion of modernization, however, must not be interpreted as process that simply "happened" to passive rural communities as change from the metropolis "penetrated" the countryside. The forces of change were internal as well as external, and rural people shaped rather than simply succumbed to them.[77]

It took a long time for Canadian historians to rediscover their rural majority, but the exciting task of recreating the rural world we have lost is well underway.

Endnotes

1. Like all social history, histories of rural life cannot be compartmentalized neatly into periods bounded by dates drawn from constitutional or political history. Because some of the best work examines the pre-Confederation period, I will range back into the seventeenth, eighteenth, and nineteenth centuries as appropriate.

2. This is a rephrasing of Richard Hofstadter's insightful comment about the United States in *The Age of Reform: From Bryan to FDR* (New York, 1955), 23.

3. The statistics are from F.H. Leacy, M.C. Urquhart, and K.A.H. Buckley, eds., *Historical Statistics of Canada*, 2d ed. (Ottawa, 1983).

4. V.C. Fowke, "An Introduction to Canadian Agricultural History," *Agricultural History* 16:2 (1942), 84; Wayne D. Rasmussen in the *Journal of Economic History* 42:1 (1981), 216-17.

5. This claim is made (also with considerable justice) for women in Susan Mann Trofimenkoff and Alison Prentice, eds., *The Neglected Majority: Essays in Canadian Women's History* (Toronto, 1977).

6. The journal's title was changed to *Annales: économies, sociétés, civilisations* in 1946.

7. Bloch's book was not translated into English until 1966 as *French Rural History: An Essay on its Basic Characteristics* (Berkeley, 1966). For a brief general discussion, see F. Roy Willis, "The Contribution of the *Annales* School to Agrarian History," *Agricultural History* 52:4 (1978), 538-48.

8. W.T. Easterbrook and Hugh G.J. Aitken, *Canadian Economic History* (Toronto, 1956).

9. W.A. Mackintosh, *Economic Problems of the Prairie Provinces* (Toronto, 1935); George E. Britnell, *The Wheat Economy* (Toronto, 1939); Vernon C. Fowke, *Canadian Agricultural Policy: The Historical Pattern* (Toronto, 1946). Fowke and Britnell: *The National Policy and the Wheat Economy* (Toronto, 1957); *Canadian Agriculture in War and Peace, 1935-1950* (Stanford, Calif., 1962).

10. Ramsay Cook, *The Maple Leaf Forever: Essays on Nationalism and Politics in Canada* (Toronto, 1977), 96-147.

11. Two examples are Helen Cowan's *British Emigration to British North America* (1928); Norman Macdonald, *Canada 1763 to 1841, Immigration and Settlement* (London, 1939).

12. Steven Hahn and Jonathan Prude, eds., *The Countryside in the Age of Capitalist Transformation: Essays in the Social History of Rural America* (Chapel Hill, NC, 1985), 4-6.

13. Robert Murchie, *Agricultural Progress on the Prairie Frontier* (Toronto, 1936); Carl Dawson and Robert Murchie, *The Settlement of the Peace River Country: A Study of a Pioneer Area* (Toronto, 1934); Dawson, *Group Settlement: Ethnic Communities in Western Canada* (Toronto, 1936); Dawson and Eva R. Younge, *Pioneering in the Prairie Provinces: The Social Side of the Settlement Process* (Toronto, 1940); A.S. Morton, *History of Prairie Settlement* and Chester Martin's *Dominion Lands Policy*, (both Toronto, 1938); W.A. Mackintosh, *Prairie Settlement: The Geographical Setting* (Toronto, 1934); A.R.M. Lower, *Settlement and the Forest Frontier in Eastern Canada* (Toronto, 1941).

14. Harold Adams Innis, *Settlement and the Mining Frontier* (Toronto, 1936).

15. J.M.S. Careless, "Frontierism, Metropolitanism, and Canadian History," *Canadian Historical Review* 35:1 (1954), reprinted in *Approaches to Canadian History*, ed. by Carl Berger (Toronto, 1967), 82. One might challenge Careless's contention by pointing out that the amount of agricultural land *per capita* is similar in both countries, and the percentage of Canada's population engaged in farming has consistently remained about the same as that of the United States, but it is significant that no one spoke up to challenge his argument. Ramsay Cook provides a much better explanation of why the frontier thesis has little applicability to Canada in "Frontier and Metropolis: The Canadian Experience," in *The Maple Leaf Forever*, 148-57.

16. Carl Berger, *The Writing of Canadian History: Aspects of English-Canadian Historical Writing, 1900-1970* (Toronto, 1976), 174-78.

17. Careless, "Frontierism, Metropolitanism, and Canadian History," *passim*, but especially 81-2.

18. George V. Haythorne, *Land and Labour: A Social Survey of Agriculture and the Farm Labour Market in Central Canada* (Toronto, 1941); Jean Burnet, *Next-Year Country: A Study of Rural Social Organization in Alberta* (Toronto, 1951); Charles Lemelin, "The Social Impact of Industrialization on Agriculture in the Province of Quebec," *Culture* 14:1 (1953), 34-46.

19. Among these articles were: John D. Croteau, "The Acadian Grain Banks of Prince Edward Island," 30:3 (1955), 127-30; H.M. Thomas, "Agricultural Policy in New France," 9:1 (1935), 41-60; Allan Bogue, "The Progress of the Cattle Industry in Ontario during the 1880s," 21:2 (1947), 163-68; J.W. Morrison, "Marquis Wheat — A Triumph of Scientific Endeavour," 34:4 (1960), 182-88; Margaret Ormsby, "Fruit Marketing in the Okanagan Valley of British Columbia," 9:2 (1935), 80-97.

20. L. A. Wood, *History of Farmers' Movements in Canada* (Toronto, 1924); Robert L. Jones, *History of Agriculture in Ontario, 1613-1880* (Toronto, 1946); Paul F. Sharp, *The Agrarian Revolt in Western Canada* (Minneapolis, 1948); E.K. Francis, "Mennonite Institutions in Early Manitoba: A Study of their Origins," *Agricultural History* 22:2 (1948), 144-55; "The Adjustment of a Peasant Group to a Capitalist Economy: The Manitoba Mennonites," *Rural Sociology* 17:3 (1952), 218-28. Jones also contributed three articles on Lower Canada/Quebec: "French-Canadian Agriculture in the St. Lawrence Valley, 1815-1851," *Agricultural History* 16:3 (1942), 137-48; "The Agricultural Development of Lower Canada, 1850-1867," *ibid.* 19:4 (1945), 212-23; and "Agriculture in Lower Canada, 1792-1815," *Canadian Historical Review* 27:1 (1946), 33-51.

21. Andrew Hill Clark, *Three Centuries and the Island: A Historical Geography of Settlement and Agriculture in Prince Edward Island* (Toronto, 1959). A professor at the University of Wisconsin, Clark also directed the graduate work of several historical geographers whose work is important to Canadian rural history, most notably R.Cole Harris, whose dissertation became *The Seigneurial System in Early Canada* (Madison, WI, 1966). Clark's influence is described in a book of essays by his students: James R. Gibson, ed., *European Settlement and Development in North America* (Toronto, 1978).

22. David P. Gagan and H.E. Turner, "Social History in Canada: A Report on the State of the Art," *Archivaria* 14 (1982), 27-35.

23. Robert P. Swierenga, "Agriculture and Rural Life: The New Rural History," in *Ordinary People and Everyday Life: Perspectives on the New Social History*, eds. James B. Gardiner and George Rollie Adams (Nashville, 1983), 93.

24. Fernand Ouellet, *Histoire économique et sociale du Québec, 1760-1850* (Montreal, 1966).

25. Gilles Paquet and J.P. Wallot first criticized Ouellet's "agricultural crisis" in 1967, but the most explicit statement of their case is "Crise agricole et tensions socio-ethniques dans le Bas-Canada, 1802-1812: éléments pour un ré-interpretation," *Revue d'histoire de l'Amérique française* 21:4 (1972), 185-237.

26. R.M. McInnis and Frank Lewis, "The Efficiency of the French-Canadian Farmer in the Nineteenth Century," *Journal of Economic History* 40:3 (1980), 497-514; Serge Courville, "La crise agricole du Bas-Canada: élements d'une réflexion géographique," *Cahiers de géographie du Québec* 24 (1980), 193-223, ?85-428; Robert Armstrong, "The Efficiency of Quebec Farmers in 1851," *Histoire sociale/Social History* 33 (1984), 149-63. The footnotes of these articles provide a running bibliography, and there is an excellent summary of the debate's implications for the history of agriculture in R.M. McInnis, "A Reconsideration of the State of Agriculture in Lower Canada in the First Half of the Nineteenth Century," *Canadian Papers in Rural History* 3(1982), 9-49; John McCallum, *Unequal Beginnings: Agriculture and Economic Development in Ontario and Quebec until 1870* (Toronto, 1980).

27. Robert Mandrou, "Primat de l'histoire sociale: propos sans paradoxes," *Histoire sociale/Social History* 1 (1968), 7-15.

28. *Histoire sociale/Social History* 1 (1968), 143-49. *Hs/SH* continues an eclectic book review policy which brings the most important European work on rural topics to the attention of historians of Canada. *Hs/SH* 34 (1984), for example, reviews four books which deal with rural France.

29. Issues 1 - 20 contained four articles and two research notes which dealt with rural topics, while issues 21 - 38 (the latest to be published) contain twenty articles and seven research notes.

30. J.M. Bumsted and J.T. Lemon, "New Approaches in Early American Studies: The Local Community in New England," *Histoire sociale/Social History* 2 (1968), 98-112.

31. The first of Swierenga's many articles on the subject was "Towards the 'New Rural History,'" *Historical Methods Newsletter* 6:3 (1973), 119. He defined rural as

"residence in an area of low population density and chief livelihood earned in agriculture," in his "Theoretical Perspectives on the New Rural History: From Environmentalism to Modernization," *Agricultural History* 56:3 (1982), 495-96.

32. Donald H. Akenson, *Canadian Papers in Rural History*, Vol. 1 (Gananoque, Ont., 1978), 9.

33. H. Mays review of *Canadian Papers in Rural History*, 4 (1984), in *Canadian Historical Review* 68:3 (1987), 488-91.

34. *Labour/Le Travail* 17 (1986), 286. Akenson includes the tables of contents of all previous volumes of *Canadian Papers in Rural History* in each volume, which greatly simplifies searches for articles.

35. Donald H. Akenson, *Canadian Papers in Rural History*, Vol. 2 (Gananoque, Ont., 1980), 7.

36. Donald Swainson in *Histoire sociale/Social History* 36 (1986), 457.

37. Examples would be Leo Johnson's *History of the County of Ontario, 1615-1875* (Whitby, Ont., 1973) and Don McGowan's *Grassland Settlers: The Swift Current Region during the Era of the Ranching Frontier* (Regina, 1975).

38. Paul Voisey, "Rural Local History and the Prairie West," *Prairie Forum* 10:2 (1985), 327-338.

39. Serge Gagnon, "The Historiography of New France, 1960-1974: Jean Hamelin to Louise Dechêne," *Journal of Canadian Studies* 13:1 (1978), 87. See the enthusiastic review by R. Cole Harris in *Canadian Historical Review* 4 (1975), 449-52.

40. The original edition (Paris, Plon; Montréal, Les Presses de la cité) was soon out of print. A new edition (Boreal, 1988) is now available, and in 1990 McGill-Queen's Press will publish an English translation in an inexpensive student edition.

41. "Manuscript census" refers to the information collected from individual handwritten questionnaires each family answered, as opposed to the aggregate data printed in the published *Census of Canada*.

42. David P. Gagan and Herbert Mays, "Historical Demography and Canadian Social History: Families and Land in Peel County, Ontario," *Canadian Historical Review* 54:1 (1978), 32, 35; Gérard Bouchard, "Le projet d'histoire de la population du Saguenay: l'appareil methodologique," *Revue d'histoire de l'Amérique française* 32:1 (1978), 41-56. For an overview, see Ian Winchester, "Review of the Peel County History Project and the Saguenay Project," *Histoire sociale/Social History* 25 (1980), 195-205.

43. David Gagan, *Hopeful Travellers; Families, Land and Social Change in Mid-Victorian Peel County* (Toronto, 1981) and as an example of the scholarly articles see Gagan's "Land, Population and Social Change: The 'Critical Years' in Rural Canada West," *Canadian Historical Review* 59:3 (1978), 293-318, and Herbert Mays, "'A Place to Stand': Families, Land and Permanence in Toronto Gore Township," *Canadian Historical Association Papers*, 185-211.

44. Gerard Bouchard et Jeannette Larouche, "Dynamique des populations locales: la formation des paroisses rurales au Saguenay (1840-1911)," *Revue d'histoire de l'Amerique française* 41:3 (1988), 363-88. Only one of the Saguenay project's articles

has appeared in English: Bouchard, "Family Structures and Geographic Mobility, 1851-1935," *Journal of Family History* 2 (1977), 350-69.

45. Séguin, *La conquête du sol au XIXe siècle* (Montreal, 1977); J.I. Little: "The Social and Economic Development of Settlers in Two Quebec Townships, 1851-1870," *Canadian Papers in Rural History* (1978), 89-101; and "The Parish and French-Canadian Migrants to Compton County, Quebec, 1851-1891," *Histoire sociale/Social History* 21 (1978), 134-43; Darrell A. Norris, "Migration, Pioneer Settlement, and the Life Course: The First Families of an Ontario Township," *Canadian Papers in Rural History* 4 (1984), 130-52; Lyle Dick, "Factors Affecting Prairie Settlement: A Case Study of Abernethy, Saskatchewan in the 1880s," *CHA Historical Papers* (1985), 11-28; Rusty Bitterman, "The Hierarchy of the Soil: Land and Labour in a 19th Century Cape Breton Community," *Acadiensis* 18:1 (1988), 33-55.

46. Allen Greer, *Peasant, Lord and Merchant: Rural Society in Three Quebec Parishes, 1740-1840* (Toronto, 1985).

47. Paul Voisey, *Vulcan: The Making of a Prairie Community* (Toronto, 1988).

48. Trevor J.O. Dick, "Productivity Change and Grain Farm Practice on the Canadian Prairie, 1900-1930," *Journal of Economic History* 40:1 (1980), 105-10; Frank D. Lewis, "Farm Settlement on the Canadian Prairies, 1898-1911," *ibid.* 41:3 (1981), 517-36; Kenneth H. Norrie: "The Rate of Settlement of the Canadian Prairies, 1870-1911," *ibid.* 25:2 (1975), 410-27 and "Cultivation Techniques as a Response to Risk in Early Canadian Prairie Agriculture," *Explorations in Economic History* 17 (1980), 386-99; William Marr and Michael Percy, "The Government and the Rate of Canadian Prairie Settlement," *Canadian Journal of Economics* 11:4 (1978), 757-67.

49. R.M. McInnis and Frank Lewis, "The Efficiency of the French-Canadian Farmer in the Nineteenth Century," *Journal of Economic History*, 40:3 (1980), 497-514; John Isbister, "Agriculture, Balanced Growth, and Social Change in Canada since 1850: An Interpretation," *Economic Development and Cultural Change* 5:4 (1977), 673-97; Robert Armstrong, "The Efficiency of Quebec Farmers in 1851," *Histoire sociale/Social History* 33 (1984), 149-63.

50. J.I. Little discusses the biases in the techniques used to compare "efficiency" in "Agricultural Progress in Canada East/Quebec," *Histoire sociale/Social History* 36 (1985), 425-31.

51. Donald Harman Akenson, *The Irish in Ontario: A Study in Rural History* (Toronto, 1984).

52. See Kathleen Neils Conzen's "Historical Approaches to the Study of Rural Ethnic Communities," in *Ethnicity on the Great Plains*, ed. Frederick C. Luebke (Lincoln, 1980), 1-17.

53. John H. Warkentin, "Mennonite Agricultural Settlement of Southern Manitoba," *Geographical Review* 49 (1959), 242-68; John T. Ryan, *The Agricultural Economy of Manitoba Hutterite Colonies* (Toronto, 1977); Royden Loewen, "Old Ways Under New Skies: Blumenort, Manitoba, 1874-1910," *Manitoba History* 9 (1985), 8-18; Robert S. Dilley, "Migration and the Mennonites: Nineteenth Century Waterloo County, Ontario," *Canadian Papers in Rural History* 4 (1984), 108-29.

54. John C. Lehr: "The Rural Settlement Behaviour of Ukrainian Pioneers in Western Canada, 1891-1914," in *Western Canadian Research in Geography*, ed. Benton M. Barr (Vancouver, 1975), 51-66; "The Peculiar People: Ukrainian Settlement of Marginal Lands in Southeastern Manitoba," in *Building Beyond the Homestead: Rural History on the Prairies*, eds. David C. Jones and Ian MacPherson (Calgary, 1985), 29-46.

55. Mary Hargreaves, "Women in the Agricultural Settlement of the Northern Plains," *Agricultural History* 50:1 (1976), 179-89; Susan Jackel, ed., *A Flannel Shirt and Liberty: British Emigrant Gentlewomen in the Canadian West* (Vancouver, 1982); Georgina Binnie-Clark, *Wheat and Woman*, (Toronto, 1914; reprinted, with Introduction by Susan Jackel, Toronto, 1979); Eliane Leslau Silverman, *The Last, Best West: Women on the Alberta Frontier, 1880-1930* (Calgary, 1984); Carol Fairbanks, "Lives of Girls and Women on the Canadian and American Prairies," *International Journal of Women's Studies* 2:5 (1979), 452-72.

56. Marjorie Griffin Cohen, "The Decline of Women in Canadian Dairying" *Histoire sociale/Social History* 34 (1984), 307-34; Rosemary Ball, "A Perfect Farmer's Wife: Women in 19th Century Rural Ontario," *Canada, an Historical Magazine* 3:2 (1975), 2-21; Veronica Strong-Boag, "Pulling in Double Harness or Hauling a Double Load: Women, Work and Feminism on the Canadian Prairie," *Journal of Canadian Studies* 21:3 (1986), 32-52; Mary Kinnear, "'Do You Want Your Daughter to Marry a Farmer: Women's Work on the farm, 1922," *Canadian Papers in Rural History* 6 (1988), 137-53.

57. David McGinnis, "Farm Labour in Transition...Alberta 1921-51," in *The Settlement of the West* (Calgary, 1977); Joy Parr, "Hired Men: Ontario Agricultural Wage Labour in Comparative Perspective," *Labour/Le Travail* 15 (1985), 91-103; J.H. Thompson and A. Seager, "Workers, Growers and Monopolists: The 'Labour Problem' in the Alberta Beet Sugar Industry," *ibid.* 3 (1978), 153-74; Cecelia Danysk, "'Showing Those Slaves Their Class Position': Barriers to Organizing Prairie Farm Workers,": in *Beyond the Homestead*, eds. Jones and MacPherson, 163-78; J.W.C. Cherwinski, "In Search of Jake Trumper: The Farm Hand and the Prairie Family," *ibid.*, 111-34.

58. Clarence Danhof, *Change in Agriculture: The Northern United States, 1820-1870* (Cambridge, Mass., 1969); David Spector, *Agriculture on the Prairies, 1870-1940*, Parks Canada History and Archaeology Series 65, (Ottawa, 1983); Claude Blouin, "Le mechanisation de l'agriculture entre 1830 et 1890," in *Agriculture et colonisation au Québec*, ed. Normand Séguin, (Montréal, 1980), 93-111; Alan E. Skeoch, "Developments in Plowing Technology in Nineteenth-Century Canada," *Canadian Papers in Rural History* 3 156-77; Ernest B. Ingles, "The Custom Thresherman in Western Canada, 1890-1925," in *Beyond the Homestead*, eds. Jones and MacPherson, 135-60.

59. Richard Pomfret, "The Mechanization of Reaping in Nineteenth-Century Ontario," *Journal of Economic History* 36:2 (1976), 399-415; Robert Ankli and John Herd Thompson, "The Adoption of the Gasoline Tractor in Western Canada," *Canadian Papers in Rural History* 2 (1980), 9-40; R. Bruce Shepard, "Tractors and Combines in the Second Stage of Agricultural Mechanization on the Canadian Plains," *Prairie Forum* 11:2 (1986), 253-72; Thomas D. Isern, "The Discer: Tillage for the Canadian Plains," *Agricultural History* 62:2 (1988), 79-97.

60. W.L. Morton, *The Progressive Party in Canada* (Toronto, 1950); Paul F. Sharp, *The Agrarian Revolt in Western Canada: A Survey Showing American Parallels* (New York, 1948).

61. Carl Betke, "The United Farmers of Alberta, 1921-1935," in *Society and Politics in Alberta*, ed. Carlo Caldarola (Toronto, 1979), 14-32; W.R. Young, "Conscription, Rural Depopulation, and the Farmers of Ontario, 1917-1919," *Canadian Historical Review* 52:3 (1973), 289-320; David Monod, "The End of Agrarianism: The Fight for Farm Parity in Alberta and Saskatchewan, 1935-48," *Labour/Le Travail* 16 (1985), 117-45; Ian MacPherson "An Authoritative Voice: The Reorientation of the Canadian Farmers' Movement, 1935-1945," *CHA Historical Papers* (1979), 164-81.

62. Garry Fairbairn, *From Prairie Roots: The Remarkable Story of the Saskatchewan Wheat Pool* (Saskatoon, 1984); J.P. Kesteman *et al.*, *Histoire du syndicalisme agricole au Québec, UCC-UPA, 1924-1984* (Montreal, 1984).

63. Ramsay Cook, "Tillers and Toilers: The Rise and Fall of Populism in the 1890s," *CHA Historical Papers* (1984), 1-20; Russell Hann, *Farmers Confront Industrialism: Some Historical Perspectives on Ontario Agrarian Movements* (Toronto, 1975); Lawrence Goodwyn, *Democratic Promise: The Populist Moment in America* (New York, 1976).

64. Alan Brinkley "Writing the History of Contemporary America," *Daedalus* 113 (1984), 124-5.

65. In, among others, C.F. Wilson's *A Century of Canadian Grain: Government Policy to 1951* (Saskatoon, 1978).

66. Margaret Conrad, "Apple Blossom Time in the Annapolis Valley," *Acadiensis* 9:2 (1979), 39.

67. D.G.G. Kerr, *An Historical Atlas of Canada* (Toronto, 1966); John Warkentin and Richard I. Ruggles, eds., *Manitoba Historical Atlas: A Selection of Facsimile Maps, Plans, and Sketches from 1612 to 1969* (Winnipeg, 1970); Geoffrey J. Mathews, *Historical Atlas of Canada*, Vol. 1, *From the Beginnings to 1800* (Toronto, 1987).

68. James M. Nyce, *The Gordon C. Eby Diaries, 1911-13: Chronicle of a Mennonite Farmer* (Toronto, 1982); Wendy Owen, *The Wheat King: Selected Letters and Papers of A.J. Cotton, 1888-1913* (Winnipeg, 1985); David C. Jones, *We'll All Be Buried Down Here: The Prairie Dryland Disaster, 1917-1926* (Calgary, 1986).

69. Hal S. Barron, "Rediscovering the Majority: The New Rural History of the Nineteenth-Century North," *Historical Methods* 19:4 (1986).

70. In Quebec this monographic material has been integrated into an excellent general text which provides the best treatment of rural history in any survey to date: P.A. Linteau, René Durocher and J.C. Robert's *Quebec: A History, 1867-1929* (Toronto, 1983). A second volume *De la crise à nos jours* (1987) is almost as good and will soon be available in English.

71. Gerald Friesen has lyrically summarized much of what has been written in "The Rural West 1900-1930: The Farm, the Village, and King Wheat", Chapter 13 of *The Canadian Prairies: A History* (Toronto, 1984).

72. In addition to the articles by Bitterman and Conrad cited above, *Acadiensis* has published Graeme Wynn's "Late Eighteenth-Century Agriculture on the Bay of Fundy Marshlands," 8:2 (1979), 80-9; there is Alan R. MacNeil's "Cultural Sterotypes and Highland Farming in Eastern Nova Scotia, 1827-1861," *Histoire sociale/Social History* 37 (1986), 39-56; and Julian Gwyn's "The Economy of Nova Scotia under Stress," *Canadian Papers in Rural History*, 6 (1988), 192-225.

73. In addition to the Ormsby article in note 17, it would contain Ormsby, "Agricultural Development in B.C.," *Agricultural History* 19:1 (1945), 11-20; and Morag Maclachlan, "The Success of the Fraser Valley Milk Producers Association," *BC Studies* 24 (1974-5), 52-64.

74. Ian Winchester, "Peel County Project and the Saguenay Project," 202; Peter Sinclair, "Agricultural Colonization in Ontario and Quebec: Some Evidence from the Great Clay Belt, 1900-45," *Canadian Papers in Rural History* 5 (1986), 104-20.

75. See, *mea culpa*, John Herd Thompson, *The Harvests of War: The Prairie West, 1914-1918*; and Ian MacPherson and Thompson, "An Orderly Reconstruction: Prairie Agriculture in World War II," *Canadian Papers in Rural History* 4 (1984), 11-32.

76. This is the framework used in John L. Shover's *First Majority, Last Minority: The Transforming of Rural Life in America* (DeKalb, Ill., 1976). The last task of the rural historian will be to study rural people as they moved to the city, a migration which has so far been ignored. In *Hopeful Travellers*, for example, David Gagan doesn't consider those who left rural Peel County for the burgeoning town of Brampton.

77. Rusty Bitterman makes this point forcefully and eloquently in "Land and Labour in a 19th Century Cape Breton Community," 54-55.

6

Writing about Business

Graham Taylor

At the end of *Northern Enterprise*, his massive narrative of business development in Canada since the sixteenth century, Michael Bliss observed — accurately — that "there are no other surveys of the history of Canadian business." He then proceeded to skewer other potential aspirants to that status. *Canadian Economic History*, a work of similarly sweeping scale by Hugh Aitken and W.T. Easterbrook published in the 1950s, had "become dated"; and its 1980 replacement, *Canada: An Economic History* by Donald Paterson and William Marr, was "almost inaccessible...to the non-specialist." Bliss adopted an even more disdainful view of Tom Naylor's two-volume *History of Canadian Business, 1867-1914*, which up to the publication of his own book, represented the only attempt to survey the entire landscape of Canadian business. It was, Bliss observed, "an eclectically Marxist work, factually unreliable and...of no use in the preparation of this history."[1]

I

Bliss's dismissal of his rivals reflects two significant developments in the fields of Canadian economic and business history over the past two decades. First, economic historians in Canada, as in the United States, have shifted

121

away from empirical studies of the evolution of specific business enterprises and government economic policies to focus more on developing methods of testing economic theories through analysis of appropriate historical data. Since much of their work emphasized the use of statistical techniques applied to questions on which reliable quantitative information was available, these "new" economic historians were often identified as "cliometricians," borrowing or building upon methods of macroeconomic analysis developed by economic theorists after the Second World War. While the more extreme advocates of "cliometrics" sometimes asserted that no serious analysis was possible for testing propositions in the absence of quantifiable data, it would probably be more accurate to characterize the "new" economic history as representing an effort to integrate economic theory with historical analysis in a more precise fashion than had been the case with traditional practitioners of economic history who "had never embraced" theory "with warmth and determination."[2]

Secondly, while economic history was striking off into the frontiers of quantitative methods, business history was developing as a distinctive field. Its adherents adopted an approach that sought to derive narrowly practical lessons from broad general theory. Before the Second World War, business history as a subject of academic research scarcely existed, although a journal was established at the Harvard Business School in 1927 under the direction of Norman S.B. Gras, a Canadian who also became the first professor of business history at the school. During the two decades after 1945, however, interest in the field expanded significantly, particularly in the United States, England, and Germany. Whereas Gras had limited the subject to a study of the administration of business enterprises — an approach that made business history useful in training corporate managers — the postwar practitioners tried to integrate the study of business into a broader social and cultural framework. As was the case with the cliometricians, the "new" business historians turned to economic theory for inspiration, but they were less concerned with methods of analysis than with the basic assumptions and concepts advanced by theorists. One group drew upon the ideas of the Austrian economist Joseph Schumpeter (who emphasized the role of entrepreneurs in economic development) and sought to trace the ways in which social institutions and values advanced, retarded, or otherwise influenced entrepreneurial behaviour. Others turned to investigating the growth and internal structures of large corporations in industrialized countries. This was an extension of Gras's approach, but one which borrowed ideas from the work of organizational theorists and economists addressing the behaviour of markets in conditions of imperfect competition. By the 1970s, business historians had not only produced a large and wide-ranging literature but had contributed significantly to broader historical analyses of the emergence of large public and private organizations in the nineteenth and twentieth centuries.[3]

The combined impact of the rise of cliometrics and the emergence of business history as an independent field appeared in Canadian scholarship about a decade ago with more dramatic results than in other countries, largely because of the unity that had prevailed in Canadian economic history up to that point. Since the 1930s the field had been dominated, if not virtually monopolized, by adherents to what was commonly called the "staple thesis" or "staple approach" associated with Harold Innis, an economist at the University of Toronto. Although Innis did not originate the "staple approach" to Canadian economic history — that status may more properly be assigned to William A. Mackintosh, a historian at Queen's University in the 1920s — he devoted a substantial part of his career to investigating the role of staple commodities in shaping social and political as well as economic development of Canada.[4]

The "staple thesis" was not precisely a theory of economic development: Hugh Aitken, a student of Innis, described it variously as "a frame of reference, a perspective," or a "powerful myth" that simplified and clarified a complex process.[5] Given this rather amorphous quality and Innis's own prolix writing style, no short description could do it full justice. Nonetheless their adherence to the staple thesis affected the way that Innis and his followers viewed the development and structure of the business community in Canada.

The central argument of the staple thesis is that the growth of the Canadian economy was determined mainly by concentration on the production and export of a series of raw material commodities or staples: fish and furs in the seventeenth and eighteenth centuries, timber in the nineteenth century, and wheat and minerals in the twentieth century. According to Innis, this dependence on staple exports affected nearly every aspect of Canada's political and economic development: "Population was involved directly in the production of the staple and indirectly in the production of facilities promoting (staple) production. Agriculture, industry, transportation, trade, finance, and governmental activities tend to become subordinate to the production of the staple...." [6] The development of the merchant community and financial institutions, the construction of canals and rail-roads, and the fashioning of government land settlement and trade policies were all harnessed to the service of the staple sector rather than reflecting the establishment of a diversified economy.

This preoccupation with staple exports also determined Canada's role in the emerging international economy. As a supplier of raw materials to Britain (and later to the United States) and as a consumer of industrial products from those countries, Canada remained economically dependent on foreign capital, technology, and markets long past the point when it secured political autonomy. In his analysis, Innis stressed the problems of dependence on foreign commodity markets, particularly when abrupt shifts in demand for Canadian staples led to recurrent boom and bust cycles in the Canadian economy, the fortunes of which were so closely linked to exports. Innis's more recent followers focused on a different penalty: Canada's reliance on foreign capital and technology restricted the development of an indigenous industrial system and perpetuated the country's status as a hinterland serving the needs of industrialized metropolitan centres abroad.[7]

Innis further believed the predominant role of staples in Canada's economic development created market conditions that promoted the growth of business monopolies or near-monopolies, often with the encouragement of government. High overhead costs involved in the transportation of staples, as well as the continuous threat of excess capacity as market demand for staples rapidly expanded and contracted, militated against the emergence (or at least the long-term survival) of many competitive firms in the Canadian business community. Canada's challenging geographic obstacles and dependence on foreign investment reinforced this tendency toward concentration on manufacturing, banking, and trade as well as the extraction of raw materials.[8]

The staple thesis in its broad formulation inspired a variety of economists and economic historians whose theoretical views diverged sharply in other respects. For example, Douglass North, a leading American cliometrician, applied a variant of the staple approach to economic development in the United States in the nineteenth century, arguing that the export of staple commodities such as cotton from the American South and wheat from the Midwest in the pre-Civil War era provided the capital and commercial infrastructure essential to U.S. industrialization. On the other side of the ideological spectrum, advocates of what is generally designated "dependency theory" generalized Innis's portrayal of Canada as a staple-based hinterland to fashion a broader argument in which the underdevelopment of Third World countries in the nineteenth and twentieth centuries was linked to their historical role as suppliers of raw material staples to the industrializing "core states" of Western Europe and North America.[9]

II

Despite the malleability of the staple thesis, by the 1970s its Canadian adherents had diminished to a relatively small and self-conscious group. They called themselves "political economists" to distinguish their approach from mainstream economists who, in their judgment, were obsessed with quantification, addressed economic issues far too narrowly, and were increasingly under the influence of American scholars committed to theories that supported the capitalist *status quo* and the absorption of Canada into a continental system dominated by the United States. Self-styled political leftists, the Canadian political economists often saw their work as complementing that of Marxist scholars on class conflict in Canada and other capitalist countries. The Marxists for their part were reluctant to accept the embrace of these would-be allies, arguing that Innis had not clearly integrated an analysis of class relations into his works, and that the critique of the Canadian economic system implicit in the arguments of the political economists derived more from bourgeois nationalism than from an understanding of the dynamics of capitalist development.[10]

While theorists from the neoclassical and Marxist traditions rejected the followers of Innis, the underdeveloped terrain of business history proved fertile ground for the political economists. Until the 1970s few Canadian academic historians of any persuasion had ventured far into this territory except for Innis himself and Donald Creighton. Most historians remained preoccupied with political and intellectual affairs. The neglect of business history also reflected the dearth of strong business archives and the ahistorical attitudes of the Canadian business community. In the United States, business-records repositories had been established at Harvard and elsewhere as early as 1910. As might be expected, German public archives and companies began maintaining records on a systematic basis even earlier. In England business archives were less developed, but companies had authorized historical research by academic scholars such as Charles Wilson and D.C. Coleman in the 1950s. There were no such parallels in Canada, and the problems of access to records continue to bedevil Canadian business historians.[11]

The political economists, however, were less restrained than business historians by the absence of primary source materials. With a methodology that emphasized analysis rather than painstaking evaluation of documentary evidence, social scientists drew eclectically on government reports, personal memoirs, newspaper articles, and the occasional historical monograph to support their arguments. Naylor's *History of Canadian Business 1867-1914*, which proceeded in this fashion, was not the only attempt by a social scientist to produce a synthetic overview of the subject, but it was one of the most intensively documented, and in many respects represented an explicit statement of the views of Canadian political economists.[12]

Naylor did not explicitly apply the staple thesis in his synthesis (indeed, in an early version he rejected Innis's "geographical determinism"[13]), but the main themes of his work elaborated on concepts implicit in Innis's interpretation of the staple thesis as applied to Canadian business development. According to Naylor's description, the Canadian business community was dominated from 1763 through the twentieth century by a "merchant capitalist" elite who acted as middle-men in the movement of staple commodities from the Canadian hinterland to the industrial centres of England and the United States. Canals and railroads were promoted to serve those ends, and investment in domestic manufacturing was deliberately neglected. When British North America lost its protected colonial status in the British mercantile empire, Canadian business leaders turned to reciprocity with the Americans "predicated on the idea that Canada would provide raw materials and the United States finished products."[14] The patent laws and trade protection provided in the "National Policy" after 1879 were intended not to encourage indigenous manufacturing but to attract foreign capital needed to exploit the resource sector which would in turn create jobs and prevent depopulation of the country. Direct foreign investment incidentally promoted some industrialization, but this industrial sector of the economy was, because of its source, largely in foreign (principally American) hands. Meanwhile, the Canadian merchant elite secured control of the banking system which financed commodity flows and channelled foreign portfolio (mostly British) investment into railroads and utilities. The Canadian business system of the early twentieth century consisted of a small industrial base largely under foreign ownership; a financial and commercial sector in which control was concentrated in the hands of the scions of the old merchant elite; and a staple resource sector where ownership was divided between foreigners and the domestic commercial group, but which continued to be the main determinant of Canada's international economic role as a raw-material hinterland.

Not surprisingly, the political economists praised Naylor's work as a significant restatement of Innis's interpretation of Canada's business evolution. Even those who challenged Naylor's assertions that the Canadian commercial elite ignored opportunities for industrial investment nevertheless drew upon his work to document their own views.[15] Canadian business historians, however, took a more skeptical view of Naylor. Their criticisms focused in part on his cavalier neglect of the growing historical literature in the field, on his tendency to accept at face value the public statements of politicians and businessmen, and on his reliance on "anecdotal evidence" (about economic trends and conditions) from newspapers. They also questioned Naylor's central argument that a "merchant capitalist" elite chose not to diversify into industrial investment, thus opening the way for an American takeover of Canadian manufacturing. Gerald Tulchinsky, author of a major study of the Montreal merchant community in the nineteenth century, dismissed Naylor's book as "an intuitive work in an area where most of the basic research has yet to be done."[16]

The mixed receptions Naylor's history received from the social scientists on the one hand and the historians on the other represented more than a disagreement over the merits of a particular book. These opposing judgments also reflected the different methods of research and treatment of documentary evidence employed in the two disciplines. For historians such as Tulchinsky and Douglas McCalla, the broad conclusions of Naylor and his colleagues lacked the solid base of sustained research essential to historical generalizations. Naylor was not alone in considering journalists' accounts and government reports on business activities to be reliable sources. Furthermore, the political economists had erected the staple thesis on a precariously small foundation. As a British business historian noted:

> From what appeared to be the overwhelming importance of a few, very large trading and transportation companies during the early stage of Canadian development came the idea that it was possible to explain the economic history of Canada by a reconstruction of entities such as the Hudson's Bay Company, the North West Company and the Canadian Pacific Railway... (F)ar too much emphasis was placed on "special" firms within certain industries, thus producing a skewed view of economic

development. Other sectors of the economy and many entrepreneurs and business firms within those sectors were almost entirely ignored....[17]

The division between the political economists and historians of Canadian business, however, rests on more than differences over methods and sources of research. Although for the most part business historians in this country have eschewed grand theorizing in order to pursue discrete empirical studies of specific individuals, industries or time-periods (so much so that one American observer warned of "a sense of drift and disunity" in the field[18]) some broad patterns of interpretation can be discerned. As Aitken suggested in the case of the staple thesis, these patterns are too diffuse to be integrated into a set of theoretical statements but they do provide a framework or perspective on the subject that many Canadian business historians share.

That framework was fashioned initially by N.S.B. Gras of the Harvard Business School in the 1930s. Although Gras limited his approach, other business historians subsequently pursued wider areas of research without fundamentally altering the structure of his theory of capitalist evolution. In his major work on the subject, *Business and Capitalism*, Gras noted in passing the existence of business enterprises in virtually every historical and contemporary society, but focused his attention on developments in western Europe and North America from the Middle Ages.

During the thirteenth to fifteenth centuries, merchant communities emerged in Europe, concentrating in towns in Italy and the Baltic and North Sea regions, and establishing market centres for the purchase and resale of agricultural surpluses. By the 1500s merchants had established a foothold in overseas trade as well and had developed techniques such as double-entry bookkeeping and joint-stock companies that were essential components of commercial growth. Over the next two hundred years merchants began to diversify and specialize their operations: some focused on particular lines of trade, others on developing banks and insurance houses, still others branched into manufacturing by financing the activities of technically innovative artisans. General and specialized merchants also migrated to the European colonies overseas, particularly to North America. By the end of the eighteenth century advances in technology and the elaboration of commercial institutions capable of mobilizing large amounts of capital laid the groundwork for industrialization in both western Europe and America.

During the 1800s industries needed increased capital in order to finance expansion and develop a transportation and marketing infrastructure; this additional requirement provided capitalists specializing in investment banking with the opportunity to control the evolving economic system. Business concentration fostered by these finance capitalists led in turn to greater economic integration, and governments began to intervene more directly in the affairs of business in response to public demands to control the abuses of power by large private enterprises, and, not incidentally, in order to acquire a larger share of the wealth created by industrial expansion.[19]

Gras thus outlined the evolution of modern business through four inter-related stages: merchant or mercantile capitalism, industrial capitalism, finance capitalism, and state or national capitalism. His successors in the field have occasionally challenged Gras's views (particularly on the development and relative importance of finance and state capitalism) and have pursued their own ideas about the role of entrepreneurship in history and other subjects, but the basic framework has remained largely intact. Perhaps the most significant contribution to the field has been the work of Alfred D. Chandler, Jr. and others on the emergence of the "visible hand" of management in large, integrated, twentieth-century corporations. This "visible hand" has supplemented the "invisible hand" of Adam Smith's market system with new instruments of internal control and long-range planning by big business. In effect this school of business historians has added another stage, managerial capitalism, to Gras's framework of business evolution.[20]

The important point here is that the framework of evolution applied generally to capitalist societies. Although the pace of the transition from mercantile to industrial to finance and managerial capitalism varied according to local economic and social conditions in different countries, the general trends could be discerned when tracing the history of business between the sixteenth and twentieth centuries. The classification of business groups did not establish absolute categories. Merchant capitalists imperceptibly melded into industrial and finance capitalists; the practices and institutions established in commercial operations became essential components of industrial organization. In large corporations, salaried managers assumed the functions of financial control, technical development and production, and marketing of goods, functions that had once been carried out by independent entrepreneurs. In those sectors of the economy not dominated by big businesses, such entrepreneurial independence continued to be the case. Competitive markets could be found alongside monopolies, and governments alternately aided and abetted or hemmed and regulated business according to circumstances.

In this context, Canadian business history could be seen as only a local variant of the general pattern of capitalist development, rather than the unique result of a staple-driven economy. As an exporter of primary materials, Canada differed from countries that specialized in industrial exports, such as Japan or England, or from the United States with its large population and internal market. But Canada experienced similar processes of industrial growth, business concentration, and state intervention. The Canadian business community likewise responded to institutional changes taking place in the international economy: the development of financial instruments, the transfer of new technologies and management practices, the establishment of regulatory and welfare policies by governments, and the emergence of multinational enterprises.

Given their penchant for empirical research and a "case study" orientation, Canadian business historians have rarely invoked Gras, or any other generalizer, as explicitly influencing their approach to the subject. Nevertheless, their selection of cases suitable for research and the kinds of questions addressed in their writings fits into the framework of business evolution and the focus of analysis that Gras and others outlined. Staple commodities, business "monopolies" such as the Hudson's Bay Co. or C.P.R., and government policies have not been major features of the work of Canadian business historians over the past two decades. Instead they have devoted their attention to the development of merchant houses and mercantile communities in the nineteenth century: Tulchinsky on the Montreal merchant-manufacturers; McCalla on the Buchanans in Toronto and Hamilton, Ontario, wholesale merchants who also invested in railways; Bruce Wilson on Robert Hamilton of Kingston, Ontario, wholesaler and land speculator; and David MacMillan on the influx of Scottish merchants into all the major centres of British North America.[21]

These studies emphasize the internal organization of enterprises, and commercial practices and innovations, an emphasis that is also to be found in some studies of financial institutions that emerged in the same era. Two examples of this kind of analysis are Ronald Rudin's book on Quebec banks, and Peter Baskerville's on the rise and fall of the Bank of Upper Canada in the mid-nineteenth century.[22] Railways and other transport modes, the development of which was as essential to the prosperity of merchant communities as banks and insurance companies, have also been examined.

But the preoccupation of the staple school with the Canadian Pacific Railway has been complemented by studies of other, less celebrated rail lines: Baskerville on railways in Upper Canada, Ted Regehr on the Canadian Northern Railway.[23]

Studies of industrial firms in Canada have been less plentiful. But this situation is due more to the paucity of accessible business records than to any theoretical convictions on the part of Canadian business historians about the inconsequential role of manufacturing. The steel industry has received attention reflecting its importance in the Canadian economy in the early twentieth century: William Kilbourn's history of Stelco is one of the few "in-house" studies commissioned to a professional historian. Duncan McDowall's *Steel At the Sault* provides both a history of Algoma Steel Company and a biography of Sir James Dunn, one of the most prominent "finance capitalists" of Canada.[24]

Other industries received more sporadic coverage. Michael Bliss's biography of Sir Joseph Flavelle encompasses a history of the William Davies Company and the growth of the Toronto meat-packing industry before World War I. Christopher Armstrong and H.V. Nelles surveyed the field of utilities (telecommunications, water, and hydroelectric power) in a sweeping fashion in *Monopoly's Moment*. In a broader context, Ben Forster in *A Conjunction of Interests* traced the role of industrial groups in the movement for protective tariffs that culminated in the National Policy. He explicitly challenged the assertions of the staple school on the dominant role of "merchant capitalists" in shaping government trade policies, much as Armstrong and Nelles implicitly challenged the views of Innis's followers on the inevitable triumph of monopolists in the Canadian economy as exemplified by the struggle over hydroelectric power distribution in Ontario.[25]

Aside from McDowall's work on Dunn, the careers of Canada's turn-of-the-century financial swashbucklers — Max Aitken, I.W. Killam, Joseph Forget, and their more recent imitators such as E.P. Taylor — have received remarkably little attention, though again this situation may reflect the limitations of accessible sources rather than lack of interest on the part of Canadian business historians. Two recent works, by McDowall and by Armstrong and Nelles, have focused on one group of financiers, the "utility entrepreneurs," who ventured into Latin America in the early years of the twentieth century.[26]

By contrast, the instruments of "state capitalism" in Canada have been chronicled in greater detail, notably by Robert Bothwell whose biography (with Kilbourn) of C.D. Howe has been followed by works on Eldorado, the uranium company, and Atomic Energy of Canada Limited, crown corporations that were offspring of Howe's interventionist policies after World War II.[27]

Curiously, Canadian business historians have not addressed the history of management to any great extent compared to their counterparts in the United States, Britain, and Germany. There is no Canadian equivalent of a Chandler. Readers of otherwise distinguished company histories such as McDowall's book on Algoma or Bothwell's on Eldorado might be pardoned for assuming that these enterprises functioned as extensions of the personalities of their chief executives rather than as large organizations dealing with complex problems of internal budgeting, production control, and marketing. Labour historians have looked into these aspects of business operations, principally in terms of shop-floor and office supervision, with a tendency to overemphasize the importance of "scientific management" techniques. Such techniques received a great deal of publicity in the early twentieth century, but were generally deployed on a piecemeal basis by managers in Canadian industries. The development of internal financial controls, advertising techniques, and related managerial tasks in the Canadian setting have had few chroniclers.[28]

Bliss's *Northern Enterprise*, which summarizes and synthesizes much of this literature, more clearly reflects the framework of business evolution enunciated by Gras. While the role of staples in the colonial period of British North America is hardly ignored, Bliss introduces the merchant communities of Montreal and the Maritimes early in his narrative and devotes much attention to the diversification of merchant enterprises into specialized lines, the growth of financial institutions, and the emergence of manufacturing in the mid-nineteenth century. The Hudson's Bay Company, the North West Company, and the Canadian Pacific Railway appear onstage in due course, but their histories are hedged about with those of a multitude of other enterprises, large and small. Indeed, the histories are so numerous that one reviewer complained that "the details become a blur of personal and corporate names, dates and commercial links whose obscurity is probably deserved."[29]

Perhaps the most striking feature of Bliss's book is the virtual absence of foreign-owned firms whose impact on the Canadian economy bulks so large in the histories of the staple school. Imperial Oil, for example, appears briefly toward the end of the book in a chapter devoted primarily to the rise of the oil industry in Alberta after World War II; its dominant role in the refining and distribution of oil and gas in Canada is alluded to in a single sentence. The coming of Ford and General Motors into Canada is buried in a chapter between remarks on railway competition in the 1920s and the rise of the Bronfmans in the Prohibition era. Other foreign multinationals, such as Canadian General Electric, rate hardly a line and many are not mentioned at all.[30]

To be fair, these omissions may be justified on the grounds that Bliss wished to provide a study of *Canadian enterprises*, but he does assert that his "subject is the whole history of business in Canada." The low profile Bliss accords foreign subsidiaries demonstrates dramatically the contrasting perspectives of the staple school and the new generation of Canadian business historians.

The two approaches present remarkably different views of the Canadian business community, past and present. The portrait that emerges from the staple school is of a Canada which resembles a Third-World country beneath a veneer of industrialization, a country dependent, throughout its history, on the exploitation of its natural resources, and dominated by subsidiaries of foreign multinationals and a native financial elite (offspring of Scottish and English merchant houses, also interlinked with foreign capital). Together these two groups have controlled the economy through large corporate concentrations in the banking, transportation, manufacturing, and resource extraction sectors.

The version offered by Bliss and other business historians envisages a far more diversified economic system than that of the staples school. Staples still bulk large, but are shown to have spawned vigorous merchant communities whose encouragement of commercial and transport networks established the foundations of an industrial society. In other words, this is a pattern similar to that of Britain and the United States. There are, however, features that are peculiar to the Canadian experience (such as the tradition of direct government intervention through crown corporations and related measures) and that are a result of Canada's political heritage and difficult environment. Beyond the sphere of government and regulated industries, competition rather than concentration has prevailed: monopolies have been short-lived, and family firms more durable than in many other industrial nations. Economic development in Canada has not been limited by a failure

of entrepreneurial vision nor the constricted attitudes of a mercantile business elite perpetually subordinated to foreign capitalists. The basic problem
has been survival in "a harsh land, difficult to extract wealth from, and
gravely handicapped by a small population... (who) desire to force the pace
of Canadian development faster than the real resource base has been able
comfortably to sustain...."[31]

For the student of Canadian business history searching for a set of
common themes or guidelines, it is hard enough to be confronted with two
virtually irreconcilable schools of thought on the subject, proceeding from
different assumptions and focusing on different areas. But these two schools
do not exhaust the literature in the field. Long before the academic scholars
turned their attention to the mundane affairs of business enterprises, the
terrain was occupied by a disparate collection of journalists, corporate
publicists, and antiquarians whose output has continued to proliferate.
These practitioners have received scant respect from the professoriate, but
their products are so numerous in quantity and range that they can hardly
be ignored, if only because without them the body of literature in the field
would be small indeed.

Commissioned corporate histories and biographies have a long, if not
always distinguished, tradition. Not surprisingly, the Hudson's Bay Company, the railroad industry, and the large chartered banks have solid institutional histories based on substantial archives.[32] Other commissioned
histories are a mixed lot: many are written by hired journalists, using a
handful of records, and, because they are anecdotal and uncritical toward
their subjects, seem to be little more than extended versions of public
relations brochures. A few, such as Kilbourn's *Elements Combined*, E.P.
Neufeld's history of Massey-Ferguson, or McDowall's history of Brazilian
Traction (Brascan), are based on systematic research by professional historians.[33] Common to almost all such works, however, is an institutional
focus that ignores or deals only marginally with the broader social and
economic context within which these enterprises evolved. Unfortunately
for Canadian business history, those writers with the best access to research
sources tend to have the most constricted approach — and vice versa.

For the most part these quasi-popular business histories are commissioned to serve particular corporate aims, usually to celebrate the achieve-
ments of their sponsors, and are generally disregarded by academic
historians. A few popularizers, however, aim to reach a wider audience.
Pierre Berton's two-volume chronicle of the building of the Canadian

Pacific Railway is probably the best known example of this genre,[34] but Peter C. Newman has been the most prolific popularizer of business history in Canada. Newman first achieved journalistic prominence for his fascinating dissections of Canadian politics in the era of Diefenbaker and Pearson. But his career has been devoted largely to extolling the virtues of Canada's business leaders, past and present, with the conscious intent (like Berton) of creating a "heroic tradition" in which diffident Canadians can take pride. An early venture, entitled *Flame of Power*, offered brief sketches of Canada's neglected business achievers. A more ambitious undertaking, *The Canadian Establishment*, appeared in the mid-1970s, followed by biographical portraits of Conrad Black and the Bronfmans, and most recently a multi-volume resurrection of the old stand-by, the Hudson's Bay Company.[35]

Newman's approach to the field has not been entirely consistent. In the first volume of *The Canadian Establishment*, he attempted a kind of sociological profile of the Canadian business community that in certain respects resembled the "corporate elite" portrayed by Clement, Naylor, and followers of the Innis tradition. In subsequent volumes, however, Newman jettisoned this approach, concentrating more on anecdotes and character sketches of a disparate collection of entrepreneurs. By doing so he implied the existence of a far more competitive and dynamic business community than had emerged from his earlier work. Yet when selecting a subject suitable for a major book on Canada's heroic commercial past, Newman turned once more to the very embodiment of the staple tradition, the fur trade.[36]

The controversy Newman's history of the Hudson's Bay Company provoked points up the differences between professors and popularizers. In preparing his history, Newman relied heavily on the writings of academic professionals, among them E.E. Rich and John S. Galbraith. But the aspects of that history which they addressed — the problems of organizing and financing a far-flung enterprise, for example, or the interlinkages of business operations and British geopolitical strategy — are at best ancillary to Newman's pageant of great men engaged in heroic deeds while creating a "northern vision" for Canada. The attempt by Newman and Berton to give weight and a measure of coherence to their treatments contrasts with many other journalistic forays into the past. Canada does not have as strong a tradition of anti-big business journalism as the United States (although Gustavus Myers, one of the original American "muckrakers" of the early twentieth century, turned a critical eye northward in *A History of Canadian Wealth*) and even those who fall into this category seldom proceed beyond the most simplistic interpretations of business behaviour.[37] On the other hand, an emerging group of journalists specializing in business reporting have produced interesting examples of "contemporary history" based on lengthy interviews with participants as well as informed use of public documentary materials. Similarly, Newman's earlier books on business are rich in details and insights about contemporary business affairs. Whatever their limitations in terms of perspective, these works may provide future historians with the best approximation of primary sources on their subjects.[38]

III

For the unwary reader, then, picking up a book on Canadian business history is much like entering a hall of offices, each one with its door firmly closed and the inhabitants therein pursuing their own version of the enterprise, deliberately ignoring the competitors next door or down the hall. The field is characterized not by "two solitudes," to use the well-worn phrase, but by a multitude of solitudes: cliometricians with their data banks, political economists fixated on the staple thesis, academic business historians linking Canada to broader capitalist evolutionary trends, labour historians eyeing bosses from the perspective of the shop floor, popularizers focusing myopically on individual entrepreneurs or companies or seeking to connect Canada business to a "national identity", and the occasional "investigative journalist" probing the wreckage of a business disaster.

Each approach exhibits virtues and flaws. Cliometricians developed techniques for effectively testing generalizations, but may not take into account the impact of particular circumstances or the role of individual behaviour in historical processes. The advocates of the staple thesis have produced a coherent and comprehensive set of arguments about Canadian economic history, but build them upon shaky foundations, ignoring a wide range of business activities that do not fit into their interpretation. The business historians, by contrast, have revealed the richness and variety of Canadian business operations, but in the process may have under-rated the role of staples and foreign investment in shaping the country. Labour historians tend to oversimplify the motives and constraints that affect business decisions and observe business behaviour from a limited vantage point, but their perspective is an important one for understanding the dynamics of industrial organizations. Popularizers like Berton or Newman may lack a sense of the larger context within which their heroes and villains posture, but their entrepreneurial epics have raised the visibility of business in the Canadian past, and may in the long term open doors to academic researchers that have hitherto been closed.

The relative merits of these assorted practitioners and the fine distinctions among them, however, are not readily apparent to the non-specialist. The field of Canadian business history is not unique in this respect: similarly wide divisions over approach and interpretation exist among social historians, analysts of foreign policy and specialists in other areas. What is perhaps most noticeable in this field is the virtual absence of a dialogue. Each group is aware of the existence of the others but regards them as hardly deserving serious debate. A dialogue among parties so far apart is unlikely to produce any consensus on the central issues that divide them. But for the puzzled outside observer, the various solitudes of Canadian business history may be a greater barrier to understanding and appreciating the remarkable outpouring of work in the field in recent years than the clash of dissident voices.

Endnotes

1.   Michael Bliss, *Northern Enterprise: Five Centuries of Canadian Business* (Toronto: McClelland and Stewart, 1987), 585-86. The other works cited are Hugh G.J. Aitken and W.T. Easterbrook, *Canadian Economic History* (Toronto: MacMillan, 1956); William L. Marr and Donald G. Paterson, *Canada: An Economic History* (Toronto: MacMillan, 1980); and R. Tom Naylor, *The History of Canadian Business, 1867-1914* (Toronto: James Lorimer, 1976).

2.   The quotation is from Thomas C. Cochran, "Economic History: Old and New," *American Historical Review* 74 (1969) 1561-72, reprinted in Cochran, *The Uses of History* (Wilmington: Scholarly Resources, 1973), 53-68. The classic presentation of the views of the "new" economic historians can be found in Robert W. Fogel and Stanley L. Engerman, eds., *The Reinterpretation of American Economic History* (New York: Harper and Row, 1971). A good selection of practitioners of the "new" economic history in Canada is contained in Douglas McCalla, ed., *Perspectives on Canadian Economic History* (Toronto: Copp Clark Pitman, 1987), which includes a useful introductory essay by McCalla.

3.   On the early development of business history as a field of study, see Ralph Hidy, "Business History: Present Status and Future Needs," *Business History Review* 44 (1970), 483-97. The orientation and work of the "entrepreneurial" school is sum-

marized by Hugh G.J. Aitken, ed., *Explorations in Enterprise* (Cambridge, Mass.: Harvard University Press, 1967). On the influence of the "organizational" school, see Louis Galambos, "The Emerging Organizational Synthesis in Modern American History," in *Men and Organizations*, ed. Edwin J. Perkins (New York: G.P. Putnam, 1977), 3-15. A somewhat dated but insightful essay is Alan Wilson, "Problems and Traditions of Business History: Past Examples and Canadian Prospects," in *Canadian Business History: Selected Studies*, ed. David R. Macmillan (Toronto: MacMillan, 1971), 302-15. A recent comparative survey that includes bibliographical references is Mansel G. Blackford, *The Rise of Modern Business in Great Britain, the United States and Japan* (Chapel Hill, N.C.: University of North Caroline Press, 1988).

4.   See Carl Berger, *The Writing of Canadian History*, 2d ed. (Toronto: University of Toronto Press, 1986), 85-111, for a review of Innis's career and an appraisal of his influence.

5.   Hugh G.J. Aitken, "Myth and Measurement: The Innis Tradition in Economic History," *Journal of Canadian Studies* 12 (1977), 98-99.

6.   Harold A. Innis, *The Fur Trade in Canada: An Introduction to Canadian Economic History* (Toronto: University of Toronto Press, 1930, reprint 1956), 385-86.

7.   Berger, *The Writing of Canadian History*, 96-97, 102-3. For the views of more recent adherents to the Innis tradition, see M.H. Watkins, "The Staple Theory Revisited," *Journal of Canadian Studies* 12 (1977), 83-95; Daniel Drache, "Harold Innis and Canadian Capitalist Development," *Canadian Journal of Political and Social Theory* 6:1 (1982), 35-60.

8.   Innis is generally seen as a "nationalist" historian in that he perceived Canada as a natural geographic entity linked together by the transport networks established to serve the staple system rather than as a "fragile political creation." This approach was more clearly developed by Donald Creighton in his classic work, *The Commercial Empire of the Saint Lawrence* (Toronto: Ryerson Press, 1938). Some of Innis's followers, however, drew upon his ideas about the tendency of the staple economy to produce monopolies to argue that the Canadian commercial elite recreated at the national level a system of regional inequalities, with the eastern and western provinces serving as dependent hinterlands to an Ontario-based metropolis. See Berger, *The Writing of Canadian History*, 97-98; and Daniel Drache, "Rediscovering Canadian Political Economy," *Journal of Canadian Studies* 11 (1976), 10-11.

9.   R.F. Neill, "The Passing of Canadian Economic History," *Journal of Canadian Studies* 12 (1977), 73-82; Daniel Drache, "Harold Innis and Capitalist Development," 49-50. The "dependency" approach was reapplied to Canada by Kari Levitt in *Silent Surrender: The Multinational Corporation in Canada* (Toronto: MacMillan, 1970), 17-26, 92-113. For an interesting recent discussion of the general application of the staple thesis by economic historians, see John T. McCusher and Russell R. Menard, *The Economy of British North America, 1607-1789* (Chapel Hill: University of North Caroline Press, 1985), 19-34.

10.   For neo-Marxist views of the political economists, see David McNally, "Staple Theory as Commodity Fetishism: Marx, Innis and the Canadian Political Economy," and Ray Schmidt, "Canadian Political Economy: A Critique," in *Studies in Political Economy: A Socialist Review* 6 (Autumn 1981), 35-63, 65-92.

11. Duncan MacDowall, "Business History As Public History: One of Canada's Infant Industries," *Journal of Canadian Studies* 20 (1985), 5-21.

12. Other examples of efforts by social scientists to synthesize Canadian business history in the 1960s and 1970s include: Wallace Clement, *The Canadian Corporate Elite* (Toronto: McClelland and Stewart, 1975); Levitt, *Silent Surrender*; Jorge Niosi, *Canadian Capitalism*, trans. Robert Chodos (Toronto: James Lorimer, 1981), 17-35. R. Tom Naylor offered another historical synthesis covering the period 1500-1900 in "Canada in the European Age," in his *Dominion of Debt* (Montreal: Black Rose Books, 1985), 23-60.

13. R. Tom Naylor, "The Rise and Fall of the Third Commercial Empire of the St. Lawrence," in *Capitalism and the National Question in Canada*, ed. Gary Teeple (Toronto: University of Toronto Press, 1972), 2.

14. Naylor, "The Rise and Fall of the Third Commercial Empire," 11.

15. See M.H. Watkins, "The Staple Theory Revisited," 89-90, for a relatively uncritical assessment of Naylor. Wallace Clement's *Continental Corporate Power* (Toronto: McClelland and Stewart, 1977) maintained that Canadian commercial and financial leaders established a mutually advantageous relationship with their American counterparts in the early twentieth century, effectively sharing control of Canadian primary and secondary industries. Niosi in *Canadian Capitalism* argued that the indigenous Canadian business elite (and an aspiring French Canadian entrepreneurial class in Quebec) manipulated growing nationalist attitudes and government policies in the 1960s and 1970s to limit the influence of American multinational corporations in Canada.

16. Gerald Tulchinsky, "Recent Controversies in Canadian Business History," *Acadiensis* 8 (1978/79), 133-39. See also Douglas McCalla, "Tom Naylor's *A History of Canadian Business 1867-1914*: A Comment," Canadian Historical Association *Papers* (1976), 249-54; L.R. Macdonald, "Merchants Against Industry: An Idea and Its Origins," *Canadian Historical Review* 56 (1975), 263-81.

17. Gregory Marchildon, "Business History in Canada," *Business History Newsletter* 16 (April 1988), 2.

18. Glenn Porter, "Recent Trends in Canadian Business and Economic History," in *Enterprise and National Development: Essays in Canadian Business and Economic History*, eds. Glenn Porter and Robert Cuff (Toronto: Hakkert, 1973), 6.

19. Norman S.B. Gras, *Business and Capitalism: An Introduction to Business History* (New York: Appleton Crofts, 1939). Gras's schema drew upon the work of a German economist, Werner Sombart, but Gras applied it distinctly to business organizations rather than to the economy as a whole. A more recent interpretation that incorporates much of the new literature in business history but retains in large measure the framework enunciated by Gras can be found in Nathan Rosenberg and L.E. Birdzell, Jr., *How the West Grew Rich: The Economic Transformation of the Industrial World* (New York: Basic Books, 1986).

20. See Alfred D. Chandler, Jr., *The Visible Hand: The Managerial Revolution in American Business* (Cambridge, Mass.: Harvard University Press, 1977); for applications of the concept in Britain, see Leslie Hannah, *The Rise of the Corporate Economy*

(Baltimore: Johns Hopkins University Press, 1976); and, for more general applications in the international business community, see A.D. Chandler, Jr. and Herman Daems, eds., *Managerial Hierarchies: Comparative Perspectives on the Rise of Modern Industrial Enterprise* (Cambridge: Harvard University Press, 1980).

21. Gerald Tulchinsky, *The River Barons: Montreal Business and the Growth of Industry and Transportation, 1837-1853* (Toronto: University of Toronto Press, 1977); Douglas McCalla, *The Upper Canada Trade, 1834-1872: A Study of the Buchanans' Business* (Toronto: University of Toronto Press, 1979); Bruce Wilson, *The Enterprises of Robert Hamilton: A Study of Wealth and Influence in Early Canada, 1776-1812* (Ottawa: Carleton University Press, 1983); David Macmillan, "The 'New Man' in Action: Scottish Mercantile and Shipping Operations in the North American Colonies, 1760-1825," in *Canadian Business History*, ed. Macmillan, 44-103. Other works in this genre include David A. Sutherland, "The Merchants of Halifax, 1815-1880: A Commercial Class in Pursuit of Metropolitan Status," Ph.D. diss., University of Toronto, 1975); and, on the merchant community of New France before 1763, Dale Miquelon, *Dugard of Rouen: French Trade to Canada and the West Indies, 1729-1770* (Montreal: McGill-Queens University Press, 1978). These references represent only a few of the large and diverse range of studies of mercantile firms and communities.

22. Ronald Rudin, *Banking en français: The French Banks of Quebec, 1835-1925* (Toronto: University of Toronto Press, 1985); Peter Baskerville, *The Bank of Upper Canada* (Ottawa: Carleton University Press, 1987). The history of banking in Canada has traditionally been the preserve of economists such as E.P. Neufeld, *The Financial System of Canada: Its Growth and Development* (Toronto: MacMillan, 1972); and journalists commissioned to write "in-house" histories of the major chartered banks. Their approach is reviewed later in this essay. The statement in the text is still applicable generally to the study of other financial service institutions such as insurance houses and the stock exchanges.

23. Peter Baskerville, "The Boardroom and Beyond: Aspects of the Upper Canada Railway Community," (Ph.D. diss., Queens University, 1973); Ted Regehr, *The Canadian Northern Railway: Pioneer Road of the Northern Prairies, 1895-1915* (Toronto: MacMillan, 1976); Albert Tucker, *Steam Into the Wilderness: Ontario's Northland Railway* (Toronto: Fitzhenry and Whiteside, 1978). While narrative histories of the C.P.R. have been left to popularizers such as Pierre Berton, business historians have introduced new approaches to the subject: see, for example, Andrew den Otter, *Civilizing the West: The Galts and the Development of Western Canada* (Edmonton: University of Alberta Press, 1982) on the role of land promoters in the development of the C.P.R.; and articles by Den Otter, John Eagle, David Breen, and Ted Regehr in *The CPR West: The Iron Road and the Making of a Nation*, ed. Hugh Demsey (Vancouver: Douglas and McIntyre, 1984).

24. William Kilbourn, *The Elements Combined: A History of the Steel Company of Canada* (Toronto: Clarke-Irwin, 1960); Duncan McDowall, *Steel At the Sault: Francis H. Clergue, Sir James Dunn and the Algoma Steel Corporation, 1901-1956 (Toronto: University of Toronto Press, 1984).* The history of the third major steel complex in Canada, in Nova Scotia, has been pieced together by several scholars working with very scattered sources. Two essays that review the history of the Cape

Breton coal and steel mills in the 1920s are: Don McGillvray, "Henry M. Whitney Comes to Cape Breton," *Acadiensis* 9 (1979), 44-70; and David Frank, "The Cape Breton Coal Industry and the Rise and Fall of Besco," *Acadiensis* 7 (1977), 3-34. The other major local steel enterprise, Scotia Steel, is examined by T.W. Acheson in "The National Policy and the Industrialization of the Maritimes, 1880-1910," *Acadiensis* 1 (1972), 3-28, which, as the title implies, casts a much broader net over industrial development in the region; and Kris Inwood, *The Canadian Charcoal Iron Industry, 1870-1914* (New York: Garland, 1986).

25.   Michael Bliss, *A Canadian Millionaire: The Life and Business Times of Sir Joseph Flavelle* (Toronto: University of Toronto Press, 1978); Christopher Armstrong and H.V. Nelles, *Monopoly's Moment: The Organization and Regulation of Canadian Utilities, 1830-1930* (Philadelphia: Temple University, 1986; Toronto: University of Toronto Press, 1988); Ben Forster, *A Conjunction of Interests: Business, Politics and Tariffs, 1825-1879* (Toronto: University of Toronto Press, 1986).

26.   Duncan McDowall, *The Light: Brazilian Traction, Light and Power Co. Ltd., 1899-1945* (Toronto: University of Toronto Press, 1988); Christopher Armstrong and H.V. Nelles, *Southern Exposure: Canadian Promoters in Latin American and the Caribbean, 1896-1930* (Toronto: University of Toronto Press, 1988).

27.   William Kilbourn and Robert Bothwell, *C.D. Howe: A Biography* (Toronto: Mc-Clelland and Stewart, 1979); Bothwell, *Eldorado: Canada's National Uranium Company* (Toronto: University of Toronto Press, 1984); Bothwell, *Nucleus: A History of Atomic Energy of Canada Ltd.* (Toronto: University of Toronto Press, 1988). Other studies of business-government linkages in twentieth-century Canada include Tom Traves, *The State and Enterprise: Canadian Manufacturers and the Federal Government, 1917-1931* (Toronto: University of Toronto Press, 1979); J.A. Schultz, "Shell Game: The Politics of Defense Production, 1939-1942," *American Review of Canadian Studies* 16:1 (Spring 1986), 41-57; and H.V. Nelles, *The Politics of Development: Forests, Mines and Hydro-Electric Power in Ontario, 1849-1911* (Toronto: MacMillan, 1974) which focuses on the role of the provincial government in the economic development of Ontario.

28.   See the recent collection of studies by Canadian labour historians in *On the Job: Confronting the Labour Process in Canada*, eds. Craig Heron and Robert Storey (Montreal and Kingston: McGill-Queens University Press, 1986), particularly essays by Paul Craven and Tom Traves on railways, Graham Lowe on office management, and Heron and Storey on the steel industry.

29.   Bruce Little, review of *Northern Enterprise* in *The Globe and Mail*, July 18, 1987, B-3.

30.   Bliss, *Northern Enterprise*, 515-20 on Imperial Oil; the auto industry in Canada is briskly covered on pp. 395-97.

31.   Bliss, *Northern Enterprise*, 11.

32.   On the Hudson's Bay Company, see E.E. Rich, *Hudson's Bay Company* (Toronto: McClelland and Stewart, 1960); and a shorter popularizing book by Douglas Mac-Kay, *The Honourable Company: A History of the Hudson's Bay Company* (Indianapolis: Bobbs Merrill, 1936). On the C.P.R., the major institutional work is W.Kaye Lamb, *History of the Canadian Pacific Railway* (Toronto: MacMillan,

1977); on the Canadian National Railway and its predecessors, see G.R. Stevens, *Canadian National Railways*, 2 vols. (Toronto: Clarke Irwin, 1960-62). On the major chartered banks, see Victor Ross and A. St. L. Trigge, *A History of the Bank of Commerce*, 3 vols. (London: Oxford University Press, 1920-34); Merrill Denison, *Canada's First Bank: A History of the Bank of Montreal*, 2 vols. (Toronto: McClelland and Stewart, 1966-67); Joseph Schull and J. Douglas Gibson, *The Scotiabank Story: A History of the Bank of Nova Scotia, 1832-1982* (Toronto: MacMillan, 1982).

33. Kilbourn, *The Elements Combined*; E.P. Neufeld, *A Global Corporation: A History of the International Development of Massey-Ferguson Ltd.* (Toronto: University of Toronto Press, 1969); McDowall, *The Light*.

34. Pierre Berton, *The Great Railway*, 2 vols. (Toronto: McClelland and Stewart, 1970-71).

35. Peter C. Newman, *Flame of Power* (Toronto: McClelland and Stewart, 1959); *The Canadian Establishment*; Volume 1 (Toronto: McClelland and Stewart, 1975); Volume 2, *The Acquisitors* (Toronto: McClelland and Stewart, 1981); Volume 3, *The Establishment Man* — a tribute to the genius of Conrad Black — (Toronto: McClelland and Stewart, 1982); *Bronfman Dynasty* (Toronto: McClelland and Stewart, 1978); *Company of Adventurers* (Markham, Ont.: Viking Press, 1985), which is the first volume of his history of Hudson's Bay Company; and *Caesars of the Wilderness* (Markham: Viking Press, 1987), which is the second volume.

36. Newman's *Company of Adventurers* prompted a protracted public debate over the merits of popular history. In an extended review, historian Jennifer Brown noted the existence of "two solitudes" on the subject: the academic historians on the one hand, and "an influential network of journalistic, media, and business people on the other." Reviews of Newman's book by journalists were extravagantly favourable, while the historians were generally critical. Historians charged that Newman perpetuated racial and sexual stereotypes. They in turn were taken to task by David Frum, a journalist, who maintained that "they are not attacking him for writing history as advocacy but for advocating the wrong causes." Brown, for her part, argued that Newman's "highlighting of certain stereotypic personalities, images and anecdotes...is not only unhistorical but ahistorical." Newman countered that "I believe that vital events...can best be portrayed through the personalities of dominant individuals working out their fates....The essence of the popular historian's craft is not only to dig up available facts but...to try to recreate the event itself, conveying the authenticity of the moment." Brown's review and Newman's response are in *Canadian Historical Review* 67 (1986), 562-78. Frum's remarks are in *Saturday Night* (February 1988), 57-58. For a comment by Bliss see *Report on Business* (February 1986), 101-2.

37. Gustavus R. Myers, *A History of Canadian Wealth* (1914; reprint James Lorimer: Toronto, 1972). Some recent examples of this genre are Walter Stewart, *Towers of Gold, Feet of Clay* (Don Mills: Collins, 1982) on Canadian banks (with hardly an allusion to the literature on the subject); and Diane Stewart, *Controlling Interest: Who Owns Canada?* (Toronto: MacMillan, 1986).

38. See, for example, Peter Foster, *The Master Builders* (Toronto: Key Porter, 1986) on the Reichmann real-estate empire; and Foster, *Other People's Money* (Don Mills: Collins, 1983) on the rise and fall of Dome Petroleum Company; and Peter Cook, *Massey At the Brink* (Don Mills: Collins, 1981) on the decline of one of Canada's largest industrial firms.

7

Writing About Labour

Greg Kealey

By international standards, Canada has arrived on the labour history scene relatively late in the day. Our sister societies and publications all date from at least a decade before the creation of the Committee on Canadian Labour History in 1971 and the initial appearance of *Labour/Le Travail* in 1976.[1] *Labour History* (the United States) commenced publishing in 1960, the *Bulletin of the Society for the Study of Labour History* (England) in 1960, and *Labour History* (Australia) in 1961. Canada's relatively late start simultaneously generated advantages and problems for the writing of Canadian labour and working-class history. The advantage lay in the fact that almost from its genesis practitioners situated the field resolutely in the orbit of social history, avoiding to some degree the narrowness of institutional labour history. The difficulty arose from the relative paucity of prior work upon which to build. The plethora of studies available to British and American historians for the construction of new interpretations quite simply did not exist in Canada.

To understand that absence, we must turn to the history of the Canadian working class itself. Even the briefest account of Canadian labour must immediately identify three themes which, when taken together, account for the national uniqueness of the historical experience of our working class.

The three are first, the geographic reality of sharing the North American continent with the United States of America, second, the deep national and regional identities which fracture the Canadian nation state, and third, the impact of the Canadian federal system which itself reflects those tensions. Taken together, all three have led to the historical fragmentation of both the Canadian working class and its labour movement. Fragmentation, however, is but part of the story. The ebb and flow of working-class development and of class conflict, in turn, affected scholarly interest. Thus waves of industrial militancy and working-class self-assertiveness produced periods of academic notice. Among these, the most important were the "progressive" era from the 1880's up to the climactic strikes of 1919, the late Depression and World War II years, and the late 1960s to the present (although some might argue pessimistically that this period has also ended). In discussing the study of the Canadian working class, a multidisciplinary perspective proves more useful than one restricted to the formal discipline of history.

Any attempt to review the product of Canadian academia must make some minimal effort to consider the history of Canadian higher education as well. Here we are most concerned with the development of the discipline of history, of the cognate social sciences, of graduate studies, and of a national research infrastructure.[2] In the colonial and early national period Canadian universities maintained a classical curriculum in which moral philosophy continued to hold pride of place well into the early twentieth century.[3] While the sciences came to play an increasingly larger role in the second half of the nineteenth century, especially at McGill, history and particularly the social sciences developed slowly.[4] By 1890, most Canadian universities had Chairs of History and many began to appoint Chairs of Economics and Political Science. Still, in the 1890s most Canadians seeking higher degrees turned south to the United States and attended the new German-influenced graduate schools at Johns Hopkins, Cornell, Harvard, and Chicago.[5]

Gradually history and political economy became well-established at all Canadian universities, but remained, until the 1920s, firmly entrenched in their humanities tradition. The orientation of curricula continued to reflect the British influence more than the American, as evidenced by a strong reluctance to allow students to choose larger numbers of electives. On the other hand, steps towards professionalization had been taken. The lead in history and the social sciences came from Toronto, McGill, and Queen's.

At Toronto, George Wrong began the annual *Review of Historical Publicaions Relating to Canada* in 1897 and in 1901 a University Press was established. Wrong's annual became the *Canadian Historical Review* in 1920 and two years later the Canadian Historical Association was founded. After an abortive first attempt in 1913, a Canadian Political Science Association was created in 1929 and the *Canadian Journal of Economics and Political Science* began publishing in 1935.[6]

The birth, in the 1920s, of a Canadian nationalism based on Canada rather than the British Empire also led to an increased concern for the development of Canadian graduate schools. Again Toronto, Queen's, and McGill played leading roles. The first Ph.D.s in history and the social sciences came in the 1920s with history again leading the way.[7] Nevertheless this development should not be exaggerated. Most Canadian students still went south or across the Atlantic to pursue graduate degrees. After World War II Canadian graduate schools grew rapidly, owing at least partially to an infusion of American money derived initially from the Carnegie, the Rockefeller, and later the Ford Foundations and administered through the new Social Research Council which was founded in 1940 as a social science equivalent of the National Research Council (1916). The nearly twenty-five year gap between the founding of the bodies suggests the Canadian government's relative lack of interest in the social sciences. In 1957, with the creation of the Canada Council, the federal government finally commenced a full-fledged program of graduate and post-graduate research funding, which in 1978 evolved into the Social Sciences and Humanities Research Council of Canada.

One unusual feature which marked the evolution of Canadian higher education was the hegemony of political economy. With the exception of McGill, where Carl Dawson developed a strong Sociology and Anthropology Department in the 1920s, most Canadian universities maintained a Department of Political Economy encompassing Economics, Political Science, Sociology, and sometimes, Anthropology, until the 1960s. Toronto, the final holdout, only split its Political Economy Department into its three component parts — Commerce, Economics, and Political Science — in 1983. The implications of this historical dominance of political economy have been much debated. Canadian nationalists and some critical scholars, unhappy with the artificiality of disciplinary divisions, lament its loss while others note that the tardy development left these fields ripe for

Americanization, which came with a vengeance in the 1960s when Canadian universities grew so rapidly that the recruitment of foreign academics became necessary.[8]

I

A delineation of roughly six periods of Canadian working-class development can help identify and, to some extent, explain the historical and related social scientific work that came about as a result of that development.[9] The first three periods include a colonial period up to the 1840s typified by staples extraction, an early industrial period from the 1850s to the 1890s which encompassed the creation of the new political state in 1867, and a period of capitalist consolidation from the 1890s to the early 1920s. This set is followed by a second set of three periods: first, the time from the mid-1920s to the immediate post-war era; second, the years from the late 1940s to the early 1960s (years characterized by American world dominance); and third, the period that commenced in the 1960s when the post-war, cold-war "consensus" (to the degree that it ever existed) broke down entirely.

During the first two periods, that is, up to the early 1890s, there was almost no academic writing. The early labour press of the 1870s and 1880s showed little interest in the colonial past and tended to look across the Atlantic or to the south for its historical lessons. The minuscule academic/intellectual community hardly noticed the emergence of the labour movement until events such as the nine-hour movement (a movement to reduce the working day to nine hours) of 1872, the rise of the Knights of Labor, and the Canadian version of the Great Upheaval of 1886 set off alarm bells among the elite. Renegade intellectuals, such as Canadian Knights of Labor "brain worker" Phillips Thompson, who had been nurtured in the bohemian world of nineteenth-century journalism rather than in the effete halls of academe, found themselves barred from speaking at Canadian universities.[10] Indeed, within the span of about twenty years the University of Toronto banned speeches by Thompson, by labour leader and free thinker Alfred Jury, and by Jane Addams; the university also, adding anti-semitism and provincialism to reaction, refused to hire Lewis Namier into its history department because he was Jewish.

The industrial crisis of the 1880s, along with the success of the Knights of Labor in central Canada and the west, and of the Provincial Workmen's Association in the east, brought the labour question prominently into federal and provincial politics for the first time. Such social and political realities found only pale reflections in the hallowed halls of Canadian universities but they did at least lead to the initial appointments of Chairs of History and Political Economy in this period.[11] From such appointments grew some of the earliest social scientific research on the "labour problem," as it was then called. Thus, at the University of Toronto, for example, William Ashley's short tenure in the Chair of Political Economy led to the publication of the *Toronto University Studies in Political Science*, which included among its initial offerings Jean Scott's pioneering, "The Conditions of Female Labour in Ontario."[12] Such work, expressing clearly the pressing concerns of moral and social reformers, illustrates the early appearance of a "social science" tied tightly to the social projects of the growing middle class and its emerging professions.

These concerns dominated the subsequent period, the 1890s to 1919, in which the "labour problem" transformed itself into the threat of Bolshevism. In the process the Canadian working class brought more attention to itself than in any previous period, and arguably helped to establish much of the legislative and repressive framework that still governs class relations in Canada. While the repressive framework, especially the Royal Canadian Mounted Police Security Service, was a uniquely Canadian solution, the legislative framework that emerged was a peculiar amalgam of a) the North American progressive interest in the Australian and New Zealand experiment with compulsory arbitration, and b) the voluntarism of the United States' system. The author of the Canadian legislation, the major component of which was the Industrial Disputes Investigation Act of 1907, was Canada's first Deputy Minister of Labour, subsequently Minister of Labour, ultimately the country's first Prime Minister to hold a Ph.D., and also its longest-serving, William Lyon Mackenzie King.

King merits our attention because he epitomized the new progressive intellectual of the early twentieth century. Educated at Toronto, Chicago, and Harvard, he rejected an academic career to become Canada's first labour relations expert, successfully transforming an initially minor appointment as editor of the *Labour Gazette* into a successful career as a civil servant, mediator, politician, industrial relations consultant, author, and then

Prime Minister.[13] His major work, *Industry and Humanity*, was published in Toronto in 1918, completing his commitment to the Rockefellers for whom he worked in the aftermath of the Ludlow Massacre.[14] In it he encapsulated his almost twenty years of labour relations experience and promoted a generally liberal view which included industrial peace among the rights of an ill-defined "community." King's extreme fear of labour unrest led him to the remarkable conclusion that "In many particulars, the horrors in international war pale before the possibilities of civil conflicts begotten of class hatreds."[15] Throughout the volume, his fascination with and admiration for industry and especially for management were patently clear.

King, while undoubtedly the most prominent, was but one of a group of generally American-educated intellectuals who came to the fore as social reformers and sometime students of Canadian labour in this period. They embraced the notion put forward by King that "the poor down trodden have more to hope from men who, having a specialized training in the operation of social forces, apply themselves to the proper remedy, than from all the windy, ultra-radical demagogues."[16] Scholars sharing these assumptions included Queen's political economists Adam Shortt, a frequent mediator for King under the terms of the IDIA, and O.D. Skelton, Shortt's successor at Queen's, whose major early work, *Socialism: A Critical Analysis*, won North American acclaim.[17]

Perhaps more important, however, than the scholars who wrote in this period were a younger group of intellectuals who attended university in these years and were heavily influenced by the rise of the labour movement, especially in the period 1917-1920. A more activist group, many of them ended up pursing careers in the United States for a variety of reasons: Louis Aubrey Wood had serious difficulties with Canadian university authorities, Bryce Stewart experienced a lack of career opportunities in Canada, and Norman Ware simply saw more attractive options in the United States.[18] Of the three, only Stewart returned to Canada, when, in 1939, he accepted King's offer to become Deputy Minister of Labour to supervise the creation of a new National Employment Service and the Unemployment Insurance Commission.[19] Wood pursued a distinguished career at the University of Oregon, and Ware, of course, became America's leading labour historian between the wars. Unfortunately, he turned his attention to Canadian labour for only a fleeting moment in the 1930s when he authored one of two essays in *Labour in Canadian-American Relations* for the Carnegie series on the interaction of the two countries. This study, based almost solely on secondary sources, shows little of the insight of Ware's major American studies, *The Industrial Worker* and *The Labor Movement in the United States*. Ware made his scholarly position clear in his preface to *Labor in Modern Industrial Society* (1935): "This book is written from the standpoint of labor. The author believes that this is a necessary and legitimate point of view."[20]

In the 1920s this generation of scholars completed a series of doctoral dissertations at American universities. Bryce Stewart, for example, after a brief stint working for the Amalgamated Clothing Workers, completed a Columbia Ph.D. published in 1926 as *Canadian Labor Laws and the Treaty*.[21] This volume, while primarily a thorough examination of the evolution of Canadian labour legislation to 1925, also contains the fullest description of the history of the Canadian labour movement published up to that date. A fellow Canadian at Columbia, Edmund Bradwin, published his thesis, *The Bunkhouse Man: A Study of Work and Pay in the Camps of Canada, 1903-1914*, two years later.[22] An active reformer, Bradwin succeeded Alfred Fitzpatrick as principal of Frontier College, an educational organization that aimed to reform conditions in the bush camps housing Canadian resource workers. Perhaps the most significant of these early efforts, however, was Harold Logan's 1925 Chicago thesis titled, "The Organized Labor Movement in Canada: A History of Trade Union Organization in Canada," published in 1928.[23] Although published after Stewart's work, it seems clear that Stewart had made use of Logan's thoroughly researched thesis.[24] Logan's work was largely chronological and descriptive. He attempted little analysis, although he did show considerable interest in the One Big Union and the events of 1919, especially the Winnipeg General Strike.

The 1920s also saw in Canadian universities the tentative initiation of research into labour; a handful of M.A.s on the subject were completed, most at McGill with a few at Toronto as well. Unlike prewar Masters' theses, which were often undocumented and extremely brief, the theses of the 1920s conform to recognizable scholarly canons. Particularly strong McGill examples, deemed to merit publication, were Eugene Forsey's study of the Nova Scotia coal industry and Allan Latham's work on the emergence of confessional unionism in Quebec.[25] There can be little question that the militancy of the Cape Breton miners in the 1920s and the rise of Quebec's Catholic unions (along with their uniqueness by North American standards) led to these particular studies.

With significant exceptions, such as the epic struggles of Cape Breton's coal miners and steel workers, the 1920s were a dismal decade for Canadian labour. The Depression, however, led to the reemergence of working-class militancy and to the revival of the labour movement. Similarly, the social problems engendered by the economic dislocations of the decade led to a rapid growth of academic study of Canadian workers. Unemployment merited most attention, but the massive slowdown in immigration also created a demographic breathing space in which significant scholarly attention was directed to the nature of western Canadian settlement and to the ethnic diversity of the Canadian labour force. These later projects derived much of their impetus from American scholarly concerns which had emerged in the 1920s as part of the debate on immigration restriction. Those controversies had led American social scientists to identify immigration and settlement as a major area of concern and eventually to focus on Canada as the readily available social laboratory for such studies. Thus, the Canadian Frontiers of Settlement series was launched. While completely funded by the American Social Science Research Council, Canadians controlled the research agenda; eventually eight volumes were published, the most significant of which, for our purposes, were Harold Innis' study of the mining frontier, A.R.M. Lower's work on the lumber industry, and Carl Dawson's on immigration.[26]

American funds, specifically Carnegie Endowment for International Peace money, also financed a second major series in the 1930s on Canadian-American relations. Launched in 1934 under the direction of Canadian-born James T. Shotwell, this series eventually resulted in the publication of some twenty-five volumes. While resolutely internationalist and pacifist in conception, the volumes vary sharply in focus. While a number condemn nationalism in general as irrational and downplay Canadian-American differences, the series also contains significant nationalist statements such as Donald Creighton's *Commercial Empire of the St. Lawrence* and Innis' *The Cod Fisheries*. Moreover, even the explicit binational conception found no support in the series' summary volume, John Bartlett Brebner's *The North Atlantic Triangle*, the thesis of which is accurately reflected in the title. The only volume specifically devoted to labour contained the short study by Norman Ware discussed earlier.[27]

The most significant American academic funding, however, at least in terms of Canadian working-class studies, was the Rockefeller Foundation's support for McGill's Social Science Research Project which commenced in

1930. To find a director to address the dual study of unemployment and the city of Montreal itself, McGill turned to those who had done similar English studies. On the recommendation of Sir William Beveridge, the University hired Leonard Marsh, who had worked on Beveridge's project to update Charles Booth's London survey. Marsh immediately set out to coordinate within the various social science departments, a series of research projects on a variety of topics related to unemployment. The Rockefeller money funded not only faculty research but, more importantly, allowed McGill to recruit almost forty social science graduate students in the 1930s, all of whom received fellowships and eventually M.A.s for their individual work on the project. Among these students was Stuart Jamieson. After his McGill degree he wrote a Ph.D. thesis at Berkeley on agricultural labourers, worked as Research Director for the Co-operative Commonwealth Federation (the social democratic predecessor of the New Democratic Party), and proceeded to an academic career at the University of British Columbia.[28] His major works, *Industrial Relations in Canada* (1957) and *Times of Trouble* (1968), represented the major surveys of labour relations and of strike activity in Canada until the late 1970s.[29] Jamieson's contribution to the Social Science Research Project was a study of the French and English presence in Montreal's institutions. Documenting carefully the dominance of the Anglo-Canadian elite, he concluded that Quebec had been conquered twice, first militarily and then economically. Prominent Yale labour economist Lloyd Reynolds also began his graduate work as a team member of the McGill project, and his own volume in the series of project publications, *The British Immigrant in Canada*, simultaneously gained him his Harvard Ph.D. and involved him in his first academic controversy.[30]

Indeed the entire project found itself in continuous political difficulty. Marsh himself and many of the students leaned significantly to the left, either aligning themselves with the CCF or, in fewer cases, the Communist Party. At a university where the Chancellor was the President of the Canadian Pacific Railway, a clash was predictable. Moreover, studies of unemployment, immigration, and French-English relations were bound to arouse controversy and they did. McGill rid itself of Marsh in 1941, when he moved to Ottawa as Research Director for the Committee on Reconstruction.[31] The product of that assignment, *The Report on Social Security for Canada*, is often taken as the Canadian equivalent of the Beveridge Report and regarded by some as a blueprint for postwar social policy.[32]

The social science activities at McGill in the 1930s were quite exceptional. Among historians, for example, the staples approach of economists Mackintosh and Innis held pride of place. Although representing an improvement on the whiggish constitutional history it replaced, it spent little time considering the men and women who produced the commodities upon which it focused. Even CCF activists, such as historian Frank Underhill, made no attempt to trace the emergence and development of the Canadian working class or its labour movement. Instead Underhill became intellectually fascinated by nineteenth-century Canadian liberalism and politically suspicious of the labour movement. His historical pursuit of radical intellectual roots led him not to the "brainworkers" of the Knights of Labor, nor to the early twentieth-century socialist movement, but rather to liberal politicians/intellectuals such as George Brown, Edward Blake, and Goldwin Smith. His socialism, while it lasted, was of the top-down variety, in which intellectuals played the major role. The Fabian intellectuals with whom he had contact while at Oxford before World War I represented an ideal intellectual elite, which he tried to create in the Canadian context.[33]

Political scientist and CCF activist Eugene Forsey, on the other hand, after failing to receive tenure at McGill, joined the labour movement as Research Director of the Canadian Congress of Labour; later, after its 1956 merger with the Trades and Labour Congress, he held the same position in the new Canadian Labour Congress. In his years in the labour movement, Forsey published a number of articles on the legal/constitutional side of labour history and subsequently, when nearing retirement, undertook to write a general history of the Canadian labour movement as the CLC's Centennial Project. While not completed in time for Canada's 100th birthday and limited to the years up to 1902, Forsey's *History of Trade Unions in Canada, 1812-1902* eventually appeared in 1982. Resolutely institutional in its focus, this is not a book to read from cover to cover. On the other hand, if you want to know the TLC's position on technical education, or on anything else for that matter, in each and every convention down to 1902, and you do not want to check the original proceedings, you will find the answer here. While Forsey's book was not published until 1982, his unedited manuscript and much of the documentary material upon which it was based had been available for a number of years at the National Archives and had been broadly consulted.[34]

The Communist Party of Canada also produced some historical writing in the 1930s. Major party intellectual Stanley Ryerson offered an interpretation of the Rebellions of 1837 on their 100th anniversary, and party journalist Bill Bennett offered a brief historical overview of Canada's most westerly province in his *Builders of British Columbia* (1937). In addition, a scattering of historical essays appeared in *New Frontier*, the party's cultural and theoretical magazine in the 1930s. The CPC's major effort, however, commenced in 1948 when it launched a People's History project. Not surprisingly, the exigencies of the Cold War and the crises of 1956 led to massive delays in the appearance of the projected multiple volumes. Nevertheless, material generated from this undertaking appeared in the late 1940s and 1950s in CPC magazines such as the *National Affairs Monthly*, *New Frontier*, and later in the *Marxist Quarterly*. In the 1960s Stanley Ryerson published two volumes of this work as *The Founding of Canada: Beginnings to 1815* (1960) and *Unequal Union: Confederation and the Roots of Conflict on the Canadas, 1815-1873* (1968). Charles Lipton's *Trade Union Movement of Canada, 1927-1959* (1966) also grew out of the original 1948 CPC conception of a people's history, although by the time of its appearance Lipton had left the party. To a considerable degree then, Norman Penner's generalizations about the relatively feeble nature of the Canadian Marxist intellectual tradition are sustainable, although somewhat overstated.[35]

Returning to the period of the late 1930s and World War II, we find yet another American "contribution" to Canadian labour studies. Foundation money was crucial to the creation of Industrial Relations institutes and departments in Canadian universities. In North America, the formal study of Industrial Relations had originated at Princeton in 1922, and had been funded by Rockefeller money. The Princeton model spread, and in October 1937 Queen's became the first Canadian university to adopt it.[36] Laval and the University of Montreal followed, setting up institutes in 1944; the following year Laval began publishing *Relations Industrielles*, which in 1964 became a bilingual journal. After World War II, Toronto and McGill also set up Industrial Relations centres.

The Queen's initiative received broad business and governmental support. Not surprisingly, labour maintained a considerable distance. J.C. Cameron, the first director of the Industrial Relations Section, fits easily into the industrial pluralist consensus emerging in the 1940s. In a 1941 paper, "Dealing with Organized Labour," he called for broader rights and recognition for unions in return for legislative restrictions to ensure "responsible" behaviour.[37]

In 1945 a group of Ontario industrialists offered a hundred thousand dollars to the University of Toronto to open an Industrial Relations Department or Centre, along the lines of the one established at Queen's. Initially Toronto resisted, owing to Innis' reluctance to set up a centre that was too clearly management-oriented. The resistance was intensified by the fact that Harold Logan, the obvious labour expert at Toronto was regarded as too pro-labour by the donors. Because the University was hungry for social science research funds, a middle way was found after visits from Harvard's John Dunlop and Chicago's Fred Harbison. On April 1, 1946, an Institute of Industrial Relations under the directorship of V.W. Bladen was created. Bladen and the Australian-born C.W.M. Hart (an important Institute member before he moved to Wisconsin in 1948) had both developed considerable interest in the work of another Australian, Elton Mayo (famous for the Hawthorne study), and so the Toronto centre developed a human relations orientation, the details of which we shall not pursue here. With the creation of a new Institute of Business Administration in 1950 under Bladen, the Industrial Relations School ceased to have a separate existence and lost much of its focus.[38]

While it existed, however, the Institute gave labour studies at Toronto an unprecedented importance. Perhaps its most important associations were with Logan, whose *Trade Unions in Canada* (1948) received its support, and with a number of graduate students who were engaged in historical research on labour, including R.L. Elliott,[39] J.T. Montague, Egil Schonning, William Martin, and especially H. Clare Pentland. Montague's doctoral dissertation on labour in meat packing, Schonning's on unionism in the pulp and paper industries, and Martin's on the history of labour legislation in the area of conflict resolution were all important contributions written in the vein of institutional labour economics.[40] The work of Clare Pentland, however, pushed beyond the limited nature of these studies. Pentland addressed directly the question of the role of labour in the colonial staples economy. His earliest published work surveyed strikes by Irish navvies and the role of labour in early capitalist development.[41] Although his doctoral thesis was not completed until 1960 and was published only posthumously in 1981, it significantly influenced scholars of the 1960s and 1970s who were seeking historical approaches outside of the Canadian mainstream.[42] More recently, some scholars have criticized Pentland's approach focusing on his failure to come to grips with the pre-capitalist nature of the early

Canadian economy and on his inability to describe adequately the transition to capitalism.[43]

In his memoirs, V.W. Bladen, Director of the Toronto Institute, drew attention to the difficulty of developing relationships with unions as well as with management. One specific incident tells us much about such problems. The presence of UAW leader Victor Reuther as a speaker at the Institute's Winter Union School in 1948 led to a vigorous protest from James Duncan, President of Massey-Harris and a Member of the University's Board of Governors. In 1949 union members wanted to invite Reuther again; Bladen sought University of Toronto President Sidney Smith's approval. He did not receive it because as Bladen recalled, Smith feared that if he took such a request to the Board it would be refused and he would have to resign. As a compromise, Reuther received an informal invitation from the union students.[44]

While the mainstream of Canadian historical writing was dominated in the 1930s by the staples school and then in the 1940s and 1950s by politics and biography in reaction against such allegedly "bloodless" economic history, there were always a few notable, if relatively uninfluential, exceptions. Two examples must suffice here, although there were others in the so-called "provincial" universities. At the University of Western Ontario, Fred Landon, a doctoral student at the University of Michigan under U.B. Phillips (who collaborated with John R. Commons on the *Documentary History of American Labor*), developed an early interest in social history, including the history of working people.[45] In an appreciation of his mentor, Landon commended Phillips for his belief that "history had been written too much upon the basis of what great men said...or wrote."[46] As Landon observed in 1944: "History has a way of disinterring the records of very humble folk.... History does not relate to the great alone but to all men, and the humble folk are always the more numerous."[47] Landon's eclectic work explored various aspects of life in south-western Ontario, including abolitionism, Black history, and the Rebellion of 1837. Among his most important contributions are: "The Common Man in the Era of Rebellion," *Western Ontario and the American Frontier* (1941), *An Exile from Canada to Van Dieman's Land* (1960), and his C.H.A. presidential address, "The Canadian Scene, 1880-1890."[48] In the latter, Landon tackled a decade and postulated that "the general pattern of Canadian affairs during the 1880's... like many other accepted patterns in history is incomplete." Why? Because,

Landon answered, "These memoirs are chiefly political in character and show little interest in other phases of national life." He then drew attention to three other important "phases," of national life; the first of these was labour's struggles, especially the rise of the Knights of Labor and the Great Upheaval of 1886-87.[49]

As part of his enthusiasm for local history, Landon played a major role in commemorating the Tolpuddle Martyrs, five of whom settled in Ontario after their pardons.[50] In addition, Landon directed students' attention to the Knights of Labor, after attempting to collect their records in the 1930s.[51] J.I. Cooper and later Douglas Kennedy wrote M.A. theses under his supervision; Cooper focused on the Knights' role in the 1887 federal election and Kennedy attempted a full narrative history of the Order in Canada.[52]

Landon, however, made little impact on Canadian historical writing. Early rejection slips from W.S. Wallace, the editor of the *Canadian Historical Review* might serve as an epitaph: "the subject strikes me as perhaps a trifle narrow" and, in a second case, "its interest is too local."[53] Landon did influence his students, however, and one of them, J.I. Cooper, went on to a long career at McGill where he authored some of the few early accounts of Canadian labour by a professional historian. His interest no doubt was also influenced by his personal background:

> The home I grew up in was working-class, C of E, and *very* conventional. My mother was an elementary school teacher; my father a railway-engine driver. He divided his time unevenly between bouts on the foot-plate and minor office jobs in *The Trainmen's Journal*, where he was a very humble associate of Eugene Debs, the American socialist.[54]

Despite Cooper's assertion, this background was quite unconventional among Canadian academics of his generation. Not a prolific author, his major contributions in the field of labour history lay in two articles, the first, on the Quebec Ship Labourers Benevolent Society, was published in 1949 and the second, on the social structure of Montreal in the mid-nineteenth century, was published seven years later.[55] In addition, he supervised early graduate work in the field including theses on the role of the Knights in the Quebec provincial election of 1886, a general study of the Knights in Canada in the 1880s, and an analysis of the Grand Trunk Railway strike of 1877.[56]

Cooper, if anything, had even less impact than Landon on Canadian historical writing. In reflecting on his career in 1979, he credited Landon as being the major influence on him, noting that "implicit in [his] teaching were the economic and social forces that operate on people." By his example even more than by his teaching, Landon convinced Cooper "that no historian is worth his salt if he does not concern himself critically and productively in the area in which he lives."[57] Such ideas remained unpopular in the 1940s and 1950s and local history was most often dismissed as the domain of antiquarians.[58]

Those four, Cooper, Landon, Pentland, and Ryerson, represent exceptions to Canadian historiography's mainstream in the late 1940s, 1950s, and most of the 1960s. While never as overtly self-congratulatory as the United States consensus-school historians, Canadian historians similarly turned away from the economic focus of the 1930s and instead concentrated on biography and political history. Even the most influential social democratic historian of the period, Kenneth McNaught, offered a biography, albeit not of a Prime Minister but of CCF founder, J.S. Woodsworth.[59]

One biography, or rather a partially biographical study, that was even farther from the mainstream than McNaught's, was Harry Ferns and Bernard Ostry's critical *The Age of Mackenzie King* (1955). Ferns, a Canadian and former Communist, who had been red-baited out of the public service and then deprived of an academic career in his own country, joined forces with Ostry to produce a slashing attack on the image of King as a pro-labour social reformer. This volume so upset the Liberal orthodoxy that the carefully orchestrated official biography which was proceeding at an appropriately magisterial pace was regarded as an inadequate response and an additional study was produced by King loyalist F.A. Macgregor.[60] Former Liberal cabinet minister Brooke Claxton, in a letter to fellow Liberal politician and former historian Jack Pickersgill, described the Ferns and Ostry volume as "tiresome emissions of Communist venom."[61] Ostry later authored two useful articles on Canadian labour and politics in the 1870s and 1880s.[62]

One other scholar of the 1950s joined Pentland in having an important underground following in the late 1960s. Frank Watt's iconoclastic Toronto Ph.D. thesis on "Radicalism in English Canadian Literature Since Confederation" and his article on proletarian ideas in late Victorian Canada enjoyed a wide New Left audience.[63] Watt's careful reading of the nineteenth-century labour press not only opened up a viable research source in ways previously unanticipated but also

identified numerous important working-class thinkers, including Phillips
Thompson, for further study.

II

By the mid-1960s considerable dissatisfaction with Canadian historical
writing began to emerge within the profession itself. In the late 1960s events
in Quebec and in English Canada provided an additional external challenge
to the national historiographic consensus.[64] A number of developments
coincided to create numerous tensions within Canadian historical writing
and from these tensions decisive new directions emerged.[65] Among these
developments were: Quebec's nationalist challenge to the existence of a
unified Canadian state and a simultaneous surge of regional sentiment from
other aggrieved components of the artificial Confederation of 1867; a liberal
challenge to all nationalisms, best reflected in the historical writing by
Ramsay Cook and in the political stances of Pierre Elliott Trudeau, and,
ironically, a coincident surge of English Canadian, (especially Ontario-
based) neo-nationalism which expressed itself most strongly as anti-
Americanism in both the economic and foreign policy realms; a resurgence
of working-class militancy, which led to a series of Royal Commissions to
investigate, yet again, the state's labour relations machinery and which
eventually resulted in a state-imposed wage freeze in the guise of an incomes
policy; and, finally, the emergence of a New Left, itself split along national
(French-English), regional, and gender lines which displayed a second
division between leftist nationalists and those they referred to disparagingly
as "Metropolitan Marxists." From this confusion emerged a Canadian social
history in which class, region, and (somewhat belatedly) ethnicity and
gender finally began to receive the attention they merited. But attempts to
integrate these diverse elements into a coherent historical whole have so far
failed. As historical reality fractured, no new syntheses emerged to replace
the older, all-encompassing views — a problem with which U.S. historians
have also tried to grapple.[66]

Broadly defined, Canadian labour and working-class history began to
appear in significant amounts in the late 1960s and early 1970s. By 1971,
enough interest existed to create the Committee on Canadian Labour
History. The Committee started a *Newsletter*, eventually upgraded to a
Bulletin (closely modelled on that of the British "Society for the Study of

Labour History") and finally to *Labour/Le Travail* in 1976. Within the Committee and on the *Labour/Le Travail* Editorial Board tension developed between two identifiable groups: on the one hand, young professors who had either just published or were about to publish their first books and, on the other hand, graduate students who had emerged from the student movement of the 1960s. What seems remarkable in retrospect was the gap which separated these two groups from more senior colleagues: for reasons that should by now be only too clear, there existed no direct line of succession from previous generations of scholars in the field. To be fair, there was an advisory editorial board filled with international luminaries (Royden Harrison, Jean Maîtron, and David Montgomery) and a number of senior Canadian scholars previously mentioned in this paper (Stuart Jamieson, Kenneth McNaught, Clare Pentland, and Stanley Ryerson). Their presence, however, was primarily promotional and the Advisory Board was allowed to lapse in 1980, its members having played no substantive role in the life of the journal. The one partial exception was Michael S. Cross (whose work in the 1960s on the Ottawa Valley timber trade went beyond the historiographic parameters of its day) who provided considerable support to the journal as a Dalhousie colleague of its editor in its first four years.[67]

The conflict reached a climax in the early 1980s, with a series of review essays by Kenneth McNaught, Desmond Morton, and David Bercuson on the one hand, and myself and Bryan Palmer on the other. Carl Berger's summary of the debate as "captious, intemperate, and confusing" suggests its flavour, and his characterization of the two sides as "the upholders of the social democratic tradition and those who had embraced a humanistic Marxism" has the advantage of offering a non-participant's viewpoint of the ideological origins of the debate. There is little to argue with in his overall assessment:

> These exchanges also obscured the very significant achievements of those who had penetrated beyond the political confines. They recovered copious and scarcely suspected details on social life in the Victorian period: they have helped move to the centre of attention the social conflict that accompanied the arrival of industrial society, and have accorded a place to ideas and attitudes in history that belied the commonplace image of Marxist scholarship as materialistic, and they have contributed far more to the ultimate clarification of class — and class in history — than the statisticians of social mobility.[68]

Indeed the debate has to a large degree quieted. Many of Bercuson's "generation" have either moved into academic administration (Ross McCormack) or into other fields of historical interest such as military (Terry Copp, Morton), diplomatic (Bercuson), public policy (Donald Avery), and immigration (Irving Abella).

The debate emerged once more in 1984, this time from an unexpected source; *Studies in Political Economy*, Canada's major socialist academic journal, published a challenge to the so-called "new labour history" by left-nationalist, political scientist Daniel Drache. Building on the critiques of Bercuson and McNaught, Drache constructed an eclectic amalgam of various labour market theories — Innis' staples model, neo-nationalism, a pinch of world system analysis, and some curiously chosen empirical facts about Canadian labour history. Identifying three crucial periods of labour market formation — canal building in the early 1830s, central Canadian industrialization in the late 1890s, and the opening of the west and growth of a resource proletariat from 1900 to 1920 — Drache argued that the "new labour history" had mistaken Toronto and Hamilton for the entire country, had misunderstood the centrality of the national question, and had insufficiently addressed colonial developments.[69] In a spirited rejoinder, Bryan Palmer reviewed the development of Canadian labour studies and especially the criticisms of Bercuson, McNaught, and others in a fashion reminiscent of his September, 1981 commentary at the Australian-Canadian-British (termed by its organizers "Commonwealth") Labour History Conference at Warwick.[70] Defending historians and their methods, Palmer assailed Drache's argument. In perhaps the most interesting part of his response, Palmer rejected the notion that labour historians' work had been too theoretical and called instead for more theory. Then, further exploring territory he had tentatively traversed in *Working Class Experience*, he redefined the terms of new labour history. It must, he argued, be "premised on the essential tenets of historical materialism," now understood as conceiving

class not in this or that particular, but as a totality resting on the essential economic relations of production, yet emerging and making itself, and being made, in an integrated series of realms that, by the very nature of bourgeois society, are divorced from one another and carved up between the public and private arenas, of an atomized social existence.

Most importantly, he called for more attention "to the structural and determining features of economic life," to the "peculiarities of place," to the state, and "above all else, to the two-sidedness of working-class life." He went on to argue that the strength of the work to date had been the description of working-class struggle and resistance; what was necessary now was equal attention to questions of accommodation in all its forms.[71]

An assessment of the two most recent attempts at synthesis in the field, Desmond Morton, *Working People* and Bryan Palmer, *Working-Class Experience: The Rise and Reconstitution of Canadian Labour, 1800-1980* also illustrates the two contrasting approaches.[72] The two books serve as core texts for most Canadian labour and working-class history courses and they could not be more different. Palmer sets out to study "the totality of working-class experience":

> It is *class*, as embedded in the structural, primarily economic context of specific social formations, that is at the conceptual root of this study, not labour as an interest group fighting its way into a pluralist society by way of its unions and its political platform. The development of distinct working and nonworking classes was a protracted and contradictory process. It grew out of the economic relations of production, but was also clarified and reproduced over time in other formal and informal ways; through ritual and revelry, culture and conflict, family and funeral and, of course, through the strengths, weaknesses, and character of the workers' movement itself. At times new initiatives — from *capital* and/or the state — drove it into retreat, but its potential was never relinquished entirely.[73]

Contrast this with Morton's assertion that his book "does not build on theories borrowed from the great English labour historian E.P. Thompson" and his sarcastic comment that "it is one of the virtues of modern social history that it gives due attention to those who say little and do nothing of historical significance."[74] Of Palmer's 300 pages almost half are devoted to the nineteenth century, while Morton devotes only 66 of 357 pages to what he clearly regards as pre-history, noting critically of Palmer's book that it devotes only one-third of its coverage to the period after 1919.[75] Moreover, Morton asserts unequivocally that

> ... the crucial decade in Canadian working class history is...the Second World War and the post war years of prosperity, full employment and expanding social justice.... For those with utopian visions of what life and

labour might be and for those who find romantic fulfillment in defeat, the prosperous post-war year have little appeal.[76]

The field of debate should be clear by now.

III

Nevertheless, a brief consideration of the three major edited collections in the field suggests that the debate of the early 1980s may itself have passed into history. Bercuson's *Canadian Labour History* includes two of the core texts of the debate and discusses in its introduction the generational differences between "democratic socialists" and Marxists. But Bercuson now describes labour history as a component of social history, which he promotes as "*the* dominant area of specialization" in Canadian historical writing. "Most historians," he argues, "now recognize that the history of workers is part of the history of employers and political leaders, and vice versa." Clearly, some ground has been gained.[77] Meanwhile, Palmer, in his introduction to *The Character of Class Struggle: Essays in Canadian Working-Class History, 1850-1985*, concedes "that there has been more to history than class war," but proceeds to demonstrate through this collection of essays how "the character of class struggle within particular political economies" has changed in the last 135 years. He concludes, "If the changing and complex character of class struggle in Canada has not consumed all of our history, it has at least occupied the centre of one of the stages on which our past had been acted out."[78]

The third reader, Craig Heron and Bob Storey's *On the Job: Confronting the Labour Process in Canada*, turns to a series of workplaces in the period from 1850 to the present and shows how workers and bosses have struggled for control, with varying degrees of respective success. In their overview, the editors remind us:

There has not been a single, permanent shift in working-class consciousness that resulted in complete submission and deference to capitalist authority.... Instead a pattern of ebbing and flowing, of surging and receding, is evident: in 1867, the dramatic rise of labour in 1872 and the mid 1880s would have seemed unimaginable; in 1905 no one would have predicted the phenomenal upheaval of 1919; in 1935, the explosion of 1946 militancy would have seemed laughable; and in the serenity of the 1950s, no one was anticipating the turbulence of the late 1960s and early 1970s.[79]

All three collections of essays demonstrate that historians have finally realized that the working class is composed of women as well as men. Heron and Storey's book contains essays on women's paid and unpaid work in the home, in the office, in garment factories, and in the newest of capitalism's "factories," the fast-food industry. Palmer's collection includes studies on textile workers and public sector workers, and an assessment of working-class feminism, while Bercuson has chosen essays on telephone operators and on the working-class family economy in nineteenth-century Montreal. Yet the integration of women's history and working-class history, as Bettina Bradbury has recently argued, still poses significant difficulties. Neverthe-less Bradbury sees cause for hope in the attempt by some labour historians to recreate a total working-class experience. In order for this hope to be realized, Bradbury believes there will need to be: first, an emphasis on working-class reproduction, both ideological and material, to match the usual attention paid to production; second, a serious examination of all aspects of the working-class family economy; third, an analysis of the process of class reproduction itself, "including marriage, childbearing, childrearing, and socialization"; and fourth, an examination of how gender has been defined, transmitted, or altered within the working class.[80] The importance of these themes has been echoed recently in U.S. historical discussion as well. Among the most intriguing of the commentaries on the late Herbert Gutman's work were those of David Montgomery and Susan Levine. Montgomery reiterated Gutman's emphasis on the role of the family in class formation and Levine pushed for further examination of how the relationships of working-class men and women influenced their interpreta-tion of their common world.[81]

The three Canadian collections of essays show little evidence of one of Gutman's major concerns in his final work, in which he raised basic questions about the specific ethno-cultural composition of the working class and its development over time. Just as his emphasis on class formation in his examination of Afro-American slaves led him to the family, Gutman had also begun before his death to analyze class development from 1840 to 1890 by asking who constituted the American working class in those years.[82] His focus on immigration, on immigrant families, and on ethnic communities in America began to reshape in a more rigorous fashion his earlier insights about the constitution and reconstitution of the American working class. These insights had been present, albeit in only a problematic postulation, in his justly famous "Work, Culture and Society in Industrializing America."[83] Gutman's work has influenced Canadian historical writing in two rather different ways. First, Canadian historians have attempted of late to eliminate the divide between immigration history and working-class history, a split that emerged (artificially to some degree) from the competition of new fields and, perhaps, from the suspicion generated by Canadian governmental enthusiasm for multiculturalism. Clearly, the work now being produced on nineteenth- and twentieth-century immigration and the role that transoceanic, continental, and regional population movements have played in fueling capitalist transformation and growth is greatly influencing our images of Canadian working-class development. To take but one example, Bruno Ramirez's work, including his forthcoming *On the Move: Agriculture, Industry, and Migrants in the North Atlantic Economy, 1860-1978*, forces us to reconsider much of Quebec history by linking a series of processes that to date have been treated as discrete — the colonization movement, migration to New England, Italian immigration, and urbanization.[84] Moreover, in the wake of this reconstruction come important insights into the nature of immigrant behaviour, insights that look far beyond the sterility of earlier conceptions of ethnic docility and ethnic radicalism (generally expressed as ethnic versus class consciousness).[85]

Ramirez's work, while focused on Quebec as simultaneous population donor and recipient, raises important questions about similar migrations elsewhere in Canada. The massive population outpouring from the Atlantic provinces to New England and to other parts of the United States is reasonably well-known, but its implications for regional working-class development remain unexplored.

Secondly, Gutman's notion of working-class constitution and reconstitution and his resolute insistence that the concept of American exceptionalism was not an appropriate historical question has led to more attention being paid in Canadian historical writing, as elsewhere, to what workers did as opposed to what they failed to do. As Gutman put it:

> We need to put aside the English model, the French model, and the Cuban model, and then ask a set of very, very tough questions about what American workers actually thought and did — and why. Once we free ourselves of the notion that it should have happened in one particular way, then we stop looking for the reasons why it didn't happen that way.[86]

This revolt against a teleological view of the working class, perhaps partially a North American variant of *The Forward March of Labour Halted*, has many reflections and echoes in recent Canadian work.[87]

As the prominence in this discussion of Bettina Bradbury and Bruno Ramirez (both of the Université de Montréal), might suggest, another positive feature of the 1980s is the developing dialogue among Canadian historians of the working class. While *Labour/Le Travail* has always been bilingual and has attempted from its inception to publish as much Quebec material as possible, the realities of academic and national politics in the 1970s made that a highly problematic goal. The changed political realities of the 1980s have led to increasing success in this realm. Quebec labour historiography has been slighted in the pages of this essay, but its direction has closely paralleled the developments described herein. If anything, there has been among Quebec labour historians a more tenacious institutional focus with most attention being devoted to trade union development, labour politics, and the national question.[88] In Quebec as elsewhere, however, this started to change in the early 1970s. Among the most prolific of the new practitioners in Quebec have been Jacques Rouilland and Fernand Harvey. In the 1980s working-class history in French and English Canada is marked by a growing congruence — a process reflected in recent issues of *Labour/Le Travail*.

As the renewed interest in migration suggests, the focus of Canadian working-class history has also begun to turn outwards in the last few years. The Warwick Conference mentioned earlier a Welsh-Canadian Labour History Conference held in 1987, and a number of other international symposia have involved Canadian scholars in the attempt to develop a broader comparative understanding of working-class development.[89] Works such as those recently published by Charles Bergquist, and Ira Katznelson and Aristide Zolberg, with their attempts at systematic comparative approaches to class formation and development, appear to be but a beginning.[90] The new project of the International Institute of Social History in Amsterdam on "Determinants of the Development of Working-Class Movements, 1870-1914: A Comparative Analysis," which at last count involves scholars from at least twenty-five countries, aims to produce a systematic comparison of national experiences. The world-wide phenomenon of capitalist development, which to date has not produced an international proletariat capable of superceding it, appears somewhat ironically to be producing a labour and working-class history attempting to comprehend it. Canadian scholars may have arrived at the study of our working class relatively late in the day, but in the last fifteen years we have made significant strides. Certainly there is no longer a vacuum waiting to be filled.

Endnotes

1. Initially named *Labour/Le Travailleur*, the French title was changed in 1983 to correct the sexism of the original. *Labour/Le Travail* appeared as an annual until 1981 and has been published semi-annually since that date.

2. Robin Harris, *A History of Higher Education in Canada, 1663-1960* (Toronto, 1976).

3. A.B. McKillop, *A Disciplined Intelligence: Critical Inquiry and Canadian Thought in the Victorian Era* (Montreal, 1979).

4. Marlene Shore, *The Science of Social Redemption: McGill, the Chicago School, and the Origins of Social Research in Canada* (Toronto, 1987).

5. Harris, *A History of Higher Education*, 190-1.

6. V.W. Bladen, "A Journal is Born: 1935," *Canadian Journal of Economics and Political Science* 26 (1960), 1-5.

7. There were exceptions such as the Ph.D. the University of Toronto awarded to James Mavor in 1912 in order, in the words of Ian Drummond, "to clothe his academic nakedness." See Drummond, *Political Economy at the University of Toronto: A History of the Department, 1888-1982* (Toronto, 1983), 27.

8. C.B. Macpherson, "After Strange Gods: Canadian Political Science, 1973" in *Perspectives on the Social Sciences in Canada*, eds. Thomas N. Guinsberg and Grant L. Reuben (Toronto, 1974), 51-76.

9. See my introduction to G.S. Kealey and Peter Warrian, eds., *Essays in Canadian Working-Class History* (Toronto, 1976), and my "The Structures of Canadian Working-Class History," in *Lectures in Canadian Labour and Working-Class History*, eds. W.J.C. Cherwinski and G.S. Kealey (St. John's, 1985), 23-26; Bryan D. Palmer, *Working-Class Experience: The Rise and Reconstitution of Canadian Labour, 1800-1980* (Toronto, 1983); Crain Heron and Robert Storey, "On the Job in Canada," in their *On the Job: Confronting the Labour Process in Canada* (Kingston, 1986), 3-46.

10. Phillips Thompson, *Politics of Labor* (New York, 1887, reprint Toronto, 1975); and R.G. Hann, "Brainworkers and the Knights of Labor," in Kealey and Warrian, *Essays*.

11. For discussion of such developments see Carl Berger, *The Writing of Canadian History* (Toronto, 1986); McKillop, *A Disciplined Intelligence*; S.E.D. Shortt, *The Search for an Ideal: Six Intellectuals in an Age of Transition* (Toronto, 1976); Drummond, *Political Economy*; Shore, *The Science of Social Redemption*; Doug

Owram, *The Government Generation: Canadian Intellectuals and the State, 1900-1945* (Toronto, 1986); and Paul Craven, *"An Impartial Umpire" : Industrial Relations and the Canadian State, 1900-1911* (Toronto, 1980).

12. Jean Scott, "The Conditions of Female Labour in Ontario," *Toronto University Studies in Political Science*, 1 (1892), 84-113.

13. The literature on W.L.M. King is immense. Among the most useful contributions are Craven, "An Impartial Umpire"; H. Ferns and B. Ostry, *The Age of Mackenzie King* (London, 1955); and Reg Whitaker, "The Liberal Corporatist Ideas of Mackenzie King," *Labour/Le Travail* 2 (1977), 137-69.

14. On the Rockefeller connection, see Stephen Scheinberg, "Rockefeller and King: The Capitalist and the Reformer," in Mackenzie King: *Widening the Debate*, eds. John English and John O. Stubbs (Toronto, 1977), 89-104.

15. W.L.M. King, *Industry and Humanity* (Toronto, 1918), 24.

16. W.L.M. King, *The Secret of Heroism* (Toronto, 1906), 114, as quoted in Whitaker, "Liberal Corporatist Ideas," 140.

17. O.D. Skelton, *Socialism: A Critical Analysis* (Boston, 1911). It was published as Volume 6 of the Hart, Schaffner, and Marx Prize Economic Essays and won the first prize of $1,000.

18. For brief descriptions of their careers, see G.S. Kealey, "Looking Backward: Reflections on the Study of Class in Canada," *The History and Social Science Teacher* 16:4 (Summer 1981), 213-22. On Woods' troubles at Western see N.S.B. Gras to Fred Landon, 2 August 1921, Landon Papers, University of Western Ontario Archives.

19. On Stewart and the demise of his original Employment Service of Canada, see James Struthers, *No Fault of Their Own: Unemployment and the Canadian Welfare State, 1914-1941* (Toronto, 1983), esp. Ch.1.

20. Norman Ware: "The History of Labor Interaction, in *Labor in Canadian American Relations*, ed. H.A. Innis (Toronto, 1937); *The Industrial Worker, 1840-1860* (Gloucester, 1959); *The Labor Movement in the United States, 1860-1895* (New York, 1964); *Labor in Modern Industrial Society* (New York, 1935).

21. Bryce Stewart, *Canadian Labor Laws and the Treaty* (New York, 1926).

22. Edmund Bradwin, *The Bunkhouse Man: A Study of Work and Pay in the Camps of Canada, 1903-1914* (Toronto, 1928; reprint Toronto, 1972).

23. Harold Logan, *History of Trade Union Organization in Canada* (Chicago, 1928).

24. Stewart, *Canadian Labor Laws*, 8.

25. Eugene Forsey, *Economic and Social Aspects of the Nova Scotia Coal Industry* (Toronto, 1926); and Allan Latham, *The Catholic and National Labour Unions of Canada* (Toronto, 1930).

26. Shore, *Science of Social Redemption*, 162-94.

27. Donald Creighton, *Commercial Empire of the St. Lawrence* (Toronto, 1937); Harold Innis, *The Cod Fisheries* (Toronto, 1954); John Bartlett Brebner, *The North Atlantic Triangle* (Toronto, 1966); Ware, "The History of Labor Interaction."

28. The thesis was subsequently published as *Labor Unionism in American Agriculture* (Washington, 1945).

29. Stuart Jamieson: *Industrial Relations in Canada* (Toronto, 1957); *Times of Trouble* (Ottawa, 1968).

30. Lloyd G. Reynolds, *The British Immigrant In Canada: His Social and Economic Adjustment in Canada* (Toronto, 1935).

31. The events at McGill in the 1930s illustrate the fragility of academic freedom in Canadian universities, a story that merits more attention than it has received. Two examples must suffice. Political scientist Eugene Forsey was denied tenure and theologian King Gordon was forced out of his position; both were prominent CCF intellectuals.

32. Leonard C. Marsh, *Report on Social Security for Canada* (Ottawa, 1943; reprint Toronto, 1975).

33. On Underhill, see R. Douglas Francis, *Frank H. Underhill: Intellectual Provocateur* (Toronto, 1986); Michiel Horn, *The League for Social Reconstruction: Intellectual Origins of the Democratic Left in Canada, 1930-1942* (Toronto, 1980); and Berger, *Writing*, Ch.3.

34. Eugene Forsey, *History of Trade Unions in Canada, 1812-1902* (Toronto, 1982).

35. William Bennett, *Builders of British Columbia* (Vancouver, 1937). Stanley Ryerson: *The Founding of Canada: Beginnings to 1815* (Toronto, 1960); *Unequal Union: Confederation and the Roots of Conflict on the Canadas, 1815-1873* (New York, 1968). Charles Lipton, *Trade Union Movement of Canada, 1927-1959,* (Montreal, 1966); Norman Penner, *The Canadian Left* (Toronto, 1978). On Ryerson, see G.S. Kealey, "Stanley Bréhaut Ryerson: Canadian Revolutionary Intellectual"; and "Stanley Bréhaut Ryerson: Marxist Historian," *Studies in Political Economy* 9 (1982), 103-71.

36. Queen's University, Industrial Relations Section, School of Commerce and Administration, *Industrial Relations: Papers Presented at 5th Conference* (Kingston, 1940), 18-21. See also: Clarence J. Hicks, *My Life in Industrial Relations: Fifty Years in the Growth of A Profession* (New York, 1941), 127, 146-7, 150.

37. J.C. Cameron, "Dealing with Organized Labour," in Queen's University, Industrial Relations Section, *Industrial Relations: Papers Presented at 6th Conference* (Kingston, 1941), 39-50, esp. 49-50.

38. On the Toronto experience, see Vincent Bladen, "Economics and Human Relations," *Canadian Journal of Economics and Political Science* 14 (1948), 301-11; and his *Bladen on Bladen: Memoirs of a Political Economist* (Toronto, 1978), 96-107; Drummond, *Political Economy*, 95-96, 105-6; and University of Toronto, Institute of Industrial Relations, *Annual Report of Director*, 1947-1950. Elton Mayo, a Harvard social scientist, conducted a series of studies for Western Electric at their Hawthorne plant outside Chicago. On Hart's interest in these, see his "The Hawthorne Experiments," *Canadian Journal of Economics and Political Science* 9 (1943), 150-63; and "Industrial Relations Research and Social Theory," *ibid.* 15 (1949), 53-73.

39. Harold Logan, *Trade Unions In Canada* (Toronto, 1948); R.L. Elliott, "The Canadian Labour Press from 1867," *Canadian Journal of Economics and Political Science* 14 (1948), 220-45, and 515.

40. J.T. Montague, "Trade Unionism in the Canadian Meat Packing Industry" (Ph.D. diss., University of Toronto, 1950); W.S.A. Martin, "A Study of Legislation Designed to Foster Industrial Peace in the Common Law Jurisdictions of Canada" (Ph.D. diss., University of Toronto, 1954); and E. Schonning, "Union-Management Relations in the Pulp and Paper Industry of Ontario and Quebec, 1914-1950" (Ph.D. diss., University of Toronto, 1955).

41. H.C. Pentland: "The Lachine Strike of 1843," *Canadian Historical Review* 29 (1948), 255-77; "The Role of Capital in Canadian Economic Development before 1875," *Canadian Journal of Economics and Political Science* 16 (1950), 457-74; and "The Development of a Capitalistic Labour Market in Canada" *Canadian Journal of Economics and Political Science* 25 (1959), 450-61.

42. H.C. Pentland: "Labour in Canada in the Early 19th Century" (Ph.D. diss., University of Toronto, 1961); and *Labour and Capital in Canada, 1650-1860* (Toronto, 1981).

43. For commentaries on Pentland see Paul Phillips, "Introduction" in Pentland, *Labour and Capital*; G.S. Kealey, "H.C. Pentland and Working-Class History," *Canadian Journal of Political and Social Theory* 3 (1979), 79-94; Bryan Palmer, "Town, Port and Country: Speculations on the Capitalist Transformation of Canada," *Acadiensis* 12 (1983), 131-9; and Allan Greer, "Wage Labour and The Transition to Capitalism: A Critique of Pentland," *Labour/Le Travail* 15 (1985), 7-22.

44. Bladen, *Bladen*, 101-2.

45. John R. Commons, Ulrich B. Phillips, Eugene A. Gilmore, Helen L. Sumner and John B. Andrews, eds., *A Documentary History of American Industrial Society* (New York, 1958).

46. Fred Landon, "Ulrich Bonnell Phillips: Historian of the South," *Journal of Southern History* 5 (1939), 364-71. Quotation from page 370.

47. Fred Landon, "Foreword," to his *Lake Huron* (Indianapolis, 1944). See also Patricia G. Skidmore, "Mind and Manuscript: A Profile of Historian Fred Landon," unpublished manuscript, University of Western Ontario Archives; F.H. Armstrong, "Fred Landon, 1880-1969," *Ontario History* 62 (1970), 1-4; and Hilary Bates, "A Bibliography of Fred Landon," *Ontario History* 62 (1970), 5-16.

48. Fred Landon: "The Common Man in the Era of Rebellion," in *Aspects of Nineteenth-Century Ontario*, ed. F.H. Armstrong *et al.* (Toronto, 1974); *Western Ontario and the American Frontier* (Toronto, 1941); "The Canadian Scene, 1880-1890," in Canadian Historical Association, *Annual Report* (1942), 5-18.

49. Landon, "The Canadian Scene," 5.

50. Fred Landon Papers, University of Western Ontario Archives, Scrapbooks.

51. Fred Landon, "The Knights of Labor: Predecessors of the CIO," *Quarterly Review of Commerce* 1 (1937), 133-39.

52. J.I. Cooper, "The Canadian General Election of 1887" (M.A. thesis, University of Western Ontario, 1933); and Douglas Kennedy, "The Knights of Labor in Canada"

(M.A. thesis, University of Western Ontario, 1945). This later work was published by Western after Kennedy's untimely death (London, 1956).

53. W.S. Wallace to Fred Landon, 22 June 1920 and 30 December 1920, Landon Papers, University of Western Ontario Archives.

54. J.I. Cooper to Carmen Miller, 3 December 1979, in author's possession. Emphasis in original.

55. J.I. Cooper: "The Quebec Ship Labourers Benevolent Society," *Canadian Historical Review* 30 (1949), 336-44; and "The Social Structure of Montreal in the 1850's," Canadian Historical Association, *Annual Report* (1956), 62-73.

56. Robert Cox, "The Quebec Provincial General Election of 1886" (M.A. thesis, McGill University, 1948); V.O. Chan, "The Canadian Knights of Labor with Special Reference to the 1880s" (M.A. thesis, McGill University, 1949); and Shirley Ayer, "The Locomotive Engineers' Strike on the Grand Trunk Railway in 1876-1877" (M.A. thesis, McGill University, 1961).

57. Cooper to Miller, 3 December 1979, in author's possession.

58. When Cooper was invited in 1980 to attend a McGill conference on "Class and Community: Perspectives on Canada's Labour Past," he wrote modestly to decline: "I am flattered, I need hardly say, to be remembered in this connection.... I don't even know the direction that labour history has taken. I should hope that it concerns itself with the men and women (and children) on the shop floor, rather than with organization and leaders." Cooper to Miller, 23 February 1980, in author's possession.

59. Kenneth McNaught, *A Prophet in Politics* (Toronto, 1959).

60. Ferns and Ostry, *The Age of Mackenzie King*; F.A. McGregor, *The Fall and Rise of Mackenzie King, 1911-1919* (Toronto, 1962). On Ferns, see his enjoyable *Reading from Left to Right* (Toronto, 1983), and on his adventures with Bernard Ostry, see 297-310.

61. Ferns, *Reading*, 305.

62. B. Ostry, "Conservatives, Liberals, and Labour in the 1870s," *Canadian Historical Review* 41 (1960), 93-127; and "Conservatives, Liberals and Labour in the 1880s," *Canadian Journal of Economics and Political Science* 27 (1961), 141-61.

63. Frank Watt: "Radicalism in English Canadian Literature Since Confederation" (Ph.D. diss., University of Toronto, 1958); and "The National Policy, the Workingman and Proletarian Ideas in Victorian Canada," *Canadian Historical Review* 40 (1959), 1-26.

64. Gregory S. Kealey, "The Writing of Social History in English Canada, 1970-1984," *Social History* 10 (1985), 347-65.

65. In addition to the Kealey article cited above, the second edition of Carl Berger, *The Writing of Canadian History: Aspects of English Canadian Historical Writing Since 1900* (Toronto, 1986), contains a new final chapter on "Tradition and the 'New' History." See also Carl Berger, ed., *Contemporary Approaches to Canadian History* (Toronto, 1987); and Terry Crowley, ed., *Clio's Craft* (Toronto, 1988).

66. Herbert G. Gutman, "Historical Consciousness in Contemporary America," in *Power and Culture: Essays on the American Working Class*, ed. Ira Berlin (New York,

1987), 395-412. For Canadian versions see William Acheson, "Doctoral Theses and the Discipline of History in Canada, 1967 and 1985," *Historical Papers* (1986), 1-10; John English, "The Second Time Around: Political Scientists Writing History," *Canadian Historical Review* 67 (1986), 1-16; and Berger, *Writing*, 317-20. The New Left arose in the 1960s and distinguished itself from both orthodox communist and social democratic parties. While taking particular shapes in different national contexts, it most often focused on civil rights, anti-Vietnam war movements, and nuclear disarmament.

67.   I should note that Eugene Forsey (after helping gain our initial funding support from Labour Canada) decided not to join the Advisory Editorial Board. His early support was crucial to the launching of *L/LT* and the first issue was dedicated to him.

68.   Carl Berger, *Writing*, 306-7. Berger's description of the sides conforms closely to Bercuson's own view in "Introduction," *Canadian Labour History: Selected Readings* (Toronto, 1987), 1-2.

69.   Daniel Drache, "The Formation and Fragmentation of the Canadian Working Class: 1820-1920," *Studies in Political Economy* 15 (1984), 43-89.

70.   Bryan Palmer, "Listening to History Rather than Historians," *Studies in Political Economy* 20 (1986), 47-84.

71.   *Ibid.*, 75-8.

72.   Desmond Morton, *Working People*, (Ottawa, 1980, 2nd. ed., 1984); and Bryan Palmer, *Working-Class Experience: The Rise and Reconstitution of Canadian Labour, 1800-1980* (Toronto, 1983).

73.   Palmer, *Working-Class Experience*, 3.

74.   Morton, "Preface," *Working People*.

75.   *Ibid.*, 326.

76.   *Ibid.*

77.   Bercuson, *Canadian Labour History*, 3 and 231.

78.   Bryan Palmer, *The Character of Class Struggle: Essays in Canadian Working-Class History, 1850-1985* (Toronto, 1986), 9-14.

79.   Craig Heron and Bob Storey, *On the Job: Confronting the Labour Process in Canada* (Kingston, 1986), 31-32.

80.   Bettina Bradbury, "Women's History and Working-Class History," *Labour/Le Travail* 19 (1987), 23-43.

81.   David Montgomery, "Gutman's Agenda for Future Historical Research" and Susan Levine, "Class and Gender: Herbert Gutman and the Women of 'Shoe City'," *Labour History* 29, (1988), 299-312, 344-55.

82.   Herbert Gutman and Ira Berlin, "Class Composition and the Development of American Working Class, 1840-1890," in his *Power and Culture*, 380-94.

83.   Herbert Gutman, "Work, Culture and Society in Industrializing America," *American Historical Review* 78 (1973), 531-88; also available in the book of the same title (New York, 1976).

84. Bruno Ramirez, *On the Move: Agriculture, Industry and Migrants in the North Atlantic Economy, 1860-1978* (Toronto, forthcoming). Also see his brief "Ethnic Studies and Working-Class History," *Labour/Le Travail* 19 (1987), 45-48.

85. For a useful, earlier exploration of these questions, albeit one posed in just these terms, see Donald Avery, *"Dangerous Foreigners": European Immigrant Workers and Labour Radicalism in Canada, 1896-1932* (Toronto, 1979).

86. "Interview with Herbert Gutman" in *Power and Culture*, 343. The debate about American exceptionalism commenced in the early twentieth century with German sociologist Werner Sombart's *Why is there no Socialism in the United States?*, which appeared in 1906 and is now most readily available in a version edited by C.T. Husbands (White Plains, New York, 1976). Recent commentaries include Eric Foner, "Why is there no Socialism in America?" *History Workshop* 17 (1984); and Sean Wilentz, "Against Exceptionalism: Class Consciousness and the American Labour Movement," *International Labor and Working-Class History* 26 (1984), 1-36, and 28 (1985), 46-55.

87. Martin Jacques and Francis Mulhern, eds., *The Forward March of Labour Halted* (London, 1981); Palmer, *Working-Class Experience*; Heron and Storey, *On the Job*; Kealey, "Structure."

88. These generalizations are derived from Kealey, Palmer, and Jacques Ferland, "Labour Studies," in *Thematic Guide to Canadian Studies*, ed. A. Artibise (Montreal, forthcoming).

89. Deian Hopkin and G.S. Kealey, eds., *Class, Community and the Labour Movement in Canada and Wales, 1890-1930* (Aberystwyth, 1989); D.C.M. Platt, ed., *Social Welfare 1850-1950: Australia, Argentina and Canada Compared* (London, 1989); C. Harzig and D. Hoerder, eds., *The Press of Labour Migrants in Europe and North America, 1880s-1930s* (Bremen, 1985).

90. Charles Bergquist, *Labor in Latin America. Comparative Essays on Chile, Argentina, Venezuela and Colombia* (Stanford, 1986); and Ira Katznelson and Aristide Zolberg, eds., *Working-Class Formation: Nineteenth-Century Patterns in Western Europe and the United States* (Princeton, 1986).

8

Writing About Women

Veronica Strong-Boag

For many years, and even today in some quarters, where history continues to be taught as if the last twenty years of scholarship did not exist, Canada's past has been dismissed as "as dull as ditchwater." Why is this so? It is because far too many texts and classes have given people only a tiny, misleading glimpse of what history is all about. To concentrate, as so many writers of history have, on the doings of a small elite group of European men leaves out the great majority of the country's inhabitants and distorts the meaning of even those few lives which have attracted attention. While all-too-familiar discussions of either the influence of imperial conferences in the 1890s on the long road to self-government or the role of businessmen in the shaping of a national energy policy in the years after World War Two can be significant and exciting, such matters are but one very small part of what it has meant to be Canadian. Events and human beings, however prominent in their own times, cannot be understood in isolation, and yet this is what many traditional historical accounts would have us believe. Interpretations of individuals and institutions only make real sense when those individuals and institutions are viewed as the expression of a variety of personal, social, and economic relationships. All too frequently, however, this richness of daily life is missing from conventional histories. No wonder students of Canada often turn their backs on the study of its past: what doesn't make sense they readily dismiss as irrelevant and boring.

Well, if too many accounts of Canada are misleading in their claims of comprehensiveness and authority, just what is history all about? From an understanding of our own family experiences, we know that history must incorporate the collective experience of past generations of women, men, and children — how they brought about and coped with change and how they achieved stability in their lives. History is concerned with all human beings, people of both sexes, every age, all classes, races, and ethnic groups; it deals with all the facets of being human, from making love to making war. To be sure, there is the question of relative importance: no one can hope to recover and understand every facet of the past. We have to make choices. Indeed that is just what traditional historical writing has done. Its choice has been to focus on a tiny group of elite white men: to know John A. Macdonald, Henri Bourassa, Joseph Flavelle, James S. Woodworth, Lionel Groulx, William Lyon Mackenzie King, Pierre E. Trudeau, we are told, implicitly if not explicitly, is to know Canada. Different choices about what is historically significant are now needed if we are to have a balanced and accurate portrait of how Canadians actually lived. This is the only way that we will move from the history of a few men to the history of human beings.

I

Many changes are needed if traditional accounts are to be remedied, but the most obvious is the inclusion of women, the half or so of the Canadian population without whom history does not exist. The move to include women as significant historical figures began in the 1960s and the 1970s, decades which saw a questioning and challenging of conventions in politics, society, and the economy. Nationalists, students, French Canadians, native peoples, poorer citizens, and women (and none of these groups were mutually exclusive) demanded a hearing from traditional white male elites. Discrimination, poverty, racism, imperialism, and misogyny were identified and criticized. In legislatures, reserves, schools, homes, and city streets Canadians demanded a better deal.

Among the strongest forces for change was the second women's movement with its wide-ranging critique of the inequities of Canadian life.

While much of the movement's effort focused on grass-roots campaigns to assist women through transition houses, union organizing, rape crisis centres, employment counselling, health collectives, the affirmation of female culture in art and music, and the like, a good part of the feminist challenge centred on Canadian scholarship which, like that elsewhere, largely ignored women.[1] The languages, sociology, anthropology, political science, economics, history, and other disciplines slowly began to be confronted with a list of their substantial shortcomings.

By the late 1980s challenges to Canada's imperfections had not disappeared. Nationalists, revived by free trade's possible threat of still greater dependence on the United States, contested the continentalism of the Conservative government. Native Canadians crusaded for land claims, local decision-making, and a voice in child welfare decisions. And the Canadian women's movement, for all the critics who regularly celebrated its demise, had expanded its membership and agenda. Feminism's progress over some two decades meant that prejudices and conventions that handicap women in a host of areas continued to be subject to critical appraisal.[2]

In particular, universities and scholarship that claim to preserve and advance human understanding have slowly been forced to address the omission of women from their ranks and from their studies. The beginnings of redress did not occur because the offenders autonomously recognized that they had excluded half of humankind. Only with resistance and reluctance have the majority of "gatekeepers" of knowledge responded to feminist demands for equity and justice. Today, a feminism naturally subversive of traditional thinking and institutions continues, through the efforts of staff, students, faculty, and the movement at large, to demand a reconsideration of the world that patriarchy has constructed so much in its own image.[3]

In particular, feminism has pointed out that not only is "the personal political," as with questions of birth control, abortion, wife battering, and incest, but "the personal is also sociological, scientific, psychological, technological, literary, and of course historical." In other words, gender or the social meaning of femaleness and maleness, is constructed and expressed in various ways and these ways lie at the heart of what it means to be human. To concern itself with human beings, and not just with a small number of men, the study of history needs to include women.

Where then, feminists asked, were girls and women in books and articles, courses, faculty and even, sometimes, in the student population?

Because it was also under attack for a host of other failings in the 1960s and 1970s, mainstream or better still, "malestream," historical scholarship was especially vulnerable to the feminist assault. Advocates of the "new social history" pointed out that families, children, minority racial and ethnic groups, and the working class were conspicuously absent from traditional texts. These presented less heterogeneous, more public, and of course less divisive accounts of what Canada has been about. Traditionalists were being told to "get it right" by a wide range of internal and external critics.

Like feminists, other questioners of the historical status quo were sympathetic to more interdisciplinary approaches that, in their use of innovative methodologies and sources, might compensate for the limitations of traditional, disciplinary scholarship. Advocates of Canadian studies, native studies, labour studies, and ethnic studies joined those of women's studies in supporting a wide range of popular and professional journals, associations, and meetings. Journals like *Atlantis* and groups like the Canadian Women's Studies Association challenged the received wisdom that denied women a fair deal.

Regular contacts among feminists in a wide variety of disciplines have been essential for constructing new ways of knowing. Women's history in Canada, as elsewhere, is supported and challenged by its close association with other interdisciplinary-minded investigators: they share the hope that a new approach to knowledge will introduce a world that better matches reality. Alliances with scholars in other fields, notably with advocates of working class history,[4] and membership in the larger women's movement has also helped keep feminists from succumbing to the hostility they meet regularly in history's traditional ranks.

Yet, if some historians still cling to the picture of a world defined by men and male prerogative, more than ever before there is a willingness to experiment and to broaden the definition of what is historically significant. Slowly the discipline of history has begun to change. At the beginning some individuals were especially influential. In the 1960s and 1970s at the University of Toronto, an Australian historian of the United States, Dr. Jill K. Conway, and an American historian of France, Dr. Natalie Z. Davis, fostered students and courses. Elsewhere historians like Stanley Ryerson, at the University of Quebec, supported feminist theses. By the mid-1970s undergraduate and graduate papers, dissertations, and courses on women were beginning to appear. At long last the "woman question" had surfaced in a significant number (although by no means all) history departments across the country.

As the early departure of both Conway and Davis to the United States (where they furthered prestigious careers) suggests, academic Canada welcomed women only reluctantly. Detractors dismissed women's history as faddish. It would go away, they hoped, once the initial fuss subsided. Surely its popularity meant it could not be good history? Still worse, women's history was overtly political: it had something to say about the contemporary world and sought to change it. By way of contrast, many liberal academics continued to believe that good (i.e., traditional) history was apolitical. Good historians must be impartial judges of the past, untouched by the perspective of their class, race, religion, ethnicity, or, of course, gender. Custodians of "truth," they oversee a world of impartial scholarship devoid of ideology. Feminist history questions the foundations of this claim to professional omnipotence. No wonder so many conventional historians felt threatened and antagonistic.

II

As suspect subversives in their discipline, feminist historians sometimes appear to be a homogeneous force, at least to their detractors. Certainly their limited numbers, shared commitment to the discovery of the full human past, and common enemies have often produced alliances and friendships that spanned Canada. In practice, however, historians of women have been characterized by a number of different perspectives. Some scholars, particularly in the early years, seemed content merely to add women to the Canadian mosaic. Mostly classic "empiricists," they were interested in including women in everything, from politics to reforms to artistic movements.[5] Others, in contrast, adopted a Marxist or class-oriented approach: women existed in society as members of classes and their behaviour was dictated by class considerations.[6] By the early 1980s a third, more "woman-centred" approach appeared that continued the interest in class but argued that gender was a key and often pre-eminent factor in shaping distinctive female consciousness and actions.[7] All three varieties of feminist history still flourish. Although membership fluctuates as historians continually rethink the specifics of their positions,[8] the first approach probably predominates among conservative amateur popularizers, late "converts" among senior faculty, and their dependent doctoral candidates. The second appeals to interpreters of the past who remain strongly attached to the masculine left. The third attracts those inspired by the women's movement of the 1970s and 1980s and now disillusioned with either Marxist interpretations or with liberal empiricism. The scholarly history with which this article is largely concerned is generally dominated by the third, woman-centred, school of analysis. Canadian history is being reconceptualized by feminist historians who argue that the inclusion of women, in discussions of everything from the labour market to popular culture, does substantially more than enlarge our picture of the past. It changes it, irretrievably, for women as for men. Whatever orientation toward female experience they favour, however, feminist historians all agree that the historical record is incomplete without serious attention to issues raised by gender. That consensus has led them to unite in such groups as the Canadian Committee on Women's History/*Le comité canadien de l'histoire des femmes* to agitate for more and better women's history across the country.

Humanizing history begins with the document record, and feminist historians have made it among their first tasks to illuminate the sources which allow a more accurate reconstruction of the past.[9] Their concerns have prompted the publication of a number of primary documents.[10] Conventional sources of information have rarely been sufficient or satisfactory. Traditionally, historical sources have been defined by a focus on the public realm, where women's influence has been more indirect. No wonder women frequently seem not to exist as historical actors. Crossing conventional disciplinary boundaries, often desirable in studying male historical figures, is inescapable when studying women. Historians of women need access to other disciplines — psychology, sociology, political science, and literature among others — both to broaden the range of questions they are accustomed to asking and to acquire data that they otherwise would not have.

Yet, while the methods and questions of other disciplines are essential, historians of women cannot abandon traditional historical sources which, when reconsidered, are also invaluable. Women's lives have intersected with men's and with the public sphere at many points, and, even if the beam of the public chroniclers has not been focused on women, historians must re-examine, from new angles if necessary, long-familiar documents. The published record — books, newspapers, and magazines — provides the most readily available sources. Considered from a new perspective, published sources are full of useful references to women's lives. Similarly, many of the abundant records generated by churches, the state, the military, and the economy, also hold promise although, despite women's participation in these sectors of Canadian life, they commonly deal with women only obliquely. A careful reading of religious sermons, royal commission reports, army regulations, labour force and demographic data, and business records frequently reveals, if not always plentiful detail on women's lives, then at least assumptions, both explicit and implied, about women and their roles. When fresh questions are asked of even traditional data, they will sometimes elicit new answers.

Yet, for all the prospect of drawing out information on women from familiar sources, historians of women have, of necessity, had to tap some previously unused, even uncollected courses. A new sensitivity to the frequency with which women's lives and beliefs have been interpreted for them by men has led to a search for documents in which the historical subjects themselves describe their own experiences. The letters and diaries of ordinary women, for instance, reveal a complex female culture that left virtually no trace in conventional historical documents.[11] In the belief that women may be their own best chroniclers, historians are now turning to oral testimony. Giving women's voices their due in this way may result in a finer appreciation for the interconnections between the public and private spheres.

Coming gradually too is a further expansion in the definition of what constitutes an historical source. Historians are now beginning to use recipes, songs, and aspects of material culture such as cooking and cleaning equipment, quilts, and wearing apparel to analyze women's positions in any given society. They look at the names women chose for their daughters — often those of their own sisters and of their close friends — to help them interpret a female culture and sense of family. Photographs and other visual materials are studied with an increasingly sophisticated eye for the clues they provide in understanding the subjects' sense of self and the patterns of interaction among individuals.[12] Domestic technology provides still other clues to the makeup and demands of women's days.

Fortunately, given the explosion of interest in new sources, there are a number of useful guides to the published and unpublished materials in Canadian women's history. A good place to start is *"True Daughters of the North": Research and Reference Bibliography of Canadian Women's History*, edited by myself and Beth Light;[13] the guide to bibliographies and historiographic essays in *Rethinking Canada*, and, the more recent publication, "The Study of B.C. Women: A Quarter-Century Review, 1960-1984" by Linda Hale and Melanie Houlden;[14] the references in *Quebec Women: A History* by the Clio Collective and those in *Canadian Women: A History* by Alison Prentice and others;[15] and *Planting the Garden: An Annotated Archival Bibliography of the History of Women in Manitoba* by Mary Kinnear and Vera Fast.[16] To keep up to date on the newest publications and discoveries the feminist journals, *Resources for Feminist Research/Documentation sur la recherche feministe* (Ontario Studies for Education), *Atlantis* (Mount Saint Vincent University), and *Canadian Woman Studies/Les cahiers de la femme* (York University) are indispensable.

III

Given the proliferation, diversity, and innovative nature of new work on Canadian women, no easy division into subject categories is possible. Nevertheless, the fact that, for many students, the introduction to Canadian history comes in post-Confederation surveys (that cover fairly predictable periods and developments) necessitates what might be termed a "counter-syllabus." Accordingly, the rest of this essay is intended to serve as a guide both to the critical issues in women's history and to the books and articles that should be included in the reading lists (usually dominated by more conventional materials) for introductory Canadian history courses. Here then are the outlines of the more human history of Canada that feminist historians are seeking to discover. Unfortunately, only the rare Canadian survey text properly integrates female experience into the whole.[17] The most notable exceptions are Susan Mann Trofimenkoff's *A Dream of Nation*[18] and, to some extent, Paul-Andre Linteau, René Durocher and Jean-Claude Robert's *Quebec: A History*.[19] In terms of general coverage concentrating on women themselves, however, three recent texts provide excellent introductions to the experience of some fifty percent of the population: the Clio Collective, *Quebec Women*; Alison Prentice *et al*, *Canada Women: A History*; and Strong-Boag and Fellman's edited collection *Rethinking Canada: The Promise of Women's History*. For individual topics within a post-Confederation survey more specialized readings are identified below.

(1) Power and Politics in Young Canada, 1867-96   Debates about the nature of the federal government, the evolution of political parties, the articulation of provincial rights, the French-English and Protestant-Catholic conflicts, and more recently the struggles of Métis and working-class peoples to defend and, sometimes, to extend their rights occupy many commentaries on early post-Confederation Canada. Women also demanded a voice in what the new Dominion was to be about. As the franchise was extended to a majority of men (with the notable exception of groups like the native population) the vote became an increasingly important symbol of full citizenship. Middle-class urban women in groups like the Toronto Women's Literary Club (founded in 1876 and by 1883 called the Toronto Women's Suffrage Club), the Woman's Christian Temperance Union (beginning in 1874), and the Young Women's Christian Association (beginning in 1870), became convinced that without the vote they could not achieve a fair hearing in a world where more and more key decisions over matters such as liquor distribution and public health lay in the hands of male legislators. Women like Dr. Emily Howard Stowe of the TWSC and Letitia Yeomans of the WCTU struggled to bring to fruition their "utopian" dreams of a "dry," more equitable Canada. Their hopes for a better world vied for popular loyalties alongside those visions offered by the Knights of Labour, John A. Macdonald and the National Policy, or the *Programme catholique*.[20]

(2) Culture and Society, 1867-1914   The setting of political agendas was not the only focus for struggle in the years after Confederation. Private and public institutions increasingly shaped the lives of Canadians. Education, both formal and informal, was fundamental to the transformation of Canada into a more modern state. Young women and their supporters fought hard for the admission of women into everything from Latin instruction (the prerequisite for the university and professional training of the day) to normal schools, classes in faculties of arts and medical programs.[21] Their hard-fought battles, not entirely won even in the present day, gave women a strong sense of their own achievement and a faith in the ability of women as a group. In many cases individuals intended to put their education to good use, both by supporting themselves and by creating a more just society. Educated women took both paid and voluntary employment in organizing,

educating, and nursing their fellow citizens. Under female management orphanages increasingly took in poor children[22] who otherwise might have been farmed out to the cheapest bidder.[23] Religious groups of every kind, made up of nuns, deaconesses, and volunteers, hurried to help and reform city-folk in particular with programs of education and charity.[24]

By World War One Canada's children, facing compulsory school attendance laws that kept them in primary classes until about age fourteen, offered important opportunities for educated women. While male teachers flourished in the relatively few high schools and universities that existed, female teachers dominated the lower grades where their poorer wages and special affinity, so it was believed, for youngsters, made them attractive to thrifty school boards.[25] Schools of nursing associated with hospitals also offered employment to ambitious girls from respectable families and began, very slowly, to alter public views of hospitals as dangerous places that served only the poor and the dying.[26] By the close of this period Canadians encountered daily a world in which women were occupying public roles essential to the efficient and humane functioning of the modern community.

(3) Waged and Unwaged Work in Industrializing Canada, 1867-1914   In 1889 the Royal Commission on the Relations of Capital and Labour warned Canadians that the world of work, bounded by traditional patterns of authority and experience, was changing. Women, mostly young and single, were increasingly active in textile, clothing, boot and shoe, and tobacco factories where their long days and low pay made high profits for Canadian industrialists.[27] Other young women, also on the leading edge of economic development, found work as clerks, typists, and stenographers in the administrative revolution that was modernizing Canadian offices.[28] To some extent the visibility of these new workers was misleading. Women had always worked, both at home and beyond. The very great majority continued to struggle with the demands of housework and child-rearing which, even for the middle class, meant coping with long days, the threat of ill health, incessant demands, and backbreaking labour.[29] Thousands of women also worked on farms of every description, often with substantial responsibilities not only for the work of the home but for the dairy and poultry as well.[30] Far more women than those employed in factories and offices continued to toil as workers at home or in small shops, and as domestic servants (who remained the largest single category of paid workers until 1941).[31] Working-class women in particular often developed elaborate

strategies, involving everything from taking in boarders, managing large gardens, tending a milch cow or pigs, and childminding for local mothers. Their financial juggling frequently kept families afloat when jobs for male breadwinners (when those breadwinners were present) were often seasonal, dangerous, and low-waged.[32]

Wherever they toiled, and their numbers were regularly severely under-counted in the census (which, for instance, did not identify housewives as workers), women discovered both independence and exploitation at the hands of employers who, while they remained unwilling to pay wages equal to men's, increasingly depended on the services of trained female staff. Not surprisingly, these years also saw the beginning of unions among working-class women. Handicapped by the hostility of business, resistance from many male unionists, the lack of female traditions of craft unionism, and diverse responsibilities on the home front,[33] women, as in the strike against Bell Telephone in Toronto in 1907, often reaped only marginal immediate benefits, but they stored up a legacy that would be important in helping women to organize more permanently in the years after the Great War.[34]

(4) Settling the West, 1867-1914   European intrusion into western lands, where tribes like the Blackfoot and the Sioux held dominion, occurred as early as the seventeenth century, but permanent white settlement awaited the founding of Red River early in the nineteenth century. While early fur-trade society offered significant opportunities to native women, its long-term heritage included a racism and sexism that would consign native and mixed-blood women to special victimization by male and white society well into the twentieth century.[35] The Northwest Company and Hudson Bay Company community combined with native and Métis populations to form the "New Nation" championed by Louis Riel in the two Northwest Rebel-lions, but this indigenous tradition was overwhelmed by heavy migrations from eastern Canada, the United States, and Europe which began in the 1880s and reach full tide a decade later. With the rise in grain prices and the fall in transportation costs in the 1890s, pioneers opened up opportunities for themselves and other Canadians on farms and in cities of the prairies. The success of agricultural settlement in particular depended very visibly on the labours of the farm wife.[36] While the significance of women's contributions was recognized by the early willingness of the western farm movement to support female suffrage, farm women, like their urban sisters, continued to face discrimination that made their world far from equal.

Canadian homestead law for example, as the English immigrant Georgina Binnie-Clark discovered, allowed men a free quarter section but ignored women.[37] The opening of the west depended on female settlers, both for their labour and for the settled community life they brought with them, but like their sisters elsewhere they found that their equal contributions brought no equality in law or social benefit.

(5) The Women and Reform, 1896-1919   Industrialization, urbanization, and the settlement of the west produced changes in society that disturbed large numbers of Canadians. Concern created a reform-minded generation who transformed old organizations and created new ones in order to manage national development according to their own preferences. Whether they worked with unions, political parties, the churches, or women's associations, women and men struggled with their special allegiances to race, class, and gender. As might be expected, very few of these so-called "progressives" were totally altruistic in their efforts to transform the Dominion.

Feminists, too, came in many guises, from those determined to impose a middle-class vision of social order on potentially dangerous aliens and workers[38] to those who espoused radical and socialist solutions to Canada's ills.[39] Historians are equally divided on the merits of the first Canadian women's movement. Some emphasize its narrow vision; others point to the radical nature of a critique that challenged unequal relations in the patriarchal family.[40] Whatever its precise persuasion, however, feminism made a difference to the reform/progressive movement of its day. Without its struggle and inspiration, the interests of women and their children, in everything from mothers' pensions[41] to daycare,[42] would have remained largely unrecognized and unaddressed by reformers of any orientation. The extent of anti-feminism and in fact real misogyny in French and English society meant that only the brave dared to embrace the women's cause.[43]

(6) Female Employment and the Canadian Political Economy, 1919-45
For girls and women in these years, maturity was increasingly associated with paid work.[44] Like their brothers, women came to expect to spend at least some of their adult life in the labour force. Whereas the authority of male heads of households rested to a significant degree on their greater ability to operate autonomously outside the home, more and more women could now hope to match at least a part of that experience. Also, more than ever before, the waged labour economy in Canada cannot be understood

without reference to women. It also cannot be understood without reference to female ghettoization in relatively few areas of employment, so that there were in reality two separate labour markets distinguished by sex. This dual or segmented labour market[45] meant that there was little competition between women and men for the same jobs, an unintended benefit of which was the persistence of some jobs for women even during the worst of the Great Depression.[46] Obvious examples of ghettoes include domestic service, teaching, nursing, waitressing, and clerical work. Jobs of every kind had their shortcomings, most particularly low wages and limited opportunities, but it was unemployment that women feared most. With themselves and others to feed, few working women, whatever their class, could afford to go without wages for any length of time. Many bitterly resented being laid off in favour of men, even those who were veterans of World War Two.[47]

There is abundant evidence that women understood and resented their vulnerability in the waged labour market. For some, especially those in the garment and textile trades, the solution was unionization.[48] Yet, for all their enhanced union involvement in the 1930s and 1940s, low-waged women tied to domestic duties, without a long tradition of organization, and often with limited help from established unions, could only make small gains.[49] Governments whose meagre relief and unemployment operations invariably favoured men were at best unreliable allies.[50] The initial optimism associated with white-collar and professional employment and the impact on women and men alike of the Great Depression and the Second World War, however, postponed recognition of and handicapped challenges to the sexual politics of the labour market. In these years most women preferred to counteract the dissatisfactions of the paid workplace by attempting to construct fulfilling private worlds with spouses, families, and friends.

(7) Women and the Family, 1919-45   Although divorce rates rose steadily in these years (though remaining far below modern figures), most Canadians continued to look to the family for emotional and economic support. The Great Depression reversed only briefly the decline in women's age of marriage which had begun in 1891. By 1941 their average age at first marriage was 23.0. Given the exigencies of the inequitable and cyclical labour market and the celebration of romantic love that marked these years it is hardly surprising that most girls and women, like many men, expected to find satisfaction, security, and purpose in marriage. Wives and husbands

were presumed to pool resources in working partnerships which would enable them to create the homes and families that signalled adulthood in their society and that would better prepare them to survive hard times. Many wives, like those of miners in the Cape Breton coal industry, quickly became family financiers, juggling a complicated combination of tasks both to save and add to income.[51] Yet, while marriage was based on practical economics, it also promised important emotional benefits. The upsurge in popular films, radio, and magazines (many coming from the U.S. in these years), encouraged young women to anticipate romantic passion.

As least as important in meeting women's desires for love were children. In their nurture mothers found many of the joys of marriage.[52] Childrearing was also influenced by the steady fall in the birthrate throughout these years as Canadians turned increasingly to contraception and abortion (despite their illegality) to regulate fertility and to achieve the desired standard of living.[53] Women who gave birth without (at least initially) benefit of clergy experienced few of the benefits of motherhood, but they came to know its dangers all too well in a society that readily pilloried unwed mothers.[54] Increasingly too from the time of delivery on[55] mothers were subject to the persistent efforts of professional advisors to dictate the course of modern parenting.[56]

Canadians' dependence on family life for emotional and economic stability, especially in worrying periods such as depression and war, made the prospect of female independence especially troublesome. No wonder many Canadians wanted desperately to believe that neither unemployment for husbands in the Great Depression nor new jobs in the Canadian Women's Army Corps during World War Two meant any permanent change in the relationship between the sexes that assigned public life to men and the home to women.

(8) Political Choices: Attempts at Integration, 1919-1960   In the forty and more years' gulf between the first and second feminist movements, many Canadian women believed that equality was won and they were free to participate in the political system as equals. They cooperated with men in searching for political solutions to the economic and social problems of modern life. They, too, joined the Progressives, the Cooperative Commonwealth Federation, the Communist Party, the Social Credit Party, as well as the Liberals and the Conservatives, not to mention more short-lived experiments like the Reconstruction Party in the 1930s.[57] These efforts at "integra-

tion"[58] produced occasional benefits, as with the election of the first female Member of Parliament, Agnes Macphail, in 1921,[59] and the 1930 appointment of the first female senator, Cairine Wilson, by William Lyon Mackenzie King,[60] but after the first receptiveness to women's issues,[61] all parties tended to benefit from women's institutional support — as fund-raisers, typists, election managers, and the like — while denying them equality of financing or office-holding.

No wonder many women continued to work independently as energetic lobbyists for causes like public health, peace, and consumers' rights. Members of the Women's International League for Peace and Freedom, for instance, struggled throughout these years, often in the face of considerable "red-baiting", to bring the need for international arbitration and demilitarization to the attention of the Canadian public.[62] The efforts of women in the WILPF, the National Council of Women, the Young Women's Christian Association, and the women's auxiliaries to the churches did much to ensure a receptive audience for Canada's postwar support of the United Nations and assumption of the role as international policeman. Waiting to be rediscovered, however, were a long list of inequities that Canadian women still faced in public and private life.

(9) Women's Place in the Post-War Economy, 1945-1980s   After the Second Great War female labour-force participation rates rose steadily, as did the numbers of married women in paid work. Increases in the desired standard of living and consumer prices combined with the buoyancy of an economy fueled by European reconstruction and Cold War spending to make more families than ever dependent on two adult wage-earners. Although the majority of married women workers were either childless or had school-age or older offspring, a substantial and growing minority had young children. There was also a steady rise in the number of lone female parents in the workplace. Despite this phenomenon, neither governments nor private enterprise had been willing by the mid-1980s to address the national daycare crisis in a significant way. There were, however, signs of change with a series of studies and reports prepared for Liberal and Conservative administrations between 1986 and 1988. By the latter date the National Strategy on Childcare,[63] which proposed greater tax benefits for parents and an increased shared federal-provincial commitment to daycare, suggested that the reality facing Canadian mothers and fathers was being addressed, albeit far too late and insufficiently.

Practical recognition of the social value of parenting was especially crucial since women's work experience, for all recurring reports of glamorous firsts and entry into previously male-dominated fields, remained very much the same. Most female workers were segregated in clerical, sales, teaching, nursing, social work, and other service occupations where they provided the critical staff for the growth of both modern corporations and the welfare state. Wherever they were employed, the majority continued to earn on average less than two-thirds of what was paid to men.[64] The fact that growing numbers of women could find only part-time work added to their financial troubles.

Solutions to women's dilemma became all the more difficult in the 1970s and 1980s when, in response to the world oil crisis and the deterioration in the American dollar, jobs with decent pay became difficult to find for all Canadians. When they could, women turned in increasing numbers to unions, particularly those in the public sector. A new generation of female activists created not only women's caucuses and committees within established labour bodies but also established, in British Columbia, an important, if short-lived, feminist precedent in the Service, Office, and Retail Workers' Union of Canada (SORWUC) which championed the cause of women among domestic and bank workers in particular.[65] Slowly, union agendas came to include at least some support for "women's issues" (daycare, equal pay for work of equal value, affirmative action, and sexual harassment policies). Working women, especially those in the clerical sector, and their supporters also paid attention to the social, health, and labour impact of the microchip revolution.[66] Governments and businesses were urged to examine carefully the implications of the introduction of computers and to ensure that retraining and job security accompanied technological innovation. Clearly, by the 1980s women, married and single, were in the labour market to stay and, inspired and supported by the modern feminist movement, were demanding equity in employment at all levels.

(10) Personal and Family Life, 1945-1980s   Between 1945 and 1960 many Canadians sought in family life the security and good times that had escaped them during the Great Depression and the Second World War. The hardships encountered by "new Canadians" (a good number of whom were "Displaced Persons") also encouraged a wide-spread determination to set one's own life in order. For many citizens, this meant attempts to purchase bungalows and split levels in the nation's rapidly expanding suburbs. In

locations like Scarborough, Ontario, and Burnaby, British Columbia, wives and husbands concentrated on establishing families in the comfortable circumstances that had so often escaped their parents.[67] In the meantime, city centres, where the poor increasingly resided, deteriorated still further. In all provinces the birthrate rose from 1941 to 1956 as Canadians both made up for postponing families and concentrated childbearing early in their marriages.[68]

Encouraged by advisors like the American "baby doctor" Dr. Benjamin Spock and Toronto Women's Hospital's Dr. Marion Hilliard, women focused on the demanding roles of wife and mother. Yet, despite transportation and childcare problems, and recurring popular and academic criticism of their actions, many married women, including those from the suburbs, took paid employment to support the rising tide of family aspirations, not only in material consumption but in education for children.[69] They also volunteered in hospitals, schools, libraries, and community centres, providing services essential to the life of communities, new and old. Their activity, waged or unwaged, was rarely publicly recognized, and the dissatisfaction, observed in American women by Betty Friedan in *The Feminine Mystique* (1963) steadily grew.[70]

In the 1960s increasing numbers of women began to question priorities that assigned them home responsibilities but little real power in society. Both as regular and as mature students, they entered colleges and universities in unprecedented numbers. They also continued their entry into the wage labour market. Some women rejected the inevitability and desirability of motherhood.[71] In some quarters there was a dawning realization that, even when women worked outside the home, they were still held responsible for domestic work of all kinds and that this assignment needed to be questioned.[72] The "discovery" of widespread poverty among the Dominion's elderly women, a population whose numbers rose steadily,[73] the extent of wife battering and incest,[74] and the dangers of pornography[75] also raised concerns about women's unequal place in Canadian society. By the end of the 1980s family life for many women had changed markedly.[76] Alternatives such as childlessness, lesbian couples, lone parenthood, divorce, househusbands, new reproductive technologies, and more egalitarian marriages, aroused ardent debates among their champions and critics.[77] These debates, perhaps best captured in the struggle between pro and anti-choice forces on abortion, suggested that Canadian women had come a long way from 1945.[78] And that they still had a substantial distance to cover.

(11) The Women's Movement and the Renewed Campaign for Equality, 1960-1980s   Until the 1960s feminism was quiescent as an organized force in Canada. In that decade it surfaced again in groups such as the Voice of Women, founded in 1960 to campaign against nuclear war but soon committed to a host of other issues including demands for the decriminalization of birth control information, opposition to the Vietnam war and Canadian uranium sales, and, with other women's groups, calls for a Royal Commission on the Status of Women.[79.] The 1970 Report of the Royal Commission on the Status of Women in Canada demonstrated that laws and institutions were still far from treating women equally and proposed 167 means to redress inequities in the economy, education, the family, the taxation system, public life, immigration and citizenship, and criminal law. While very few of its recommendations were enacted, the Report soon came to be the liberal measure of how far women had come on the long road to the fair deal espoused by Nellie McClung and the first generation of feminists. Modern feminism, however, turned out to be a good deal more than demands for simple changes in law, politics, or institutions.

Moved by feminists such as Germaine Greer (*The Female Eunuch*), Shulamith Firestone (*The Dialectic of Sex*), and Simone de Beauvoir (*The Second Sex*), as well as home-grown publications such as *Women Unite: An Anthology of the Women's Movement* (1972) and Margaret Anderson's *Mother was Not a person* (1973), Canadians questioned and criticized the very functioning of society itself.[80] Beginning in the late 1960s Women's Liberation groups sprang up from Victoria to St. John's to raise women's consciousness and propose concrete solutions to women's oppression.[81] In Quebec women's liberation was allied with the nationalist movement in protesting the place of francophones in Canadian society, but feminists went on to identify and protest the subordinate role of women in the nationalist movement and in society generally. They, along with women elsewhere in the country, ended up questioning the family, sexual conventions and roles, language, and the distribution of power. Such emphases differ from those of "first-wave" feminism, reflecting contemporary women's greater participation in the labour force, the separation of sexuality from reproduction, the higher divorce rate, and the incursion of the state into ever more aspects of women's lives.[82]

Like their earlier counterparts, contemporary feminists have been divided as to how to effect the changes they would like to see in women's lives. Some have created alternative institutions, run by women themselves, to deal with the unmet needs of female Canadians. Women's health collectives, feminist bookstores and newspapers, houses for battered women and their children, and feminist labour unions are all attempts to compel modifications in the terms by which conventional institutions deal with women. To alter the impoverished symbolic representation of women, feminists have analyzed and criticized all forms of media as well as traditional bodies of knowledge, and, where possible, have begun creating their own art, literature, and scholarship, taking women's points of view into account. All such activity has made an impact. Many more Canadians have become self-conscious about language, support equal pay for work of equal value, and acknowledge that men ought to take their share of domestic responsibilities. Labour unions have begun tackling subjects such as sexual harassment and day care for members' children. In their quest to see the world through women's eyes, feminists, while not convincing everyone, have identified issues that have touched a nerve in most citizens.

Institutions tend to be resistant to change, however, and the state has been far from an unqualified advocate of equality for women, especially where such reforms would challenge vested interests.[83] Lobbying, one traditional way of inducing legislators to adopt a specific group's point of view, has been given more attention by women in recent years. The National Action Committee on the Status of Women continuously prods legislators to pay attention to women's issues, while other groups such as the Legal Education and Action Fund (LEAF), have emerged to ensure the enshrinement of equal rights in the Canadian Charter of Rights and Freedoms and the Meech Lake Accord, to inform government commissions of the impact of pornography on women, and to pressure crown corporations into hiring females for "male" occupations and positions.

Yet, outsiders to the political system suffer substantial disadvantages and women cannot afford to leave the politics of the public sphere solely to male direction. Decisions taken within city councils, provincial legislatures, and the House of Commons critically influence women's lives. More women than ever before are seeking political office.[84] Experience in every party from the Social Credit to the Parti Québécois indicates that an independent feminist lobby within the party is essential if women and their particular interests are not to be subsumed to the demands of a male agenda.[85] Current political issues such as daycare and abortion lie at the centre of many of the debates now agitating Canadian government and politics. Even more so than at the turn of the century the feminist vision of a better world is challenging citizens of both sexes.

As these brief introductions to problems in the history of post-Confederation Canada suggest, the human past is coming into clearer focus. A woman-centred approach is providing an overdue corrective to blinkered accounts that concentrated on elite males. Yet, if much has been accomplished, much remains to be done before the complex variety of Canada's human history will be recovered. Feminist scholars have identified issues — among them (1) the origin and practice of misogyny, including but not limited to anti-feminism, (2) the legal system as it addresses gender, (3) the sources of gender identity and anxiety, (4) the expression of heterosexuality and homosexuality, (5) the psychological consequences of parenting, (6) the evolution and entrenchment of a segmented labour market, (7) the nature and evaluation of domestically-based labour and its gender identification, (8) the relationship among ethnic, racial, class, and gender identities, and (9) feminist visions of the future and the confrontation with patriarchy — an understanding of which, in the past as in the present, will illuminate not only female but male experience. Slowly but surely we are learning that, despite the teaching of so many texts, a small group of men constitute neither Canada nor its past. History is about human beings, women and men, their relationships, their hopes, and their struggles. Once history is understood in its rich complexity, it is never as "dull as ditchwater," or to adopt a metaphor more appropriate to this article, never as "dull as dishwater."

Endnotes

1. Margrit Eichler, "The Relationship Between Sexist, Nonsexist, Women-Centred, and Feminist Research," in *Gender and Society: Creating a Canadian Women's Sociology*, ed. Arlene Tigar McLaren (Toronto: Copp Clark Pitman, 1988).

2. Angela Miles and Geraldine Finn, eds., *Feminism in Canada: From Pressure to Politics* (Montreal: Black Rose Books, 1982); and Roberta Hamilton and Michele Barrett, eds., *The Politics of Diversity: Questions for Feminism* (Montreal: Book Center Inc., 1987).

3. Roberta Hamilton, "Feminists in the Academy: Intellectuals or Political Subversives?" *Queen's Quarterly* 92 (Spring 1985), 3-20.

4. Bettina Bradbury, "Women's History and Working-Class History," *Labour/Le Travail* 19 (Spring 1987), 23-48.

5. As good examples of this "inclusion" tendency see Veronica Strong-Boag *The Parliament of Women: The National Council of Women of Canada, 1893-1929* (Ottawa: National Museum, 1976); and many of the essays in *The Neglected Majority: Essays in Canadian Women's History*, eds. Susan Mann Trofimenkoff and Alison Prentice (Toronto: McClelland & Stewart, 1977).

6. Janice Acton, Penny Goldsmith, Bonnie Shepard, eds., *Women at Work, Ontario, 1850-1930* (Toronto: Canadian Women's Educational Press, 1974); and Carol Lee Bacchi, *Liberation Deferred? The Ideas of the English-Canadian Suffragists, 1877-1918* (Toronto: University of Toronto Press, 1983).

7. Sylvia Van Kirk, "What Has the Feminist Perspective Done for Canadian History?" in *Knowledge Reconsidered: A Feminist Overview* (Ottawa: Canadian Research Institute for the Advancement of Women, 1984); and many of the essays in *The Neglected Majority: Essays in Canadian Women's History*, Vol. 2, eds. Alison Prentice and Susan Mann Trofimenkoff (Toronto: McClelland & Stewart, 1985).

8. See, for example, my shift from position 1 to 3: "Pulling in Double Harness or Hauling a Double Load: Women, Work and Feminism on the Canadian Prairies," *Journal of Canadian Studies* 21 (Fall 1986), 32-52.

9. Veronica Strong-Boag, "Raising Clio's Consciousness in Canada: Archives and Women's History," *Archivaria* 6 (Summer 1978), 70-82.

10. See the series *Documents in Canadian Women's History* which includes Beth Light and Joy Parr, eds., *Canadian Women on the Move, 1867-1920* (Toronto: New Hogtown Press and The Ontario Institute for Studies in Education, 1983).

11. Margaret Conrad, "'Sundays Always Make Me Think of Home': Time and Place in Canadian Women's History," in *Rethinking Canada. The Promise of Women's History*, eds. Veronica Strong-Boag and Antia Clair Fellman (Toronto: Copp Clark Pitman, 1986).

12. For a longer discussion of the use of documents with specific examples see Veronica Strong-Boag and Anita Clair Fellman, "Introduction," *Rethinking Canada*.

13. Veronica Strong-Boag and Beth Light, eds., *"True Daughters of the North": Research and Reference Bibliography of Canadian Women's History* (Toronto: Ontario Institute for Studies in Education, 1980).

14. Linda Hale and Melanie Houlden, "The Study of B.C. Women: A Quarter-Century Review, 1960-1984," *Resources for Feminist Research* (July 1986), 58-68.

15. The Clio Collective, *Quebec Women: A History* (Toronto: Women's Press, 1987); and Allison Prentice *et al.*, *Canadian Women: A History* (Toronto: HBJ-Holt Publishers, 1988).

16. Mary Kinnear and Vera Fast, *Planting the Garden: An Annotated Archival Bibliography of the History of Women in Manitoba* (Winnipeg: University of Manitoba Press, 1987).

17. Even recent publications do not reflect the change in the literature. Particularly flawed are: R. Bothwell, J. English, and I. Drummond, *Canada Since 1945: Power, Politics,*

and Provincialism (Toronto: University of Toronto Press, 1981); and G. Friesen, *The Canadian Prairies: A History* (Toronto & London: University of Toronto Press, 1985).

18. Susan Mann Trofimenkoff, *A Dream of Nation* (Toronto: Gage, 1983).

19. Paul-Andre Linteau, René Durocher and Jean-Claude Robert, *Quebec: A History* (Toronto: James Lorimer, 1983).

20. On women's vision of the new Dominion see Catherine Lyle Cleverdon, *The Woman Suffrage Movement in Canada*, with an introduction by Ramsay Cook (Toronto: University of Toronto Press, 1970); Carol Lee Bacchi, *Liberation Deferred? The Ideas of the English Canadian Suffragists, 1877-1918* (Toronto: University of Toronto Press, 1982). Wendy Mitchinson: "The YWCA and Reform in the 19th Century," *Histoire sociale/Social History* 12:24 (November 1979), 368-84; and "The WCTU: 'For God, Home and Native Land': A Study in Nineteenth-Century Feminism," in *A Not Unreasonable Claim: Women and Reform in Canada, 1880s-1920s*, ed. Linda Kealey (Toronto: The Women's Press, 1979). Nancy Sheehan, "The WCTU on the Prairies, 1886-1930: An Alberta-Saskatchewan Comparison," *Prairie Forum* 6:1 (Spring 1981), 17-33.

21. On the entry of women into universities see Margaret Gillet, *We Walked Very Warily* (Montreal: Eden Press, 1982). On women in medicine see the account of an early female doctor, *A Woman With a Purpose: The Diaries of Elizabeth Short*, edited and introduced by Veronica Strong-Boag (Toronto: University of Toronto Press, 1980); and Charlotte Hacker, *The Indomitable Lady Doctors* (Toronto and Vancouver: Clark, Irwin and Co., 1974).

22. With the conspicuous exception of emigrant children who continued to be turned over to strangers without even the minimal protection offered Canadian youngsters. See Joy Parr, *Labouring Children* (London: Croom-Helm, 1980).

23. Bettina Bradbury, "The Fragmented Family: Family Strategies in the Face of Death, Illness, and Poverty, Montreal, 1860-1885," in *Childhood and Family in Canadian History*, ed. Joy Parr (Toronto:McClelland & Stewart, 1982); and Patricia Rooke and R.L. Schnell, "The Rise and Decline of British North American Protestant Orphans' Homes as Woman's Domain, 1850-1930," *Atlantis* 7:2 (Spring 1982), 21-35.

24. Marta Danylewycz, *Taking the Veil: An Alternative to Marriage, Motherhood, and Spinsterhood in Quebec, 1840-1920* (Toronto: McClelland and Stewart, 1987); Micheline Dumont-Johnson, "Les garderies au XIXe siècle: les salles d'asile des Soeurs Grises à Montréal," *Revue d'histoire de l'Amérique française* 34:1 (June 1980), 27-55; John Thomas, "Servants of the Church: Canadian Methodist Deaconess Work, 1890-1926," *Canadian Historical Review* 65:3 (September 1984), 371-95.

25. Marta Danylewycz and Alison Prentice, "Teachers, Gender and Bureaucratizing School Systems in 19th Century Montreal and Toronto," *History of Education Quarterly* 24 (Spring 1984), 75-100; Alison Prentice, "The Feminization of Teaching," in *The Neglected Majority*, Vol. 1, 49-65; Nadia Fahmy-Eid and Micheline Dumont, eds., *Maitresses de maison, maitresses de l'école: femmes, famille et éducation dans l'histoire du Québec* (Montréal: Boréal Express, 1983).

26. Judy Coburn, "I See and Am Silent," in Acton, Goldsmith and Shepard, *Women at Work*, 127-163.

27. Susan Mann Trofimenkoff, "One Hundred and Two Muffled Voices: Canada's Industrial Women in the 1880s," *Rethinking Canada*; and Gregory Kealey, *Canada Investigates Industrialism* (Toronto: University of Toronto Press, 1973).

28. Graham Lowe: "Women, Work and the Office: The Feminization of Clerical Occupations in Canada, 1901-1931," *Rethinking Canada*; and *Women in the Administrative Revolution* (Toronto: University of Toronto Press, 1987).

29. Veronica Strong-Boag, "Keeping House in God's Country: Canadian Women at Work in the Home," in *On the Job*, eds. C. Heron and R. Storey (Toronto: McGill-Queen's University Press, 1986).

30. Marjorie Griffin Cohen, "The Decline of Women in Canadian Dairying," *The Neglected Majority*, Vol. 2; and her extended discussion in *Women, Work and Markets* (Toronto: University of Toronto Press, 1988).

31. Claudette Lacelle, "Les domestiques dans les villes canadiennes au XIXe siècle, effectifs et conditions de vie," *Historie sociale/Social History* 15 (1982), 181-207.

32. Bettina Bradbury: "The Family Economy and Work in an Industrializing City, Montreal, 1871," Canadian Historical Association *Historical Papers* (1979), 71-96; and "Pigs, Cows, and Boarders; Non-Wage Forms of Survival Among Montreal Families, 1861-91," *Labour/Le Travail* 14 (1984), 9-46.

33. For problems with union support see, for instance, Ruth Frager, "No Proper Deal: Women Workers and the Canadian Labour Movement, 1870-1940," in *Union Sisters: Women in the Labour Movement*, eds. Linda Briskin and Lynda Yanz (Toronto: The Women's Press, 1983); and Marie Campbell, "Sexism in British Columbia Trade Unions, 1900-1920," in *In Her Own Right. Selected Essays on Women's History in British Columbia*, eds. Barbara Latham and Cathy Kess (Victoria: Camosun College, 1980).

34. Joan Sangster, "The 1907 Bell Telephone Strike: Organizing Women Workers," *Rethinking Canada*; and Star Rosenthal, "Union Maids: Organized Women Workers in Vancouver 1900-1915," *BC Studies 41* (1979), 36-55.

35. Sylvia Van Kirk, *"Many Tender Ties": Women in Fur-Trade Society, 1670-1870* (Winnipeg: Watson & Dwyer Publishing Ltd., 1980); and Jennifer Brown, *Strangers in Blood: Fur Trade Company Families in Indian Country* (Vancouver: University of British Columbia Press, 1980).

36. Sara Brooks Sundberg, "Farm Women on the Canadian Prairie Frontier: The Helpmate Image," in *Rethinking Canada*; and Eliane Silverman, *The Last Best West: Women on the Alberta Frontier, 1880-1930* (Montreal and London: Eden Press, 1984).

37. Georgina Binnie-Clark, *Wheat & Woman*, with an Introduction by Susan Jackel (Toronto: University of Toronto Press, 1979).

38. Bacchi, *Liberation Deferred?* and her "Divided Allegiances: The Response of Farm and Labour Women to Suffrage," in *A Not Unreasonable Claim*.

39. Linda Kealey, "Canadian Socialism and the Woman Question, 1900-1914," *Labour/Le Travail* 13 (1984), 77-100.

40. On this division see Strong-Boag, "Pulling in Double Harness or Hauling a Double Load."

41. Veronica Strong-Boag, "Wages for Housework: Mothers, Allowances and the Beginnings of Social Security in Canada," *Journal of Canadian Studies* 24 (1979), 24-34.

42. Christina Simmons, "'Helping the Poorer Sisters': The Women of the Jost Mission, Halifax, 1905-1945," in *Rethinking Canada.*

43. Unfortunately, we are still waiting for an extended treatment of anti-feminism as an intellectual force in the period. The first steps in this direction are found in Susan Mann Trofimenkoff, "Henri Bourassa and 'the Woman Question'," *Journal of Canadian Studies* 10 (November 1975), 3-11. See also Stephen Leacock, *Essays and Literary Studies (New York: John Lane, 1916);* Andrew MacPhail, *Essays in Fallacy* (New York: Longmans, Green and Co., 1910); and Goldwin Smith, *Essays on the Questions of the Day* (New York: Macmillan, 1893).

44. For an assessment of the role of paid work in the female life cycle and in Canada generally, see Veronica Strong-Boag, *The New Day Recalled: Lives of Girls and Women in English Canada, 1919-1945* (Toronto: Copp Clark Pitman, 1988), Ch. 2.

45. See Lowe, "Women, Work and the Office," 111-112.

46. Gail Cuthbert Brandt, "The Transformation of Women's Work in the Quebec Cotton Industry, 1920-1950," in *The Character of Class Struggle: Essays in Canadian Working-Class History*, ed. Bryan D. Palmer (Toronto: McClelland & Stewart, 1986); and Joy Parr, "The Skilled Emigrant and Her Kin: Gender, Culture, and Labour Recruitment," *Canadian Historical Review* 68 (December 1987), 529-551; and her "Rethinking Work and Kinship in a Canadian Hosiery Town, 1910-1950," *Feminist Studies* 13:1 (Spring 1987), 137-162.

47. Ruth R. Pierson, *"They're Still Women After All": The Second World War and Canadian Womanhood* (Toronto: McClelland & Stewart, 1986).

48. Strong-Boag, *New Day*, 69-70.

49. Elaine Bernard, "Last Back: Folklore and the Telephone Operators in the 1919 Vancouver General Strike," in *Not Just Pin Money: Selected Essays on the History of Women's Work in British Columbia*, eds., Barbara Latham and Roberta Pazdro (Victoria: Camosum College, 1984).

50. Rebecca Coulter, "Young Women and Unemployment in the 1930s: The Home Service Solution," *Canadian Woman Studies* 7:4 (Winter 1986), 77-80.

51. See David Frank, "The Miner's Financier: Women in the Cape Breton Coal Towns, 1917," *Atlantis* 8:2 (Spring 1983), 137-43.

52. Strong-Boag, *New Day*, Ch(s). 3, 4, and 5.

53. Angus McLaren and Arlene Tigar McLaren, *The Bedroom and the State: The Changing Practices and Politics of Contraception and Abortion in Canada, 1880-1980* (Toronto: McClelland & Stewart, 1986); and Mary F. Bishop, "Vivian Dowding: Birth Control Activist 1892-," in *Rethinking Canada.*

54. Andrée Levesque, "'Deviant Anonymous': Single Mothers at the Hôpital de la Miséricorde in Montréal, 1929-1939," Canadian Historical Association *Historical Papers* (1984), 168-84.

55. Veronica Strong-Boag and K. McPherson, "The Confinement of Women: Childbirth and Hospitalization in Vancouver, 1919-1939," *BC Studies* 69-70 (Spring/Summer 1986), 142-74.

56. Veronica Strong-Boag, "Intruders in the Nursery: Childcare Professionals Reshape the Years from One to Five, 1920-1939," in *Childhood and Family*; and Norah Lewis, "Reducing Maternal Mortality in British Columbia: An Educational Process," in *Not Just Pin Money*.

57. Strong-Boag, *New Day*, Ch. 6.

58. On this strategy see Sylvia Bashevkin, *Toeing the Lines: Women and Party Politics in English Canada* (Toronto: University of Toronto Press, 1985), Ch. 1.

59. Margaret Stewart and Doris French, *Ask No Quarter: A Biography of Agnes MacPhail* (Toronto: Doubleday, 1959).

60. Franca Iocavetta, "The Political Career of Senator Cairine Wilson, 1921-62," *Atlantis* (Fall 1985), 108-23; and Valerie Knowles, *First Person: A Biography of Senator Cairine Wilson* (Toronto: Dundern Press, 1988).

61. See Diane Crossley, "The B.C. Liberal Party and Women's Reforms, 1916-1928," in *In Her Own Right*.

62. Veronica Strong-Boag, "Peace-making Women: Canada 1919-1939" in *Women and Peace: Theoretical, Historical and Practical Perspectives*, ed. Ruth Roach Pierson (London: Croom Helm, 1987).

63. Health and Welfare, *National Strategy on Child Care* (Ottawa: Minister of Supply and Services, 1988).

64. S.J. Wilson, *Women, The Family and the Economy* (Toronto: McGraw-Hill Ryerson, 1982); and Pat and Hugh Armstrong, *The Double Ghetto: Canadian Women and their Segregated Work* (Toronto: McClelland & Stewart, revised 1984).

65. Briskin and Yanz, eds., *Union Sisters*; and Julie White, *Women and Unions* (Ottawa: Canadian Advisory Council on the Status of Women, 1980).

66. Marion Pollock, "Under Attack: Women, Unions and Microtechnology," in *Union Sisters*; and Pat Armstrong, *Labour Pains: Women's Work in Crisis* (Toronto: Women's Press, 1984), Ch. 7.

67. S.D. Clark, *Suburban Society* (Toronto: University of Toronto Press, 1968).

68. McLaren and McLaren, *The Bedroom and the State*, Ch. 6.

69. Patricia Connelly and Martha MacDonald, "Women's Work: Domestic and Wage Labour in a Nova Scotia Community," in *The Politics of Diversity*, eds. Roberta Hamilton and Michèle Barrett (Montreal: Book Centre Inc., 1986).

70. Betty Friedan, *The Feminine Mystique* (New York: Norton, 1963).

71. J.E. Veevers, "The Child-free Alternative: Rejection of the Motherhood Mystique," in *Women in Canada*, ed. Marylee Stephenson (Toronto: General Publishing, 1977).

72. Martin Meissner, E.W. Humpreys, S.M. Meis and W.J. Scheu, "No Exit for Wives: Sexual Division of Labour and the Cumulation of Household Demands," *Canadian Review of Sociology & Anthropology* 12 (1975), 424-39; and Penney Kome, *Somebody Has to Do It: Whose Work is Housework?* (Toronto: McClelland & Stewart, 1982).

73. Louise Dulude, "Getting Old: Men in Couples and Women Alone," in *Women and Men: Interdisciplinary Readings on Gender*, ed. Greta Hoffmann Nemiroff (Toronto: Fitzhenry & Whiteside, 1987); and Ellen M. Gee and Meredith M. Kimball, *Women and Aging* (Toronto: Butterworth, 1987).

74. Lee Chalmers and Pamela Smith, "Wife Battering: Psychological, Social, and Physical Isolation and Counteracting Strategies," in *Gender and Society*.

75. Sara Diamond, "Pornography: Image and Reality," in *Gender and Society*.

76. Marilyn Porter, "'Women and Old Boats': The Sexual Division of Labour in a Newfoundland Outport," in *Gender and Society*; Meg Luxton, "Two Hands for the Clock: Changing Patterns in the Gendered Division of Labour in the Home," in *Politics of Diversity*; and her *More Than a Labour of Love. Three Generations of Women's Work in the Home* (Toronto: Women's Press, 1980).

77. *Inter alia* Katherine Arnup, "Lesbian Mothers and Child Custody," in *Gender and Society*; Louise Vandelac, "Mothergate: Surrogate Mothers, Linguistics, and Androcentric Engineering," *ibid.*.

78. Margrit Eichler, *Families in Canada Today* (Toronto: Gage, 1983).

79. Kay Macpherson and Meg Sears, "The Voice of Women: A History," in *Women in the Canadian Mosaic*, ed. Gwen Matheson (Toronto: Peter Martin Associates Ltd., 1976); and Kay Macpherson, "Persistent Voices: Twenty-Five Years with the Voice of Women," *Atlantis* 12 (Spring 1987), 60-72.

80. Germaine Greer, *The Female Eunuch* (New York: McGraw-Hill, 1971); Shulamith Firestone, *The Dialectic of Sex* (New York: Bantam, 1971); Simone de Beavoir, *The Second Sex*, trans. H.M. Parshley (New York: Knopf, 1953); *Women Unite: An Anthology of the Women's Movement* (Toronto: Canadian Women's Educational Press, 1972); Margaret Anderson, *Mother Was Not a Person* (Montreal: Black Rose, 1973).

81. See Maureen Fitzgerald, Connie Guberman, and Margie Wolfe, eds., *Still Ain't Satisfied! Canadian Feminism Today* (Toronto: The Women's Press, 1982).

82. Nancy Adamson, Linda Briskin, and Margaret McPhail, *Feminist Organizing for Change: The Contemporary Women's Movement in Canada* (Toronto: Oxford University Press, 1988).

83. Jane Ursel, "The State and the Maintenance of Patriarchy: A Case Study of Family, Labour, and Welfare Legislation in Canada," in *Gender and Society*.

84. Josephine Payne-O'Connor, *Sharing Power: Women in Politics, Vancouver Island Profiles* (Victoria: Kachine Press, 1986).

85. Sylvia Bashevkin, *Toeing the Lines*.

9

Writing About Ethnicity

Roberto Perin

Multiculturalism has become a permanent fixture in Canadian political culture. Enshrined in the Charter of Rights and Freedoms and given additional legislative recognition through an Act of Parliament, the concept nevertheless remains elusive, and the objectives which it purports to espouse are even more so.[1] Like the central idea informing a Greek myth, multiculturalism is capable of infinite variation and interpretation and, one might add, manipulation.

Some of its subscribers see it as an instrument of ethnic self-esteem, serving to wipe away the shame which unfortunately newcomers all too often were made to feel for deviating from the cultural norm. In this view, multiculturalism not only fosters pride in one's ethnic origins, but also breaks down the subtle and the not so subtle signs of exclusion that are consciously or unconsciously devised by groups and institutions in the country of adoption.

Others go further, seeing multiculturalism as a very effective means of challenging the bilingual accommodation established over time by Canada's two charter groups. Some years ago, a member of the Royal Commission on Bilingualism and Biculturalism recommended that languages other than English and French be accorded official status at the regional level. Commissioner Jaroslav Rudnyckyj added that the federal government should provide for the use of such languages in education, in the mass media, and in those public services where a demand for them existed.[2] More recently, a number of prominent Italian Canadians from Toronto objected to the "distinct society" clause in the Charter of Rights, arguing that giving special recognition to Quebec was tantamount to downgrading the status of other ethnic groups in Canada.

Sceptics (or, some would say, realists) provide yet another view of multiculturalism, one opposed to those discussed so far, which focuses primarily on its use as a crude instrument of patronage. According to this interpretation, multiculturalism allows the party in power to co-opt successfully entire immigrant groups by raising seemingly under-qualified members of such groups to social prominence through political favouritism.

These different views of multiculturalism reflect differing conceptions of ethnicity in the context of New World societies. Some maintain that ethnicity is an objective force identified by such tangible markers as language, religion, and custom. Others contend instead that ethnicity is a subjective phenomenon: individuals are ethnics because they identify themselves as such, irrespective of whether they exhibit any of the tangible markers defining ethnicity. If so, then in a cosmopolitan environment like Toronto, the boundary separating a religiously indifferent Italo-Canadian who does not speak his heritage language from an Anglo who regularly eats *spaghetti alla carbonara* and takes his daily *cappuccino* in the neighbourhood cafe is fragile indeed! Among those who consider ethnicity in purely subjective terms, there are some who argue that it "concerns privilege, not primarily culture...."[3] Ethnicity then becomes the basis on which to build a strategy for individual or group mobility.[4] Whatever the definition, most social scientists marvel at the persistence of ethnicity, even though they are not quite sure what is persisting. Some even proclaim it to be as significant a social category as social class itself.[5]

I

It may be helpful at this point to examine the context in which the recent ethnic revival in North America took place. For although ethnically mixed populations have been a fact of North American life since the latter half of the last century, ethnicity only became the object of serious concern during the civil rights movement in the United States and the Quiet Revolution in Canada. Is it mere coincidence that ethnic groups were "discovered" officially at a time when each state faced a serious threat to its integrity from a large, restless, and distinct group within its borders? As Blacks and Québécois demanded their place in the sun, ethnic communities pressed their claims to social prominence.

But ethnic demands did not end there. Ethnic representatives in Canada insisted that their culture no longer be confined to the private sphere. It was time, as some put it, for Ukrainian Olga to be let out of the closet to share the limelight with Anglo Alice.[6] Seizing on the rhetoric of French-Canadian nationalism, they pressed the state to extend the same recognition and protection to their own culture as it had to French Canadian culture. Such demands ignored Quebec history, which might have provided ethnic revivalists with a realistic perspective. If French Canada, with its three hundred years of history, its large territory and population, and its articulated social structure and institutions, experienced problems maintaining cultural integrity, what hope was there for cultures with little institutional expression and with small populations scattered over the length and breadth of the country (a portion of which had only the vaguest notions of their ancestral heritage)?

One's view of ethnicity inevitably conditions one's approach to writing ethnic history. Are we to assume that in the process of migration, immigrants carry their ancestral culture with them, that they transplant it in the new soil,[7] and that it survives, largely unaltered, so that successive generations faithfully live what is essentially a local variant of this culture? "Institutional completeness" is the term coined by sociologists to denote individuals living an ethnically self-contained existence without reference to the receiving society. They maintain that this is possible because of the proliferation and diversification of voluntary organizations and services.[8] If such were the case, writing ethnic history would be no different from writing the history of French or English Canadians with their distinct and complete cultures.

There are, however, flaws in this view. Ethnic intellectuals occasionally notice, with embarrassed dismay, that their community's culture and that of the Mother Country do not coincide. The overwhelmingly peasant background of most immigrant groups has coloured the way they speak their native tongue. Their vocabulary is, by bourgeois urban standards, impoverished and their knowledge of grammar, limited; their speech over time has become studded with Anglicisms and English grammatical structures.

They have had little contact with high culture and have clung tenaciously to cultural forms long discarded in their homeland and ill-suited to a sophisticated environment. Ethnic intellectuals, who were their community's first historians, either glossed over these anomalies, or worse, whitewashed the immigrants' past.[9] For their part, ethnic groups were very much aware of their "shortcomings" and suffered from what Robert Harney has termed "self-disesteem."[10] Over the years, they experienced assimilation, to the extent that inside observers frequently express serious doubts about the future viability of many ethnic cultures.[11] The reality of the immigrant experience is generally far removed from the theorizing of the sociologists of ethnicity, from the celebrations of ethnic revivalists, or from the mental gymnastics of government officials busily devising new cultural policies based on such intangibles as subjective perceptions, private preferences, or the importation of metropolitan cultures.

That reality is best understood by discarding concepts such as persistence and completeness. Granted that the classical notion of ethnicity is rooted in these concepts: an ethnic group may well emerge and grow from a long and intimate association with a geographical space, from shared experiences and memories transmitted to successive generations, and from a sense of autonomy and cohesion. If so, we are not dealing in North America with classical ethnic groups. The notion of geographic space is basic to ethnicity. Without it, there can be no shared experience or memories, nor can a sense of autonomy or cohesion emerge. An ethnic culture cannot survive simply on memories of a distant space. To maintain its distinctiveness and to flourish, it must interact with a real, an immanent space. In North America, however, immigrant groups do not have a space they can claim exclusively for themselves. They are dispersed across a continent and must contend with the ever-present receiving culture. Consequently, their experience is not that of an ethnic group. The terms "immigrant communities" and "immigrant cultures" are therefore preferable to those of "ethnicity" and "ethnic cultures" because they capture the changing and evanescent character of the immigrant experience through successive generations.

How is the historian to understand immigrant communities? Robert Harney, who has been in the forefront of such efforts, emphasizes the need to study them on their own terms. Although his comments refer specifically to Little Italies, they have universal validity. "Perhaps nothing...epitomized the marginality of being immigrant, more than the fact that while the immigrant enclave was being treated as an aberrant and temporary problem for North American scholars, Italian intellectuals dismissed them as an embarrassing misrepresentation of Italian civilization."[12]

These immigrants, Harney insists, are not stereotypical Italians who happen to be living in North America. To begin with, their native culture is particular, bounded by class and region. In some way, it shares in the overall metropolitan culture of the Mother County, but cannot be seen as synonymous with it.[13] In fact, Old World intellectuals often have regarded this particularistic culture as an aberration in their own society. When this culture is exposed to the New World environment, it becomes profoundly North American in a way which social gospellers and their modern successors, the theorists of multiculturalism, cannot fathom because they define the term "North American" by the standards of the host society. The institutions and culture which immigrants established here were a response to specific North American conditions and, while they may have retained Old World forms, their content had a peculiarly New World meaning. The immigrants' "American-ness" was immediately apparent to their Old World relatives, but not to North Americans, who dismissed them as aliens while at the same time expecting them to behave as Anglos.

In this context, Frances Swyripa's provocative critique of *All of Baba's Children* raises a false methodological problem. "What is the dividing line," she asks, "between Ukrainian Canadian history and Canadian history?"[14] Is Two Hills, Alberta, any different from any other prairie town? Doubly ironic is the fact that this perspective leads Swyripa to a conclusion, tentative though it be, that ultimately undermines the legitimacy of immigrant history. "In future, will Ukrainian Canadian history be increasingly restricted to the ever-narrowing, visible, vocal community, the guardian and spokesman of a distinct Ukrainian cultural identity?"[15] At that point, we may well ask, will anyone care? Swyripa's point of view betrays the conscious or unconscious assumptions that Ukrainians in Canada are the remnant faithfully living the true Ukrainian culture as defined by "proper" speech, preferably by adherence to Orthodoxy (though Uniate Catholicism will do), and by other such formal characteristics.

Instead, the concept of culture must be broadened to encompass aspects of everyday life which, after all, are its very basis. Immigrant history, it must be stressed, is not about "national" culture, but about popular culture. Fortunately, historians have begun to identify these North American forms, rituals, and institutions which, together with the formal structures, give immigrants a sense of themselves and of the world around them. Whether or not these are short-lived is immaterial. The fact remains that they help us to understand key aspects of the immigrant experience as long as there continue to exist, in one form or another, observable communities (not Swyripa's visible and vocal remnant which is self-consciously Ukrainian and disdains things Ukrainian-Canadian). Immigrant culture therefore may not be a permanent historical category, but it is a useful tool to penetrate the complexity of industrial society and to elucidate important chapters of Canadian history.

The historiography of Canadian immigrant groups has mushroomed in the past fifteen years.[16] In fact, some observers term it the "new ethnic history" to distinguish it from earlier filio-pietistic writings. It remains true, however, that there is a lot of old wine in these new wineskins.

II

The most visible contribution to the field is the Generations series of monographs commissioned by the Department of the Secretary of State. This project arose out of a legitimate concern expressed by the Royal Commission on Bilingualism and Biculturalism that Canadian historical writing had neglected the contribution of many immigrant groups to their country of adoption. The government decided to correct this imbalance by funding the research and publication of monographs dealing with some twenty-five such groups. The quality of the work varies considerably. Of the fifteen books published so far, few can be regarded as important contributions to the field. Some, mostly of earlier vintage, are unmitigated failures, while others contain only the odd good chapter.[17]

Most studies begin with an outline of the political history of the Mother County, devoid of any historiographical reference. Two books focus instead on early contacts between Canada and the Mother Country. A more fitting and relevant introduction to these books might have been an examination of the social and cultural conditions of the peasantry in the Mother Country during the nineteenth century, since most non-English-speaking immigrants came from these ranks. In this regard, Paul Body's chapter in *Struggle and Hope* which discusses the macro- and micro-determinants of emigration is a model to be emulated, drawing as it does from migration studies in Hungary and American immigration history.[18]

The core of many of these studies consists of several chapters, as dry as they are static, describing the ethnic culture. Predictably, culture is defined as family, religion, ethnic organization, and language. But instead of considering the family as an economic unit, which might eventually have encouraged comparative analyses, most authors present it in structural terms, emphasizing its supposedly unique characteristics. The topic of religion is presented largely as a set of beliefs and rituals revolving around a litany of feast days. David Higgs diverges briefly from this model to make insightful comments on popular religion and levels of religious practice, which underscore the importance of viewing religion not as a formal and ossified structure, but as an essentially popular and living phenomenon.[19] The chapters on ethnic organizations, enumerations of professional, business, press, sport, and political associations, invariably depict a monolithic community. Those not fortunate enough to find themselves in that conceptually elusive but very real "mainstream" are either ignored or relegated to the outer reaches of society. Another symptom of this eviscerated kind of history are the perfunctory references to Quebec, even though many groups have important concentrations in that province. It seems obvious that their presence in a French-speaking milieu would give rise to particular, if not interesting, problems, but these are not investigated.

These books exhibit the serious methodological pitfalls discussed at the beginning of this article. The authors of the Generations series are not responsible for conditions imposed upon them — the notion, for example, that a standard-sized text should be the format suited to each of the twenty-five groups. And yet, many of these works betray a blithe disregard for the rich literature on American immigrant history, as well as the innovative and stimulating research produced by urban, labour, or family history in North America. More surprising still is their insensitivity to the Canadian context in describing immigrant culture. Even discussions of the work-place in most of these studies are little more than catalogues of jobs leading ever onward and upward. The authors do not attempt to analyze what kind of labour market their immigrants entered, nor how they took advantage of particular growth sectors in regional and local economies to better their circumstances. Little wonder that these studies fail to come to terms with the immigrant experience.

Fortunately, there are exceptions within this mediocre collection. The books on the Chinese and the Ukrainians (both of which, significantly, are the fruit of a collective effort), as well as those on the Hungarians and the

Croatians, stand out as honest, mature, and stimulating syntheses which will serve as springboards for further research. The authors marry social and cultural themes within specific periods of study so that discussions of formal culture are neither abstract nor belaboured. They use a wide range of primary and secondary documentation, including the Canadian census, government documents, and parish and newspaper records. They generally show more than a perfunctory acquaintance with Canadian historiography and with the literature of immigration studies. These books thus provide a broad picture of immigrant life in Canada. Their subjects are not cardboard cut-outs, but real people with an historical presence. They move on a Canadian stage and are shaped by and interact with their Canadian environment.

The Generations series is by no means a barometer of the state of the art in Canada. Small and unpretentious monographs, the special issues of *Polyphony*, and the conference papers published by the Multicultural History Society of Ontario have on the whole contributed more to the history of immigrants in Canada than the Generations series. Also useful are a series of pamphlets written by a number of well-known historians and published by the Canadian Historical Association with the help of the Multiculturalism Directorate, Ottawa, under the general title "Canada's Ethnic Groups." For the past fifteen years, scholars and writers have been examining different aspects of the immigrant experience, from its earliest manifestations in the phenomenon of migration, to the creation of immigrant communities and their participation in the socio-cultural life of Canada. Their work has lent seriousness and sophistication to a field which Canadian historians can no longer afford to ignore.

The period of the first major immigration, from 1896 to 1913, and the decade of the 1920s, has been better researched. With few exceptions, the later period, following the Second World War, is still dominated by analyses of public attitudes to immigration, government policies, mobility, and voter behaviour patterns.[20] In other words, for this more recent era, most scholars have not considered the immigrants on their own terms. No one has attempted to apply the concepts developed for the earlier era; nor has anyone measured with success the impact of later immigration on existing communities.[21] Having said this, we can look at the various components of the immigration experience and assess the contribution of the many authors to the field.

For many immigrants, abandoning their homeland was an involuntary act. Initially, it took the form of migration and was considered to be a temporary leave-taking. In two excellent essays, Robert Harney looks at the topic both as an individual experience through the eyes of the migrant,[22] and as a process, a business, to be exact.[23] He evokes the rural Old World milieu, with its failing economy, its family-centred life, and its strong sense of place. At the same time, he illustrates the extreme porosity of peasant societies at the turn of the century when labour recruitment literature and *padrone* business cards penetrated the most "backward" and inward-looking villages. In this world, illiterate migrants sought out "educated men" to mediate between themselves and the alien world outside their familiar space. A succession of go-betweens entered the picture — from the parish priest, to the notary, the local notable, the steamship agent, the labour bosses — each of whom exacted his pound of flesh.

Harney dispels the romantic image of the migrants as latter-day Robinson Crusoes. Theirs was not an exciting adventure in which they remade life in the New World without reference to the Old. The go-betweens and the migrant's work companions, who more likely than not came from the same area, ensured that the home town was omnipresent in America. Psychically too, migrants were prisoners of their objectives. The urgency of acquiring cash and the possibility of failure haunted them constantly. Harney movingly describes the migrant's decline into brutishness which was caused by the deplorable working conditions in the Canadian bush. While there is no reason to idealize the life of the peasantry in the late nineteenth century, the contrast between this closely-knit, settled, immanent society and the raw exploitation, the barren isolation of the Canadian North, could not have been greater for the migrant. Yet migrants lived through this experience in a state of suspended animation, knowing that it was temporary and that somehow their objectives would be achieved. Harney's pieces are undoubtedly a high point in the literature of immigrant groups.

The factors drawing this surge of immigrants to Canada at the turn of the century were first examined by Donald Avery.[24] His approach revolutionized our perception of Canadian immigration policy. Avery clearly identified the immigrant's place in the Canadian economy during the Laurier era, as well as the pre-eminent role played by capitalists in fashioning immigration policy. He subsequently published an expanded version of this study which appeared as *Dangerous Foreigners.*[25] Whatever the defects of this book (the lack of thematic unity being its most notable), it stands as an important contribution to immigrant studies. Based on solid and wide-ranging documentation, the work successfully challenges many of the myths surrounding the immigrant.

Avery does not, however, deal with the life of the immigrant either in the bush or in the city. Writing about the immigrant's experience on the northern fringes, however, presents a certain challenge because of the underdevelopment of Canadian local history and the dearth of readily available documentation. While Edmund W. Bradwin's remains the classic study,[26] new work is slowly appearing. Anthony Rasporich has encouraged and has himself carried out solid research in this important area, with reference to the Croatians.[27] Scholarly attention has also focused on immigrants, particularly Italians and Finns, in the extractive industries of Northern Ontario.[28] These studies feelingly reveal how immigrants in these more remote centres and in the face of harsh and tyrannical employers managed to rekindle the sense of cohesion and solidarity which they had known in the Mother Country.

A key figure linking immigrant workers to the labour needs of the frontier was the *padrone*. Harney also sensitized Canadian historians to this figure.[29] The *padrone* was considered by the receiving society to represent the archetypal immigrant: slippery, furtive, ruthless, and violent. He also served as an effective scapegoat for their residual guilt feelings. In assessing this character, Harney has tried to break away from the moralism of American and Italian historiography by placing the *padrone* in the overall context of the commerce of migration. The historian emphasizes the *padrone's* vulnerability, dependent as he was on the good graces of Canadian capitalists, on a state of non-belligerence and of grudging co-operation with the many *padroni* of North America, and on the forebearance of government. Although the precarious world of the *padrone* is well illustrated, Harney does tend to downplay the exploitative relationship between labour boss and migrant. No matter how grateful the latter might be for the *padrone's* protection, no matter how content with his remittances, no matter how exploitative the whole commerce of migration, the *padrone* remained an integral and insidious part of that system.

Jobs in the bush were seasonal and if, at the end of the season, migrants had not reached their financial goals, they would look for extra work in the cities. Historians have now begun to study some of the urban institutions of the migrant's sojourning culture. The boarding-house was one of these.

Harney has drawn us away from seeing it simply as a folksy institution which allowed the transplanted culture to thrive.[30] It was, he insists, an enterprise, and a very organized one at that. For the owner, it formed part of a set of strategies to increase family income, allowing the wife to earn money while she raised her family. For the boarder, the benefits were also primarily financial, but there were also intangible advantages, such as home-cooking and the re-creation of the ambience of home. The boarding-house was so crucial that for many migrants no reality existed outside of it.[31] It also proved vital to the whole immigrant community since it spawned a host of institutions which became mainstays of the New World culture.

Migrants soon became immigrants and the period of sojourning gave way to that of settlement. When this transition occurred is unclear. It may be, as Harney suggests, that once questions of marriage and inheritance were settled back home, the sojourner put down roots in the new country. At the community level, it may have happened when women joined their menfolk and children began to be born in Canada. Still, the concept of sojourning remains illusive because within many immigrant groups it was an ongoing phenomenon, even after the community got settled. Historians too often think of the transition from sojourning to settlement as linear when in fact it is dynamic. However, at some point in the immigrant's odyssey ethnic neighbourhoods began to emerge.[32] These were found in areas of cheap housing, usually the urban core, and they were not the exclusive preserve of any one ethnic group.

Ethnic neighbourhoods expressed the immigrant culture. They were neither static nor monolithic, but rather a curious amalgam of pre-industrial and modern. They were, for example, fragmented by an intense *esprit de clocher* because the peasants' primary loyalty was to their village or town. So strong was this feeling that, as John Zucchi indicates, the Italians of Toronto only patronized merchants from their home town. Immigrants formed organizations based on this intense localism of which the *landsman-shaften* (Jewish Mutual Aid Societies based on regional origin) are but an example.

It is impossible to say when a broader identification with the Mother Country developed.[33] Undeniably, however, this wider identity arose out of specifically Canadian circumstances. In part, it may have been a response to nativism. A much stronger force was undoubtedly the participation of immigrants from the same country in common institutions. Still, in communities where immigration is ongoing, the narrower allegiance persists to this day side by side with the larger sense of identity. Ethnic neighbourhoods were divided not only according to region, but also by rank and status. To some extent, these divisions reflected the peasant society back home, with its hierarchies and its sense of deference. But they were also the product of specifically Canadian circumstances. A barely literate rustic like Antonio Cordasco could, by artful manipulation, become a *prominente* in his community. The range of services he provided as a labour boss, banker, food provisioner, and boarding-house keeper made him indispensable to migrants. Yet, as Bruno Ramirez and Michael Del Balso skillfully demonstrate, this prominence without pedigree co-existed with a more genteel and established one based on Mother Country standards. The two sometimes clashed, using different sets of symbols and honours to establish their primacy.[34] Whether status was inherited from the Old World or established as a result of cunning, stratification was very real in the immigrant neighbourhood.

How one became a *prominente* is still unclear. But the ability to exploit the needs of recently arrived immigrants, and particularly to control part of the labour market, was important. For example, an immigrant who opened a grocery store moved out of wage labour and took the first tentative steps to prominence. If, as Franc Sturino has shown for the twenties, a grocer could through his contacts with market gardeners provide migrant farm labourers with their first jobs, his rise to prominence was secured.[35] Nor should we neglect contacts with important members of the receiving culture. Jacob Cohen, for example, greatly enhanced his status in the Jewish community in Toronto through his links with the Conservative party and with Colonel Denison, who got him a judicial appointment.[36]

Prominence was not the itinerary of most immigrants. They struggled instead against the vicissitudes of the wage system vividly described in recent Canadian social histories. They devised various strategies to cope with this situation. The immigrants were above all "polyvalent" workers prepared to take on a variety of odd jobs to see them through slack periods. Even their houses expressed this adaptability and resourcefulness since very often there was no clear distinction between living and working space. The pictures in Robert Harney and Harold Troper's *Immigrants* are very eloquent in this regard. Wives and children were integral parts of the family economy. In a stimulating and imaginative article, Bruno Ramirez explored some of the devices which made immigrants less responsive to the inducements of the market-place. Keeping vegetable gardens and one or two farm animals, processing food at home, exchanging skills and services among kinsmen, building one's house in stages using material discarded (or not) from one's work-place: immigrants used these and other techniques to make life more settled and pleasant at a time when, as Terry Copp showed, real wages were falling.[37] This extra-market production, as Ramirez termed it, formed a part of the immigrant's culture.

Slowly material conditions improved. It may be best at this point to consider the concepts of class and social mobility as used in some of this literature. Doubtless it is important to study how immigrants perceived their position within the neighbourhood. There is a danger, however, that the historian will transform these perceptions into absolutes. Harney, for example, is so anxious to move away from the view of the ethnic neighbourhood as the rubbish heap of the American dream that he exaggerates its autonomy with respect to the social structure of the receiving culture. The switch from being a ditchdigger to a grocer may indicate relative mobility, but may not change (perceptions notwithstanding) the immigrant's position in the Canadian class structure. Harney further abuses a much-abused term by referring to the ethnic middle-class as a "bourgeoisie." It is one thing to note that stratification existed within immigrant neighbourhoods; it is quite another to argue as if these differences in rank were somehow unrelated to an overall class system.[38]

As material circumstances got better, so did the ambience of the neighbourhood. Immigrants began to make for themselves a familiar landscape soon after their arrival in Canada. Varpu Lindstrom-Best, for example, captures the Finns' spirit of inventiveness as they created a garden out of the cultural wilderness with their temperance societies, their "fist presses," and their theatre.[39] Eventually, they institutionalized these early creative impulses by building halls which became centres of political and artistic expression.[40] But most settled communities looked to more formal symbols of their "arrival."

For many immigrants, the church was one of these. What this symbol actually meant to them, however, is not always obvious. Historians too often interpret it as proof of the peasants' innate religiosity.[41] But North America altered the conditions under which Old World churches operated: here they were voluntary institutions deprived of the coercive power of the state and subject to intense competition from indigenous churches.[42] Moreover, the phenomenon of religion as a bond between the individual and the local community no longer existed. Harney vividly illustrates this point by citing the example of immigrants from two different villages in Italy fighting in Toronto to see which group would carry in procession the statue of St. Roch who happened to be the patron saint of both home towns.[43] Somehow the environment had altered, not to say debased, the meaning of a primitive and vital Mother Country ceremony. Finally, the most telling point on the religiosity of peasants is made by Ramirez and Del Balso, who looked at the annual reports prepared by the pastors of two Italian parishes in Montreal. These indicated that the immigrants generally neglected their Christian duties.[44] In the early stage of settlement at least, the church was certainly a gathering place and a focal point for the immigrant community; what it was beyond that, however, requires further investigation.

Ethnic schools were another accoutrement of a settled community, a bridge between the first and second generations. Eleoussa Polyzoi strongly portrays the tension between the Old World curriculum, often filio-pietistic, and the New World pupils, underlining the point that these schools, just as other ethnic institutions, were not merely "transplants" of the culture of the Mother Country.[45]

But formal structures like churches and schools should not mask the more informal institutions of an established community. For example, Italian grocery stores, which doubled in number in Montreal between 1911 and 1916, not only contributed to the ambience of the immigrant neighbourhood, but were important centres of community life, serving as meeting-places where news and gossip were exchanged.[46] More attention must be given to these informal structures, which might be as important as churches and schools for immigrant cultures.

Because *The Jews of Toronto* is an extensive study of an immigrant community in an urban setting, it warrants particular attention here. This book is both a social and institutional account. But the two perspectives are not well integrated; the latter soon takes precedence, to the detriment of the study's vitality. The pages dealing with the immigrants from eastern Europe, their entry into Toronto's industrial life, and their confrontation with the older "white" Jewish community over ritual, social assistance, and labour issues are vividly reconstructed by the author. Stephen Speisman in fact touches many of these themes. However, the book abruptly shifts attention away from the working-class Jews who, the author insistently reminds us, comprised the bulk of the community, to the elite and their organizational activities. It also concentrates almost exclusively on observant Jews and their religious life, making only brief references to the secularists and their organizations. And yet Speisman never indicates clearly how significant an element the religious Jews were within the community. In short, part of the study will be of interest to Canadian social historians; the rest has a much narrower appeal.[47]

While urban immigrants have been the subject of some excellent work, their country cousins predictably have suffered neglect. Examinations of the rural immigrant experience are neither considerable nor substantial.[48] *Canadian Ethnic Studies* devoted an issue to immigrant settlement patterns and the way government regulations undermined their distinctiveness.[49] There is, however, no rural equivalent to the studies of the urban immigrant experience discussed above.

Two books on Ukrainians in the West move in that direction, but both are flawed.[50] Helen Potrebenko adopts a crudely Manichean style, pitting the capitalist exploiters and their Ukrainian lackeys against the hapless, but not helpless Ukrainian workers and farmers. Her narrative is also marred by a lack of focus: in her frequent accounts of Albertan social and political history, she does not indicate the specific Ukrainian presence. The book constantly alternates between happenings within the Ukrainian-Albertan communities and broader events in Albertan history without connecting the two. Myrna Kostash, for her part, writes a popular history based on her own experience as a second-generation Ukrainian growing up in small-town Alberta. The anecdotal style and the presentation of events without reference to historical context and in romanticized tones diminishes this study.

Yet both accounts have their moments of lucidity and impact. Particularly evocative are descriptions of the difficult settlement years at the turn of the century.[51] The terrible isolation of the prairies caused by the ban on block settlement, and the policy of reserved lands which dispersed immigrants even more, contrasted sharply with the rural village life of eastern Europe. These peasants, however, were as resourceful as their urban cousins in confronting difficult circumstances. To see hardship through, they adopted many of the co-operative strategies of urban immigrants. Yet neither Kostash nor Potrebenko succumbs to a facile Whiggism: a view of immigrant history as inevitable progress. Settlement was not uniformly successful and many farms had to be forfeited because settlers could not meet their obligations. Further, both authors describe the almost total absence of social services in these communities: the early settlement years left a legacy of high infant mortality, poor nutrition, substandard housing, and inadequate clothing. What is never clear from these accounts, however, is whether the Ukrainians' experience differed from that of other settlers.

Of the two writers, Kostash is both more courageous and insightful. She does not hesitate to broach the anti-Semitic and anti-native attitudes of early Ukrainian Canadians, a subject which seems to be taboo in this era of cultural tolerance. She also alludes to Liberal party patronage in the Laurier years and efforts to co-opt prominent members of the community, a theme echoed by Martin Kovacs in his study of prairie Hungarians.[52] Kostash deplores as well the other-worldliness, the cult of a mystical Ukraine which permeated cultural expression in the West. Nevertheless, in her own chapter on culture, she still tends to depict Ukrainian-Canadian culture as folklore: painted Easter eggs, merry wedding feasts, religious holidays and their elaborate celebrations. A broader perspective on this topic has yet to be developed.

The experiences of rural and urban immigrants come together under the topic of labour. Almost every newcomer to this country was a worker, toiling in the primary sector before settling on the farm or moving on to jobs in the city. Historians have begun to study both the immigrant as worker and the complex relationship between ethnicity and labour. It is clear, however, that there will be no proper appreciation of the place occupied by the immigrant in Canadian society without a close examination of the exigencies of the labour market. In an admirable study, sociologist Peter Li has shown how the low entry status of the Chinese worker and his marginality in the Canadian economy was maintained through institutional racism. Official discrimination facilitated a split labour market in which Oriental labourers were paid substandard wages. This mechanism not only increased the profit margin of the Canadian employer but also the wages of white employees who benefited directly from Chinese exploitation. In the long run, however, this situation undermined the white workers' bargaining position. As a result, they forced the Chinese out of the manufacturing sector into job ghettoes like laundry and restaurant work. These menial jobs merely served to reinforce the contempt with which the receiving society viewed the Chinese in their midst.[53]

Women were the largest category of workers to be victims of a segmented labour market. The system hit immigrant women particularly hard since many of them sought work to augment an otherwise inadequate family income. They found jobs in insular sectors of the economy like domestic service and piece work, or in manufacturing industries where they served as a reserve army of cheap labour. In these circumstances, the ability to organize for collective action was very narrow. Ruth Frager has underlined the unusual character of the 1912 Eaton's strike where Jewish male workers supported their women against management's labour-saving devices. In this case, ethnic cohesion was the main reason for the strikers' disciplined response. The strike failed, however, because of ethnic antagonisms within labour, and class distinctions within the women's movement. Frager's study provides a fascinating example of the intersection between class, ethnicity, and gender.[54] In the absence of collective action, individual women simply took matters into their own hands, often leaving an uncongenial work situation to seek employment elsewhere. Franca Iacovetta and Varpu Lindstrom-Best have shown that women as ethnically diverse as Southern Italians and Finns could, within limits, control their working environment and so were hardly an infinitely exploitable work-force.[55] These studies confirm an increasingly clear picture which is emerging from the literature of immigrant women as active participants in the overall process of immigration.[56] Like their husbands, these women were actors rather than victims. They may not have controlled the circumstances in which they found themselves, but within the constraints of their immigrant existence, they actively shaped strategies to improve their condition.

Defiant Sisters is the first major treatment of a particular group of immigrant women in Canadian historiography.[57] And what women they were! Anti-bourgeois, anti-clerical, socialist, and feminist: these were neither typical Finnish women, as the author concedes, nor typical immigrant women. Many of them were single and remained so. Those who married did so in later life. They obtained jobs mostly as domestics and camp cooks. Some became bootleggers and prostitutes. Despite the isolated working conditions, they created a solid support network for themselves; there were even attempts at unionization. Above all, they took pride in their work and remained defiant in the face of exploitation and condescension. Lindstrom-Best is to be commended for her vivid portrayal of these women and her novel treatment of such themes as health, welfare, marriage, and childbirth. Her study, however, remains theoretically weak. Class, ethnicity, and gender are categories conveniently invoked, but the connection between them is never really explained, either at the conceptual level, or concretely, in the act of writing about her subject.

Split and segmented labour markets have become central concerns in Canadian working class and immigrant history, as has the lack of a genuine and enduring socialist culture in North America. In a very suggestive essay, Ramirez relates this phenomenon to the labour market itself.[58] Attention is focused specifically on Italians employed by the CPR as casual labourers in turn-of-the-century Montreal. These immigrants encountered a market characterized by a variety of temporary dead-end jobs which required them to be spatially mobile. In this context, it was unlikely that collective strategies of emancipation would emerge. Such strategies were redefined in individualistic terms as Italians sought escape from their marginality in the labour force through self-employment, particularly as shop-keepers. Ramirez provides a fascinating hypothesis which will have to be tested by longer-term and cross-cultural studies.

The absence of a socialist culture did not imply passivity. Although Gabriel Kolko depicts immigrants as an amorphous and rootless *lumpenproletariat* who presumably made the American labour movement what it is today,[59] this stereotype is now being challenged. Foreign workers may not have had the opportunity or the inclination to participate steadfastly in trade unions, but they did not hesitate to use force when pushed to the limit by their employers.[60] Some immigrants displayed a remarkable sense of solidarity which overrode their diverse origins, as Allen Seager recently showed. Was this because such immigrants worked in rather isolated communities which allowed for "a substantial measure of cultural autonomy?"[61]

Ethnic rivalry, however, undoubtedly existed among workers, and employers constantly manipulated it to advantage. Labour historians eventually will have to determine whether such divisions were centripetal or centrifugal forces within the working class. To what extent did groups of workers play on these rivalries to promote their own interests? In the Lakehead strikes at the turn of the century, Jean Morrison contrasts the British workers and their parliamentary methods with southern European labour and its traditions of spontaneous revolt. Morrison is not clear on what part cultural determinants played in these different reactions. But more fundamentally, in the violent atmosphere characterizing labour relations at the Lakehead, was not the advocacy of due process a way of ingratiating oneself with management? Did not the English-speaking workers have most to gain by this approach? Were "foreign workers" marginalized by an accommodating indigenous working class or must other factors, such as repression by employers and the police or the Americanization of Canadian trade unions, be considered?

A related question involves the role of immigrants in radical labour movements. Avery, Rasporich, Radforth, and Seager have documented the participation and even the leadership of immigrants in unions from the IWW to the Workers' Unity League.[62] Were these people an insignificant minority in their own communities and among immigrants as a whole in Canada? The question will doubtless have to await further research. But the image of the acquiescent immigrant now must be qualified.

Closely allied to the theme of labour is that of the political immigrant. Recent research has transformed our perception of early Canadian socialism.[63] The important presence of Finns and Ukrainians in Canadian socialist parties is now well established. Lindstrom-Best describes the political culture of Finnish immigrants: their commitment to self-improvement through the establishment of libraries and the dissemination of handwritten newspapers, their earnestness in opposing drink and church-sanctioned weddings, and their discipline. She emphasizes as well the active role of women in socialist politics. Norman Buchignani and Doreen Indra, for their part, show the high degree of politicization on the part of East Indians in turn-of-the-century British Columbia.[64] For these immigrants, politics were not only to be talked about but to be acted on. They established institutions based on egalitarian or socialist principles, such as co-operatives, credit unions, and mutual aid societies, most of which endured long after the parties and sects had disappeared.[65]

The individual immigrant radical has attracted a good deal of attention, much of it perhaps unwarranted.[66] A peculiar breed of immigrant, well-born, highly educated, and politically committed, these radicals were in most cases forced to flee to the New World because of repression at home. North America made them into misfits. The conservative intellectual climate prevailing in Canada, their own difficulties with the English language, the cultural gap between themselves and their immigrant communities — all these factors conspired to make them marginal. Among Canadian socialists, they were different, outsiders; among their fellow immigrants, they were sophisticated urbanites; in the wider Canadian society, they were just more aliens. The message which they delivered with such conviction in the Mother Country somehow lost its impact in the new environment, and they seemed incapable of adjusting it to changed circumstances. In some ways, they had never immigrated because spiritually they remained children of the Mother Country; yet in other ways, emigration abruptly cut them off from rapidly changing and critical events at home. This explains their restlessness, their undisciplined activity, and their eclecticism — a striking example of which is Ole Hjelt, the self-professed Norwegian socialist who nevertheless supported Quisling's right-wing government during the Second World War. Only Tomo Cacic does not fit this stereotype. A self-educated worker of peasant origins, he never wavered in his commitment to revolutionary ideology and paid the price, eventually being deported to Yugoslavia as one of the celebrated victims of the infamous Section 41 of the Immigration Act. But Cacic aside, is there not in the fascination with the radical immigrant more than an element of romanticism? These intellectuals were atypical immigrants, and they did not, as a whole, participate in the life of their local community. Most in fact regarded their fellow countrymen with condescension, if not contempt. Why then accord them such significance? One is reminded here of Kostash's remark: "Is it really necessary to see picturesqueness...in the perfectly mundane in order to accord [immigrants] dignity and personality? It is only necessary if you imagined them otherwise."[67]

Immigrants were heavily involved in the Communist party of Canada during the twenties and thirties.[68] It was a passionate affair, blowing alternately hot and cold. Avery attributes the party's success among immigrants partly to its advocacy and use of violence, which appealed to their peasant traditions (although this should not be taken to mean that immigrants were attracted to violence by their nature). Moreover, in the early years, Canadian communism was very much part of the fibre of immigrant culture. Its federated organizations like the Ukrainian Labour-Farmer Temple Association, the Finnish Organization of Canada, and other associations such as the Hungarians' Independent Sick Benefit Association offered immigrants a wide variety of cultural and social services.

Historians have not tried to measure with any accuracy the popularity of the Communist party in various immigrant communities. Certain indices exist,[69] but this scattered evidence only seems to corroborate the conclusion which John Kolasky substantiated for Ukrainians[70] — the party appealed consistently only to a small minority of the immigrant population.

The party's setbacks among new Canadians were partly self-inflicted, but also resulted from external factors. Most noteworthy of these was the repression unleashed during the "Red Scare," which reached its apogee in the thirties. But this cannot mask the party's own mistakes. In an important and well-written book, Kolasky documents how communism lost its vitality and its appeal for Ukrainian Canadians of the Left. He portrays a leadership stolidly following the Moscow line, repressing dissent and criticism, gradually becoming a self-satisfied gerontocracy leading an organization without members. The study's only important shortcoming is its failure to situate post-war events in the context of the Cold War, which makes Kolasky's account stilted and one-sided.

The Depression saw strong political and ideological polarization develop within many immigrant communities. In part, these divisions were caused by consular personnel who exploited "their" immigrants in order to advance the diplomatic or political interests of their respective govern- ments. To this end, they organized umbrella organizations which claimed to speak on behalf of the whole community. These should not be seen as unmistakeable signs of the growing maturity of immigrant groups since the impetus for their establishment in many cases came from outside. The consulates of Finland, Italy, Hungary, Poland, Japan, and Germany took a variety of other initiatives which marked a willingness to intervene in the affairs of the community.[71] Of course, some consular activities were more harmful than others. Finnish diplomats, for example, created a repressive apparatus which sought to isolate Finnish radicals in their work and com- munities. As well, the actions of zealous consular officials from Italy and Germany cast long shadows over these immigrant groups during the war. Overall, this diplomatic presence reinforced the organizational structure and the influence of the Right in many communities.

To imagine, however, that all immigrants became willing accomplices for consular propaganda, as Lita-Rose Betcherman suggests of the Italians,[72] is to share the consul's wildest fantasies. There was resistance, more successful in some cases than in others, to these attempts to monop- olize community life.[73] But more common than active resistance was the generalized apathy of the immigrant population in the face of their Mother Country's diplomatic manoeuvrings.[74] Consuls could expect large and enthusiastic audiences at picnics and other such festivities. Properly politi- cal meetings, however, only brought together the faithful few. Immigrants were, after all, rooted in a Canadian reality. Those who remained especially blind to this fact were the self-appointed immigrant elite, flattered and seduced by consular attention and favours. More research must be devoted to this group, which emerged from the immigrant community, but were not part of it. Ambivalent in their identity and allegiances, the elite were aberrations rather than representatives of the immigrant experience.

An ironic fate awaited these umbrella organizations so carefully put together by diplomats. During the Second World War, the Canadian government discovered the immigrants' overall lack of enthusiasm for the war effort. Through the Nationalities Branch of the Department of National War Services, these umbrella organizations once again became propaganda vehicles, this time for the Canadian government. In this way, Canada's first multicultural policy saw the light of day. It was born, as was the second, of crisis and neglect.

Studies on nativism are not within the purview of this article since they really concern the host society. However, scholars have recently paid some attention to the immigrants' response to nativism.[75] In both the Jewish refugee crisis and the evacuation of Japanese Canadians during the Second World War, two communities were helpless in confronting the overwhelming hostility of the host society and powerless because they did not have access to those in authority. Unfortunately, they were also incapable of overcoming their own internal divisions. Many members of these communities continued during the bleakest moments to have an abiding faith in government, a faith which for some Jews was cemented by partisan ties. Others sought personal exemptions from the harsh injunctions of government. Still, as Irving Abella, Harold Troper, and Ann Gomer Sunahara show, these communities were not leaderless. Energetic and dedicated leaders did emerge from these crises, but they were effective only insofar as they could recruit Canadian opinionmakers to their cause. These studies underline the fragility of minority groups and the all-too-human responses of their members in times of crisis. This theme, which has barely been explored, needs further study.

The history of immigrant groups in Canada has come of age. It is not a tale ringing with drums and bugles; neither a stage filled with noble families, intellectuals, or revolutionaries, nor an edifying homily about economic and cultural miracles. The story of immigrants is much more ordinary than the distorted and censored version served up by filio-pietists. What it loses in tawdry brilliance, it gains in vitality and realism. This history is an integral part of the Canadian past. It has emerged because of new trends in social, labour and urban history. Its future development depends as well on the rapidly expanding area of migration studies.

The non-English-speaking immigrants who came to Canada were, as noted above, overwhelmingly of peasant origin. They brought with them a particularistic culture which they adapted to the Canadian environment.

Their communities were neither static, nor monolithic, nor submissive. This is probably not the type of history which "professional ethnics" want to hear recounted. But they should be reminded that self-proclaimed immigrant leaders have not traditionally been the best interpreters of the needs of their communities. Immigrants, like many other important groups, have been largely ignored in the past by Canadian historians. It would be a pity if, after these years of neglect, they should again be swept under the carpet by their official historians, anxious to present a favourable image of their group to a wider public.

Harney has observed that the attempt to write a pan-Canadian synthesis of an immigrant group would, given Canada's intense regionalism, reflect more of an intellectual construct than a reality.[76] Certainly, as this article has suggested, local and regional studies have best depicted the immigrants in their total socio-economic and cultural context. However, two regions have yet to be much explored by the historian of immigrant groups: the Atlantic provinces and British Columbia (which continues to be dominated by studies of nativism). As well, Quebec, outside of Montreal, and small-town Ontario remain largely uncharted territories. Still, the history of immigrant groups can only be as good as Canadian history itself. Without more of a regional focus, without more attention being given to popular culture, without more studies of local communities, Canadian history will fail to provide the context which the study of immigrants requires to be fully meaningful. The futures of the two areas are intimately bound up in the same way that the immigrants' fate is tied to that of their country of adoption.

Endnotes

1. Jean Burnet, "The Policy of Multiculturalism within a Bilingual Framework: A Stock-taking," *Canadian Ethnic Studies* 10:1 (1978), 107-113. This very insightful article highlights the ambiguities underlying the policy of multiculturalism.

2. Jaroslav Rudnyckyj, "Separate Statement," *Report of the Royal Commission on Bilingualism and Biculturalism* 1 (Ottawa 1967), 158. This demand is echoed by J. Dahlie and T. Fernando, "Reflections on Ethnicity and the Exercise of Power: An Introductory Note," in *Ethnicity, Power and Politics in Canada*, eds. J. Dahlie and T. Fernando (Toronto, 1981), 1.

3. Kogila Moodley, "Canadian Ethnicity in Comparative Perspective," in Dahlie and Fernando, *Ethnicity, Power*, 9. Although disagreeing with this view, Moodley says that it is the current wisdom among sociologists. The author maintains instead that ethnicity is both an objective and a subjective phenomenon and that the interaction

between the two needs to be explored, rather than simply asserting the primacy of one over the other.

4. Karl Peter has called for the creation of ethnic social movements to force a reallocation of power in favour of the "third force." See his "Myth of Multiculturalism and Other Political Fables," in Dahlie and Fernando, *Ethnicity, Power,* 62. Giving ethnic collectivities more power is also a theme in A. Anderson and J. Frideres, *Ethnicity in Canada* (Toronto, 1981).

5. Nathan Glazer and D. P. Moynihan, eds., *Ethnicity: Theory and Practice* (Cambridge, 1975), 3.

6. Wsevolod Isajiw, "Olga in Wonderland: Ethnicity in Technological Society," *Canadian Ethnic Studies* 9:1 (1977), 77-83.

7. Rudolph Vecoli, "Contadini in Chicago: A Critique of the Uprooted," *Journal of American History* 51 (1964), 404-17.

8. Raymond Breton, "Institutional Completeness of Ethnic Communities and the Personal Relations of Immigrants," *American Journal of Sociology* 70 (Sept. 1964). That "Institutional Completeness" said more about the geographical, social, or cultural isolation of the individual than about the institutions' vitality is not immediately apparent to these theorists.

9. Myrna Kostash, *All of Baba's Children* (Edmonton, 1980). Kostash has identified the process of whitewashing and attempts to deal with its consequences.

10. Robert Harney and Vincenza Scarpaci, *Little Italies in North America* (Toronto, 1981), 4. Apologies for not being able to speak "proper" Italian are a manifestation of this ethnic self-disesteem. The present climate of ethnic triumphalism has not been propitious for doing research on this vital topic.

11. Many of the authors in the Generations series voice this concern.

12. Harney and Scarpaci, *Little Italies,* 3.

13. For a succinct discussion of this theme, see Franc Sturino, "Family and Kin Cohesion among South Italian Immigrants in Toronto," in *The Immigrant Woman in North America,* eds. B. Caroli *et al.* (Toronto, 1978), 288-311.

14. Frances Swyripa, "Perspectives on an Ethnic Bestseller," *Canadian Ethnic Studies* 10:1 (1978), 60.

15. *Ibid.,* 60.

16. Other historiographical articles include Howard Palmer, "Canadian Immigration and Ethnic History in the 1970s and 1980s," *Journal of Canadian Studies* 17 (Spring 1982), 35-50; Robert Harney, "Frozen Wastes: The State of Italian-Canadian Studies," in *Perspectives in Italian Immigration and Ethnicity,* ed. S. M. Tomasi (New York, 1977), 115-31; Bruno Ramirez, "La recherche sur les Italiens du Québec," *Questions de culture* 2 (1982), 103-11; Sylvie Taschereau, "L'histoire de l'immigration au Québec: une invitation à fuir les ghettos," *Revue d'histoire de l'Amérique française* 41:4 (printemps 1988), 575-89.

17. Stanford Reid, *The Scottish Tradition in Canada* (Toronto, 1976); Peter Chimbos, *The Canadian Odyssey* (Toronto, 1980); Baha Abu-Laban, *An Olive Branch on the*

Family Tree (Toronto, 1980); Gulbrand Loken, *From Fjord to Frontier* (Toronto, 1980); Grace Anderson and David Higgs, *A Future to Inherit* (Toronto, 1976); Henry Radecki with Benedykt Heydenkorn, *A Member of a Distinguished Family* (Toronto, 1976); Ken Adachi, *The Enemy That Never Was* (Toronto, 1976); N.F. Dreiziger *et al., Struggle and Hope* (Toronto, 1982); E. Wickberg, ed., *From China to Canada: A History of the Chinese Communities in Canada* (Toronto, 1982); A. Rasporich, *For a Better Life: A History of Croatians in Canada* (Toronto, 1982); M. Lupul, ed., *A Heritage in Transition: Essays in the History of Ukrainians in Canada* (Toronto, 1982); N. Buchignani *et al., Continuous Journey: A Social History of South Asians in Canada* (Toronto, 1985); K. Aun, *The Political Refugees: A History of the Estonians in Canada* (Toronto, 1985); H. Ganzevoort, *A Bittersweet Land: The Dutch Experience in Canada, (1890-1980)* (Toronto, 1988); Jean Burnet with Howard Palmer, *"Coming Canadians": An Introduction to a History of Canada's Peoples* (Toronto, 1988). To these can be added a recent work of mediocre quality not in the Generations series, on the Portuguese in Quebec, see Antonio Alpalhao and Victor da Rose, *Les Portugais du Québec* (Ottawa, 1979).

18. "Emigration from Hungary, 1880-1956," in Dreisziger *et al., Struggle and Hope*, 27-60. Equally worthy of mention is Bruno Ramirez, *Les premiers Italiens à Montréal: l'origine de la petite Italie du Québec* (Montréal, 1984), 26-36.

19. Anderson and Higgs, *Future to Inherit*, 147-50.

20. Milda Danys, *Lithuanian Immigration to Canada after the Second World War* (Toronto, 1986) is a notable exception to this generalization.

21. Radecki and Dreisziger have observed that post-Second World War immigration provided a shot in the arm to their communities, as articulate professionals became available to take up leadership positions in various organizations. They allude to tensions between old and new immigrants, as does Jeremy Boissevain, who probed the attitudes of the two waves of immigrants to each other. See Boissevain's *The Italians of Montreal: Social Adjustment in a Plural Society* (Ottawa, 1970).

22. Robert Harney, "The Commerce of Migration," *Canadian Ethnic Studies* 9:1 (1977), 42-53.

23. Robert Harney, "Men without Women," in *The Immigrant Woman*, ed. B. Caroli, 79-101.

24. Donald Avery, "Canadian Immigration Policy and the 'Foreign' Navvy, 1896-1914," Canadian Historical Association, *Historical Papers* (1972), 135-56.

25. Donald Avery, *"Dangerous Foreigners": European Immigrant Workers and Labour Radicalism in Canada, 1896-1932* (Toronto, 1979).

26. Edmund W. Bradin, *The Bunkhouse Man* (Toronto, 1972).

27. Anthony Rasporich, "South Slavs on a Northern Margin: The Frontier Experience of Croatian Migrants during Canada's Great Depression," in *Ethnic Canadians: Culture and Education*, ed. M. L. Kovacs (Regina, 1978), 399-410. See as well his monograph on the Croatians in the Generations series cited above.

28. J.L. DiGiacomo, *They Live in the Moneta: An Overview of the History and Changes in Social Organization of Italians in Timmins, Ontario* (Downsview, 1982); Ian

Radforth, "Finnish Lumber Workers in Ontario, 1919-1946," *Polyphony* 3:2 (Fall 1981), 23-34; Allen Seager, "Finnish Canadians and the Ontario Miners' Movement," *ibid.*, 35-45.

29. Robert Harney: "The Padrone and the Immigrant," *The Canadian Review of American Studies* 5:2 (Fall 1974), 101-18; "Montreal's King of Labour: A Case Study of Padronism," *Labour/Le Travailleur* 4 (1979), 57-84; "The Padrone System and Sojourners in the Canadian North, 1885-1920," in *Pane e Lavoro: The Italian American Working Class*, ed. G. Pozzetta (Toronto, 1980), 119-37.

30. Robert Harney, "Boarding and Belonging," *Urban History Review* 2 (1978), 8-37; Carmela Patrias, "Hungarian Immigration to Canada before the Second World War," *Polyphony*, 2:2-3 (1979-80), 17-26; Robert Harney and Harold Troper, *Immigrants: A Portrait of an Urban Experience* (Toronto, 1975).

31. Lillian Petroff, "Macedonians in Toronto: From Encampment to Settlement," *Urban History Review* 2 (1978), 53-73.

32. Robert Harney, "Toronto's Little Italy, 1885-1945," in Harney and Scarpaci, *Little Italies*, 41-62; Varpu Lindstrom-Best, *The Finnish Immigrant Community of Toronto, 1887-1913* (Toronto, 1979); John Zucchi, *The Italian Immigrants of St. John's Ward, 1875-1915* (Toronto, 1981); Paul Voisey, "Two Chinese Communities in Alberta: A Historical Perspective," *Canadian Ethnic Studies* 2 (December, 1970), 14-57. See as well the excellent collection of essays edited by Robert Harney, *Gathering Place: Peoples and Neighbourhoods of Toronto* (Toronto, 1985).

33. John Zucchi deals with this problem in his thought-provoking article "Italian Hometown Settlements and the Development of a Italian Community in Toronto, 1875-1935," in Harney, *Gathering Place*, 121-46.

34. Bruno Ramirez and Michael Del Balso, *The Italians of Montreal: From Sojourning to Settlement* (Montreal, 1980). An expanded version of this piece has appeared as Ramirez, *Les premiers italiens de Montréal* already cited above.

35. Franc Sturino, "Italian Immigration to Canada and the Farm Labour System through the 1920's," *Studi emigrazione\Études migrations* 22:77 (marzo 1985), 81-97.

36. Stephen Speisman, *The Jews of Toronto: A History to 1937* (Toronto, 1979), 249-50.

37. Bruno Ramirez, "Montreal's Italians and the Socio-Economy of Settlement, 1900-1930: Some Historical Hypotheses," *Urban History Review* 10:1 (June 1981), 39-48; Terry Copp, *Anatomy of Poverty* (Toronto, 1974).

38. Robert Harney, "Ambiente and Social Class in North American Little Italies," *Canadian Review of Studies in Nationalism* 2:2 (Spring 1975), 208-24. For a view of post-Second World War mobility, see Franc Sturino, "A Case Study of a South Italian Family in Toronto, 1935-1960," *Urban History Review* 2 (1978), 38-57. Sturino defines mobility too eagerly in residential and generational terms without taking into account the overall expansion of the Canadian economy in this period. Moving from "dirty work" to self-employment may not reflect upward mobility but only structural changes in the Canadian economy. He has since refined his views in "The Social Mobility of Italian Canadians: 'Outside' and 'Inside' Concepts of Mobility," in F. Sturino and J. Zucchi eds., *Italians in Ontario*, special issue of *Polyphony* 7:2 (Fall-Winter 1985), 123-27.

39.   See in this regard the excellent special issue of *Polyphony* dedicated to Finns cited above. It illustrates how regional studies perhaps can better represent the life of an immigrant community than can a pan-Canadian approach.

40.   Taru Sundsten, "The Theatre of the Finnish Canadian Labour Movement and Its Dramatic Literature, 1900-1939," in *Finnish Diaspora*, ed. Michael Karni (Toronto, 1981), 77-91.

41.   "The churches were still the Old World institution to which immigrant workers were most likely to turn in the first instance in an alien environment," *Dangerous Foreigners*, 46. As for Zucchi's reference in *Italian Immigrants* (15-16) to Sidney Sonnino's depiction of the parish priest as the peasant's friend in the exploitative world of rural Italy, one could cite eloquent passages in the novels of Carlo Levi and Ignazio Silone where the priest forms part of the local notability and oppresses the peasant.

42.   Varpu Lindstrom-Best, *Defiant Sisters: A Social History of Finnish Immigrant Women in Canada* (Toronto, 1988), Ch. 6; L. Petroff, "Macedonians: From Village to City," *Canadian Ethnic Studies* 9:1 (1977), 29-41; F. Grunier, "Hebrew-Christian Mission in Toronto," *ibid.*, 18-28. Chapter 2 of Paul Yuzyk, *The Ukrainian Greek Orthodox Church of Canada* (Ottawa, 1981) is useful, although the study on the whole is turgidly institutional, triumphalistic, and narrowly ethno-centred, pitting his protagonists against "foreigners" like Archbishop Langevin of St-Boniface. For the response of the Catholic Church to Protestant proselytizing among immigrant groups, see Roberto Perin, "Religion, Ethnicity, and Identity: Placing the Immigrant Within the Church" *Religion/Culture: Comparative Canadian Studies*, special issue of *Canadian Issues/Thèmes canadiens* 7 (1985), 212-29.

43.   Harney and Troper, *Immigrants: Portrait*, 147.

44.   Ramirez and Del Balso, *Italians of Montreal*, 28-33.

45.   Eleoussa Polyzoi, "The Greek Communal School and Cultural Survival in Pre-War Toronto," *Urban History Review* 2 (1978), 74-94.

46.   Ramirez and Del Balso, *Italians of Montreal*, 34-35.

47.   Speisman, *The Jews of Toronto*.

48.   Harold Troper, *Only Farmers Need Apply* (Toronto, 1972), looks at the efforts of the Immigration Department in attracting American farmers during the Laurier era. Robert Painchaud, *Un rêve français dans le peuplement de la Prairie* (Saint-Boniface, 1987), gives some attention to the recruitment of Francophones in Europe and the role played by the Catholic Church in this regard. Bernard Pénisson, *Henri D'-Hellencourt: un journaliste français au Manitoba, 1898-1905* (Saint-Boniface, 1986), gives us some tantalizing glimpses of life among Francophone immigrants in Manitoba and the battle between the Liberal party and the Catholic Church to win their hearts and minds. The role of political patronage is alluded to, but not pursued in any great depth. Howard Palmer, *Land of Second Chance* (Lethbridge, 1972), is a popular, but now dated account of immigrant groups in southern Alberta. See also Howard and Tamara Palmer, "The Hungarian Experience in Alberta," *Hungarian Studies Review* 7:2 (Fall 1981), 149-203.

49.   John Lehr, "The Government and the Immigrant: Perspectives on Ukrainian Settlement in the Canadian West," *Canadian Ethnic Studies* 9:2 (1977), 42-52; in the same issue, Donald Gale and Paul Korocsil, "Doukhobor Settlements: Experiments in Idealism," 53-71; Richard Friesen, "Saskatchewan Mennonite Settlements: The Modification of Old World Settlement Patterns," 72-90. See as well Hildegard Martgens, "Accommodation and Withdrawal: The Response of Mennonites in Canada to World War II," *Histoire sociale/Social History* 8:14 (November 1974), 306-27.

50. Helen Potrebenko, *No Streets of Gold: A Social History of Ukrainians in Alberta* (Vancouver, 1977); Kostash, *All of Baba's Children.*

51. Primary documents as well as some excellent photographs on this period have been collected in Harry Piniuta, ed., *Land of Pain, Land of Promise: First Person Accounts of Ukrainian Pioneers, 1891-1914* (Saskatoon, 1978). Piniuta's Ukrainians, however, are uniformly unsullied by radicalism.

52. Kovacs, *Struggle and Hope*, 80-82. See also Nadia Kazymyra's mediocre article, "Aspects of Ukrainian Opinion in Manitoba during World War I," in *Ethnic Canadians*, ed. Kovacs, 117-34.

53. Peter Li, *The Chinese in Canada* (Toronto, 1988).

54. Ruth Frager, "Sewing Solidarity: The Eaton's Strike of 1912," *Canadian Woman Studies* 7:3 (Fall 1986), 96-98.

55. Franca Iacovetta, "From *Contadina* to Worker: Southern Italian Immigrant Working Women in Toronto, 1947-62," 195-222; Varpu Lindstrom-Best "'I Won't Be a Slave': Finnish Domestics in Canada, 1911-30," 33-53, in *Looking into my Sister's Eyes: An Exploration in Women's History*, ed. J. Burnet (Toronto, 1986); on Finnish working women, also see Joan Sangster, "Finnish Women in Ontario, 1890-1930," *Polyphony* 3:2 (Fall 1981), 46-54.

56. Burnet, *Looking into* contains a series of essays (some much better than others) which shows the active role of women in the decision to emigrate, in the settlement process, and in assuring cultural continuity within the community.

57. Varpu Lindstrom-Best, *Defiant Sisters: A Social History of Finnish Immigrant Women in Canada* (Toronto, 1988).

58. Bruno Ramirez, "Brief Encounters: Italian Immigrant Workers and the CPR, 1900-1930," *Labour/Le Travail* 17 (Spring 1986), 9-27. Ramirez was fortunate to have had access to CPR company records for this research. A similar use of company records was made by Gabriele Scardellato, "Italian Immigrant Workers in Powell River, B.C.: A Case Study of Settlement Before World War II," *Labour/Le Travail* 16 (Fall 1985), 145-163.

59. Gabriel Kolko, *Main Currents in Modern American History* (New York, 1976), 95.

60. Avery, *Dangerous Foreigners*. For Ukrainian involvement in labour disputes see Potrebenko, *No Streets of Gold*, 43-45, 149-57. For immigrant participation in the Rouyn-Noranda strike, see Evelyn Dumas, *The Bitter Thirties in Quebec* (Montreal, 1975), Ch. 2; and A. Rasporich, "South Slavs on a Northern Margin," in Kovacs, *Ethnic Canadians*. For the Finnish presence in strikes see the articles by Radforth and Seager cited above. Strikes in the needle trade are briefly described in Speisman, *Jews of Toronto*, 192-95. For violent labour confrontations in which immigrants were

involved, see Jean Morrison, "Ethnicity and Violence: The Lakehead Freight Handlers before World War I," in *Essays in Canadian Working Class History*, eds. G. Kealy and P. Warrian (Toronto, 1976), 143-60; Antonio Pucci, "Canadian Industrialization Versus the Italian Contadini in a Decade of Brutality, 1902-1912," in Harney and Scarpaci, *Little Italies*, 182-207.

61.   Allen Seager, "Class, Ethnicity, and Politics in the Alberta Coalfields, 1905-1945," in *"Struggle a Hard Battle" : Essays on Working Class Immigrants*, ed. Dirk Hoerder (DeKalb, IL, 1986) 320.

62.   For Ukrainian involvement in these radical movements, see Kostash *All of Baba's Children*, Ch. 12; Potrebenko, *No Streets of Gold*, Ch. 6; Jaroslav Petryshyn, *Peasants in the Promised Land: Canada and the Ukrainian, 1891-1914* (Toronto, 1985), Ch. 11.

63.   Avery, *Dangerous Foreigners*, 59-62; Edward Laine, "Finnish Canadian Radicalism and Canadian Politics: The First Forty Years, 1900-1940" in Dahlie and Fernando, *Ethnicity, Power*, 94-112. In the same volume, see Varpu Lindstrom-Best, "The Socialist Party of Canada and the Finnish Connection, 1905-1911," 113-11; Norman Buchignani and Doreen Indra, "The Political Organization of South Asians in Canada, 1904-1910," 202-32.

64.   The authors appear quite hostile to Indian nationalism and often put a favourable interpretation on the Indian policies of British officials in India and Great Britain. Their article depends quite heavily on the reports of a British spy. For a different interpretation, see Hugh Johnston, *The Voyage of the Komagata Maru: The Sikh Challenge to Canada's Colour Bar* (Calcutta, 1979).

65.   Mauri Jalava, "The Finnish Canadian Cooperative Movement in Ontario," in Karni, *Finnish Diaspora*, 93-100; Kostash, *All of Baba's Children*, 160-62.

66.   Jorgen Dahlie, "Socialist and Farmer: Ole Hjelt and the Norwegian Radical Voice in Canada, 1908-1918," *Canadian Ethnic Studies* 10:2 (1978), 55-64; in the same issue, D. Wilson, "Matti Kurikka and A.B. Makela: Socialist Thought among the Finns in Canada, 1900-1932," 9-21; Nadia Kazymyra, "The Defiant Pavlo Krat and the Early Socialist Movement in Canada," 38-54; Anthony Rasporich, "Tomo Cacic: Rebel without a Country," 86-94; Jorgen Dahlie, "From Ringsaker to Instow: A Norwiegan Radical's Saskatchewan Odyssey" in Kovacs, *Ethnic Canadians*, 97-107; Donald Wilson, "Finns in British Columbia before the First World War," *Polyphony* 3 (Fall 1981), 55-64; and by the same author "'Never Believe What You Have Never Doubted': Matti Kurikka's Dream for a New World Utopia," in Karni, *Finnish Diaspora*, 131-53.

67.   Kostash, *All of Baba's Children*, 41.

68.   Avery, *Dangerous Foreigners*, Ch. 5. E. Laine: "Finnish Canadian Radicalism," in Dahlie and Fernando, *Ethnicity, Power*, 94-112; "The Finnish Organization of Canada, 1923-1940 and the Development of a Finnish Canadian Culture," *Polyphony* 3 (Fall 1981), 81-90; John Kolasky, *The Shattered Illusion: The History of Ukrainian Pro-Communist Organizations in Canada* (Toronto, 1979).

69.   Donald Avery, "Ethnic Loyalties and the Proletarian Revolution: A Case Study of Communist Political Activity in Winnipeg, 1923-36," in Dahlie and Fernando,

Ethnicity, Power, 68-93; Leonard Sillanpaa, "Voting Behaviour of Finns in the Sudbury Area, 1930-1972" in Karni, *Finnish Diaspora*, 101-16; and in the same book, Reino Kero, "The Canadian Finns in Soviet Karelia in the 1930s;" Jules Paivio, "Finnish Canadians during the Spanish Civil War, 1936-1939," *Polyphony* 3 (Fall 1981), 77-80.

70. Kolasky, *Shattered Illusion*, 22.

71. Varpu Lindstrom-Best, "Central Organization of Loyal Finns in Canada," *Polyphony* 3 (Fall 1981), 97-103; Roberto Perin, "Making Good Fascists and Good Canadians: Consular Propaganda and the Italian Community in Montreal in the 1930s," in *Minorities and Mother County Imagery*, ed. Gerald Gold (St. John's, 1984), 136-158; Carmela Patrias, *The Kanadai Magyar Ujsag and the Politics of the Hungarian Elite, 1928-1938* (Toronto, 1978); Benedykt Heydenkorn, *The First Polish Umbrella Organization: The Federation of Polish Societies in Canada* (Toronto, 1978); Jonathan Wagner, "The Deutscher Bund of Canada, 1934-1939," *Canadian Historical Review* 58 (June 1977), 176-200.

72. Lita-Rose Betcherman, *The Swastika and the Maple Leaf: Fascist Movements in the Thirties* (Don Mills, 1975).

73. See for example, Angelo Principe, "The Italo-Canadian Press of Toronto, 1922-1940," Italian Section/Northeast Modern Languages Association Conference, *Proceedings* 4 (1980), 119-37.

74. Robert Harney has captured the essence of this spirit in "Toronto's Little Italy," in *Little Italies*. See as well, Perin, "Making Good Fascists."

75. This issue is addressed pointedly in Irving Abella and Harold Troper, "The Politics of Futility: Canadian Jewry and the Refugee Crisis, 1933-1939," in Dahlie and Fernando, *Ethnicity, Power*, 233-53. See also Abella and Troper *None is Too Many* (Toronto, 1982); Ann Gomer Sunahara, "Historical Leadership Trends among Japanese Canadians, 1940-1950," *Canadian Ethnic Studies* 11:1 (1979), 1-16. See also Sunahara, *The Politics of Racism: The Uprooting of Japanese Canadians during the Second World War* (Toronto, 1981), especially Part IV.

76. "Frozen Wastes," in *Perspectives in Italian Immigration*, 115-31.

10

Writing About War

Donald M. Schurman

Canadian soldiers, sailors and airmen, led by competent officers, have engaged in the two world wars, Korea, and various peace-keeping activities; and they have done so in a manner that has elicited favourable international comment on their worth. Although the Canadian military has not produced spectacular effects on a world level (no native Frederick the Great or Napolean blazes across our military horizon), it has, at times, played very significant roles indeed, on both the Canadian and the world stage. And yet, in spite of the undoubted competence of Canadian military personnel (as evidenced by their performance in two large twentieth-century conflicts), their concerns have often been ignored by politicians and policy makers.[1] Further, the record of Canadian military achievement seems to have attracted little interest, aside from that of a small group of specialists in the field. Military history, for instance, rarely figures very largely in the typical introductory survey course in Canadian history. This state of affairs is due, in part, to Canadians' general lack of enthusiasm for military matters, but it also reflects the approach and focus of Canada's military historians.

All writers depict their chosen subject within some framework, conscious or unconscious, and military historians are no exception. Historians are influenced by both external circumstances and personal outlook or bias as they try to order and to interpret the raw material of the past. It is impossible for them to merely recount facts and events (and even if such bald chronicling could be achieved it would be repellant to the reader). Hence, those who would examine the work of Canadian military historians must ask themselves certain questions. What constraints and freedoms (both internal and external) have affected the work of these historians? What features of being a Canadian have influenced the military in general and the military historian in particular? Related to these two questions are two further interconnected complexities for the military historiographer. First, since the patterns of military tradition were formed long ago (before 1867 and even before 1763), and since these traditions helped form the thinking of later military historians, one must investigate those traditions if one would understand modern military commentators writing since 1930. Second, although writing about Canada's military past may have begun and developed quite recently, the material being examined and analyzed needs to be understood in the context of its own time, whether that time is the age of George III or even Louis XIV.

I

The history of Canada's military activity (like its political, economic, and social history), has evolved under the heavy shadow of its European antecedents and latterly of its pro-American gravitation. Most actions that the Canadian military has engaged in have been undertaken as part of either a colonial or an alliance obligation. Before the conquest (the defeat of New France in 1759), the struggle appeared to be clear-cut: France against England. Colonials on both sides could, even in retrospect, identify fairly readily with at least local aspects of the aims of the Mother Countries (except when France surrendered Quebec in 1760 and this sense of solidarity was questioned). But as early as the War of 1812, British needs and colonial needs had different emphases. During the nineteenth century, these growing colonial concerns could be easily subdued when British North America seemed threatened by an increasingly powerful United States. Later still, during the overseas wars of the twentieth century, the sense of a direct threat was absent; in these circumstances Canadian military concerns became less straightforward and more difficult to define. Defence policy, for example, became progressively less directed toward the defence of geographical frontiers. As a result of this greater complexity, it is difficult to construct an interpretation by simply applying to Canadian actions the usual rules of military strategy developed by Jomini and Mahan.[2] Population, geography, and history demand Canada's participation in alliance politics (once with Britain, now with the United States), but leave the scale and nature of the participation uncertain and therefore difficult to analyze within a purely military framework. The debate over nuclear submarines in 1988 offers a recent case in point.

This basic situation has meant that those who write about the Canadian military have found their themes restricted. It may, for instance, be more congenial to write about the brave Canadians, either as units or individuals, than to delineate the genesis and positioning of a Canadian force as a part of a colonial or alliance grouping.[3] It is even more congenial to write about the basic stuff of war; since heroism remains part of our pantheon of virtues, Canadians may usefully be given their due. Hence, a blow-by-blow account of a desperate action has a sort of self-justification. But writing a military history which attempts to examine and explain the size or nature of a force in a theatre or theatres of action is not such a straightforward matter. Why, for instance, did Canada raise a large volunteer army in World War One and send hundreds of thousands of men overseas? Why did she do this instead of creating and using a naval force, or alternatively contributing directly to the naval defence of the Empire? Such questions have seldom been raised by military historians. Leaving aside the individual motives of the volunteers themselves, there are larger political, social, and military answers to these questions. But the choices actually made (by politicians, policymakers, and their military advisors) in the case of the Great War, and in most other cases, reflected the fact of Canada's client status in military affairs.

The point needs to be made because the general theme of a formative generation of Canadian political historians has been that Canada has progressed, as Arthur Lower put it, from colony to nation. The Canadian military writer has no such apparent progress to record. Junior partners, or even acolytes, cannot generally afford the luxury of large military expenditures in peacetime, nor is their role in wartime fixed and clear. In these circumstances the philosophically-inclined military chronicler, or even the addict of smooth narrative history, finds it difficult to write with such absolute conviction. This is not to say that military affairs have not had a tremendous effect on Canada's national development — 1759 (the capture of New France) is the obvious example and Vimy seems another. But to determine the connection between, on the one hand, valour, victories, and defeats and, on the other hand, state purposes, with any sense of proportion and degree of consistency, is very difficult.

In World War One Canada's contribution in manpower was disproportionate to its size. One need only make the familiar comparison with American casualties on the Western Front. The nation of over one hundred million, which supposedly "won the war," suffered about the same number of casualties (fifty thousand) as did Canada with a population of merely eight million. Casualties aside, and by any reckoning except perhaps by comparison with other British settlement colonies (Australia or Newfoundland, for instance), Canadian participation in that war represented an extraordinary effort.[4] Such sacrifices turned Anglo-Canadians against war at the same time, paradoxically, that they gradually came to appreciate the accomplishments of their military practitioners. Their perception of the significance of those accomplishments reflected to a great extent the approach taken in retrospect by those who attempted to analyze the decisions, the actions, the battles, and the outcomes.

Before 1918, or even 1945, Canada was not a country bristling with historians, and few of those concentrated on the military. Military history made its debut as an international professional discipline in the period after 1880, principally in the United States and Great Britain, and Canadian scholars followed the lead established there. Prior to World War One, military history was a branch of the historical discipline much like any other. But after 1914-18, it was tainted with the barbarity of the Great War and, to an extent, shunned by the mainstream of Anglo-American historians. Academics also disliked the preoccupation with battlefield details occasioned by the war, which required a familiarity with technical and tactical matters outside their experience.

Thus the influence of the brooding shadow of World War One was profound and pervasive, with significant consequences for military history. Because of the horrors of this war many writers shifted their attention to the causes of the war, and to a general consideration of war, rather than to the details of the fighting. Conversely, most of the remaining material published in Canada on World War One was confined to locale, personal, or regimental history. Military history, strictly speaking, languished. Meanwhile, by 1935 there was a dramatic increase in British published material on World

War One. Official histories began to appear, and this trend continued and simply embraced Hitler's war. Indeed, World War Two served as a great catalyst. A new school of Canadian military historians who had formed their attitudes in the inter-war period emerged not only to describe military events but to emphasize continually the link between policy and war. As its official history of World War One Canada had produced only Duguid's first volume, which dealt mainly with supply.[5] But after World War Two the Directories of History, led by the disciplined, determined, and prolific Charles Stacey, began to prepare and eventually to publish, the history of the Canadian Army in the Second World War.[6] Stacey also included in his goals the publication of a suitable record of World War One. As the official histories progressed, interest was sparked at the universities about military affairs.

Stacey was himself university-trained but he also knew and wrote for soldiers. His influence actually predated the setting up of the Historical Directorate. During World War Two he had been appointed Historical Officer at Canada's military headquarters in London.[7] George Stanley, Gerald Graham, and others were associated with him in the painstaking collecting, arranging, and writing of the history of the Canadian army and navy.[8] The writing of the air and naval histories proceeded more slowly than that of the army although the naval history finally emerged from the Navy's own plan as *The Naval Service of Canada* in 1952.[9] In many ways it was a helpful book, but one which did not in its coverage of World War Two meet the needs of either the general reader or the naval veteran.

The seeds of the war-time work done by Stacey, Graham, and Stanley matured as each acquired disciples who were not confined in scope to the narration of military combat but could extend the general framework of analysis into a broader context. Stacey, Graham, and Stanley shared a common view which underpinned their approach: they interpreted the Canadian military situation in terms of Canada's imperial relationship. Stacey, who held the senior appointment, had had his perception of military affairs shaped by his experience at Princeton (where he taught) and by his research experience at Oxford and London. His *Canada and the British Army* showed how a change in British imperial policy had led Canada to develop her own military responses.[10] Stacey understood how the British official mind worked, and understood as well the limitations and pretensions of the colonial responses to it. Stanley, who also did graduate work at Oxford and was associated with Stacey for a time in London, was a westerner who made a considerable mark in the scholarly world with his unique and perceptive work, *The Birth of Western Canada.*[11] Stanley had some knowledge of the military; he also understood the people, history, and culture of French Canada. His special contribution, after two wars in which French and English Canada were divided against each other, was to elucidate a joint Canadian heritage that dealt reasonably and even-handedly with the soldiers of both founding cultures. Although the research on which he based his later book, *Canada's Soldiers*, was admittedly shared with others, it was Stanley's mind that perceived, and his hand that arranged, the significant events in the story, and expressed it in the distinguished prose style that was his hallmark. He eventually became head of the history department at the Royal Military College of Canada and gave the study of history there a great impetus. Gerald Graham was, for a time, also a member of the London headquarters team during the war. Like Stacey he gained American experience (in his case at Harvard) before the war. Unlike the other two, however, he took his graduate degree from Cambridge. In 1949 he became Rhodes Professor of Imperial History at the University of London (King's College). In his London seminar, Graham trained a great many Commonwealth historians from a wide variety of backgrounds and consequently had a wide influence. Underlying all his work was a keen sense of the importance of the sea and sea-power in imperial and colonial history.

II

Of course Stacey, Stanley, and Graham did not invent military history in Canada, but they gave it decisive shape and direction. Most earlier writing had been concerned with Canadian military activity before 1763. A good deal of history had been done concerning both New France and New England, most of it anchored on personalities. The approach reflected the influence of the American historian Frances Parkman, who shaped the general form of recording the conflict in North America in a way that stood for at least sixty years. Post-war scholars began to re-examine the earlier period along the lines suggested by Stacey and his colleagues, and Parkman is now read "if at all for his prose rather than his history".[12] W.J. Eccles' works on Frontenac and New France, for example, destroyed many of the Parkman myths and changed our appreciation of French Canadian history.[13]

Also, like much other modern scholarship, Stacey, Stanley, and Graham
tended to confirm that crucial events in North America were determined
more by activity in France and England than in the New World. Despite the
fact that fierce land conflicts raged between New France and New England,
these did not finally decide matters in North America. Before the final war
that brought about the conquest of Canada, the defeat of Louisbourg in the
campaign of 1745 was a harbinger of the future. A great fortification fell to
an amateur, colonial army, and a naval force sufficient to isolate it. The
details have been imaginatively described by George Rawlyk.[14] Guy
Frégault's interpretation of what caused the fall of Louisbourg illustrated
the changing perspective on such events; referring to the campaign of 1758,
he saw the loss of Louisbourg as caused not by British prowess but by a
French failure in nerve, interest, and response.[15] Frégault made the point
that the fort had held on long enough to save Quebec, but what would happen
in 1759?[16]

Although the role of sea-power in shaping the military affairs of North
America in the past received more attention, the subject was developed with
considerable sophistication by the generation of post-war scholars. The
campaigns of the Seven Years War had been given their first sea-oriented
treatment by Julian Corbett in 1907.[17] William Wood developed this theme
in his *Logs of the Ships* in 1909; he was the first Canadian to put these
arguments forcefully. No doubt he was encouraged by Corbett, whom he
had met in 1908.[18] Gerald Graham was the direct heir of Corbett and Wood.
His work covering the conquest showed the long-term effects of sea-power
and its application. Following the capture of Jamaica in 1665 there were
nearly always ships of the Royal Navy stationed in North America. Graham
examined the connection between state policy and sea-power over long
periods of time; this focus gave Graham's work its distinctive perspective.[19]
The siege and capture of Quebec as a significant episode in the Seven Years
War was carefully reconstructed by Charles Stacey.[20]

Meanwhile, Graham showed seapower's wider significance in his
Empire of the North Atlantic.[21] He demonstrated that the pressure that
provided decisive margins of force at various places — Louisbourg in 1758,
Quebec and Montreal in 1760 — was supplied by fleet dispositions in
Europe, which allowed the British to dispose their forces so as to effect their
designs overseas and prevent decisive enemy reinforcements from disrupt-
ing operations as they developed. By reading Graham one could see that
these results were not certain simply because they were planned.

Consummation had to be striven for in the light of shifting priorities and the availability of means. He described one such consummation when the exhausted and semi-defeated British were holding out in 1760 against Lévis' besieging forces. When the frigate *Lowestoft* arrived in the basin and showed her colours, it signalled the end of the Empire for the French in the St. Lawrence. Of course *Lowestoft* was only a harbinger; a few weeks later more vessels joined her as Frégault and Stanley have pointed out.[22]

The effect of this juxtaposition of forces was decisive. Canada had really always been hanging from a halyard. This fact was demonstrated again, at least in the short run, during the American Revolution. Perhaps few knowledgeable people really believed that, while fighting a coalition in Europe, Britain had the resources to subdue a quarter of a continent three thousand miles away. It proved too much for her. With sea-power choked at its source in Europe, Admiral de Grasse's victory off the Chesapeake sealed the fate of Lord Cornwallis' army. The result was a critical turning point in the fortunes of the First British Empire.

The balance of naval power also played a decisive role in the War of 1812. The land operations of this war have been described by many, including Stanley, Pierre Berton, and J.M. Hitsman.[23] But it was A.T. Mahan who had earlier suggested the key to the war.[24] Nobody expected, Mahan said, that the British could or would reconquer America. The question was, could they protect effectively what they had? As on previous occasions when they were heavily extended in Europe, the task was daunting. But when Napoleon was defeated in Spain the fleet supporting British operations there could be moved westward to deal with Napoleon's friends. The Royal Navy swiftly gained the initiative along the American seaboard, burned Washington, and thereby supplied the pressure necessary for the peace treaty.

The strategic thinking which resulted from the war has been perceptively outlined by Bourne and Hitsman.[25] Both emphasize the key role played by sea-power in shaping the "Pax Britannica" during the early nineteenth century, especially as it applied to Canada. With the War of 1812 in mind, Britain felt able to protect Canada. The Americans would be blamed should war break out. This was to be followed by a short period of sharp attack, followed by a judicious withdrawal to strong points like Quebec, Kingston, and Halifax. There the forces would hold out until the fleet was able to cross the ocean and apply the kind of pressure that would induce the Americans to make peace.[26] Fort Henry was built at Kingston, and British garrisons were supplied to Canadian forts. This was the British plan under which Canadian independence was guaranteed; it remained in place at least until World War One. Clearly a great war in Europe would place the plan at risk, but the withdrawal of the garrisons after Confederation in no way altered the promise of general fleet support. The Canadians would handle local defence on their own, although certainly they were not to be denied land support in an emergency. In any event, the American threat gradually receded.

It was in this supporting role that Colonel Garnet Wolseley was sent out to lead a combined expedition of colonial militia and imperial troops to put down the Riel Rebellion in 1870. In 1885, Riel returned. This time a British general, General Middleton, led colonial volunteers. According to Desmond Morton, Middleton's professionalism helped redeem his troops.[27] The Canadian participants drew other conclusions: that Canadians were equal to British regulars and needed no instruction from Englishmen. Those were dangerous deductions. A detailed description of Canada's uneasy relationship with imperial military authorities has been written by Richard Preston of R.M.C. and, latterly, Duke University.[28]

The South African War, to which Canada contributed roughly eight thousand men and financing for a third of them, maintained this trend toward the identification of self-confident colonial independence with soldiering. This war, of course, again brought into focus the deep divisions that service in British wars could create between French and English in Canada. English Canadians seemed to find it increasingly congenial to measure their sense of national worth by comparing Canada's *military* performance with British military officers, individuals, and units. Morton mentions the sense of patriotism which the war seemed to enhance. However, Canadians' colonial situation demanded that when they gauged themselves against the British, *the measuring took place in wars where the British made the rules as well as the ultimate strategic and political decisions.* It was the conquest scenario all over again and not easily escaped. Unfortunately for military historians who might wish to emulate the colony-to-nation school of political historians, it is by no means certain that the Canadian military *wished* to escape from a dependent status — partly because the militia created a convenient expression of social status in the country generally.

The army's preoccupation with its British connections, reinforced by the support of a militia spread across the country in a politically governed network, was superficially challenged by naval problems in the years before

World War One. The armament burden imposed by increasing German naval expansion prompted the British to seek colonial help in creating a more powerful navy. They wanted either money or ships and they wanted ultimate control to rest with the Admiralty in London. After some discussions and political manoeuvring, the Canadian government finally decided to form a Canadian navy.[29] However, it obscured its purpose by attempting to secure political authority to provide support for the Royal Navy. In the end, Canada formed a minuscule navy and refused support for the Royal Navy. The whole matter caused acute political division in Canada, but the debate was only marginally concerned with the seriousness of the military danger in Europe and with the approach of war.[30] The attitude seemed to justify Admiral Fisher's dictum that Canadians were "an unpatriotic grasping people who only stick to us for the good they can get out of us."[31] He was wrong. The Canadian response in 1914 surprised everybody, but Canada's naval policy was consistent with the growing sense of self-confidence in its soldiering ability and it paved the way for Canada's massive effort in France and Flanders in 1914-1918. So many Canadians volunteered for army service in the war that the Royal Navy was hard put to provide escorts to see them safely from the Gulf of St. Lawrence to England.[32]

Nevertheless, the successes, such as Vimy Ridge, and the losses, especially at Passchendale, only seemed to confirm the tendency of Canadians to measure themselves against other countries according to the value and expertise of their troops.[33] This tendency was, if anything, reinforced when a Canadian Corps finally began to fight as a unit under Canadian leadership, from June, 1917 onward. For an understanding of a war that cost Canadians nearly fifty-five thousand dead, Nicholson's very accomplished official history should be consulted.[34] The little-known but significant role played by Canadian airmen in World War One has been described by Sidney Wise, Stacey's successor at the Directorate of History, in the first volume of what is to be the complete History of the Royal Canadian Air Force.[35]

To some extent, the army's achievement had begun to generate a professional pride that translated itself into a generalized awareness of national status; Morton's powerful book laid bare most of the political processes that operated behind the work of Canadians at the Front.[36] In a sense, Sir Sam Hughes, the Minister of Militia, represented those who were determined not to get caught in the British trap,[37] just as Mackenzie King was to represent that viewpoint much more suavely in civilian terms during the ensuing decades. Yet there seemed to be virtually no escape from the colonial situation and its subordinate, "gentlemen's" mentality.

Significantly, popular war-protest literature of any quality was practically absent from the Canadian scene. Writers like Siegfried Sassoon and Robert Graves did not appear in Canada; neither, after the war, did writers of the pungency of Eric Maria Remarque or Vera Brittain surface.[38] Instead Canada produced John McRae, who died at the Front and left "In Flanders Fields," a poignant poem, inspirational and dedicated to the cause.[39] It is indeed almost impossible to imagine Canadian writers protesting in print, either against World War One or its successor. Support for the military goals of the war was a hallmark of the colonial English Canadian. That the French Canadians rejected the war reflected tradition, inept recruiting, and the lack of a national consensus on war aims. Extremely heavy casualties overseas led to the conscription crisis that split the country and embittered its politics for at least sixty years — a tragedy that matched the war's casualties in ultimate national significance. Canadians could not be united behind a military solution, because people viewed the manpower problem differently.[40] The negative French Canadian response that so angered anglophones was no doubt defensible on the grounds of *Canadien* history. It certainly provided an alternative idea for politically-hawkish anglophones to consider. But whatever anglophones and francophones may have thought, they were both victims of Canada's colonial status whereby the parent state virtually set the terms for Canadian military activity and largely defined the method and arena of that activity.

In World War Two, Canada again sent large numbers of men abroad. They served, this time, in more varied ways and on different fronts. Economic development, surpassing that of World War One, was accompanied by the growth of the Royal Canadian Navy and the tremendous expansion of the Royal Canadian Air Force.[41] This expansion drew upon civilian air development and the existence of people with air experience from World War One (during that war Canadians made up about one-quarter of the Royal Flying Corps), as Wise has shown in detail.[42] The writing of the official military history of Canada's participation in World War Two is still in process. The history of the Army Campaigns has been completed; the history of the Royal Air Force is well-advanced; and plans and work are going forward for the production of a history of the Royal Navy under the present Director, W.A.B. Douglas.

In all of these services, Canadians played significant roles. The army was given priority on Stacey's production timetable, but this arrangement reflected the facts well enough. After the war, the naval history was prepared by Tucker, as noted above.[43] However, this did not turn out to be a satisfactory treatment of the World War Two period, despite the usefulness of its background material. A history of the R.C.A.F. in World War Two was produced almost immediately, which filled a need for a time but dealt gingerly with the bombing campaign.[44] It was years before the British began to deal with the concept of strategic bombing, and their hesitancy affected Canadian historians. Some in the United Kingdom might raise doubts about the policy of mass bombing, but Canadians who had been badly bruised in this campaign were, and remain, uneasy with the notion that the basic policy might be questioned. Not until 1961, when the British official history dealt with the subject, were Canadians able to re-examine the whole subject.[45] Once again Canadians had been forced to conform to objectives in wartime that they had not chosen. There is no evidence of any heavy regrets about these policy decisions amongst Canada's politicians; her airmen during the war had not time for anything but to play out their assigned role. The airmen simply strove for competence within their theatre, as did the sailors in their theatre. Within that assigned responsibility they saw their importance to Canada and the war. By 1944, R.C.N. ships made up a third of the convoy escort routes where their abilities were sorely tested.[46] A problem for the historian has been to establish the significance of the Canadian contribution. The bombing of Germany, for example, cost the Canadian Air Force some nine thousand killed, yet the relevance of the bombing campaign to winning the war is still in doubt.[47] The fact is that Canadians, including many of those writing military history, felt comfortable with the status their support role forced them to adopt in all three services. The problem of Canadianization and autonomy, that seemed such a vital matter from other historical perspectives, almost vanished when both the military and their civilian sponsors were happy in their restricted roles.

Nevertheless, those roles linked military operations to broader questions of national politics and policymaking. Behind the growth of Canada's military activity lay the question of support and sustenance. As in World War One, manpower demands loomed large by 1944. Army pressure for increased replacements placed heavy stress upon the Minister of National Defence.[48] Stacey and J.L. Granatstein have covered this "conscription crisis" in a measured way.[49] Anglo-Canadians accepted with equanimity the notion that Canada could make strong war contributions in *three* service arms, whereas one had dominated in World War One. Meeting those demands was a strain. For a long period air and naval casualties exceeded those of the army; meanwhile the pressures of alliance politics aimed for maximum output. When working under such pressure, anglophones found it easy or at least expedient to blame any failures on the manpower response of French Canada. Yet the High Command of the Navy was, even during the war, busy planning for expansion in the post-war period.[50] Air Force personnel were prepared to carry out, almost without question, whatever Air Marshall Arthur Harris might decree, meanwhile losing personnel on a staggering scale. With all these drives toward expansion, it is hardly surprising that a manpower crisis developed. Canada was in a total war situation, perhaps created by events over which the politicians and military did not have control, but one which they found congenial. Few would suggest that the enemies did not earn the enmity they generated, the reaction they provoked, or the attacks they sustained. However, a policy based on almost blind expansion could hardly be described as a sensible guide to future policy in a country whose strength was limited and whose population was divided over foreign policy.

The basic situation changed little after World War Two. Through the vehicle of the Korean War, Canada found a new "big-brother." The North American Treaty Organization was an almost perfect vehicle to facilitate the transition from domination by Britain to domination by America. The new arrangement seemed to mean that wartime industrial growth could be retranslated into "peacetime" prosperity and dynamic economic adjustment. However, predictably, Canada attempted to expand on *all* military fronts as the new American relationship developed. The transition was also masked by the temporary eclipse of Germany's economy, so that Canada was able to contemplate substantial economic expansion as the concomitant of military development. A great influx of British aircraft designers, scientists, and electrical wizards encouraged the prospect of significant industrial development. The demise of the Avro Arrow, however, brought this dream to an end. At almost the same time the Germans resumed their natural industrial role, and the Americans, changing their technical policies, insisted upon unloading some of their old equipment (including the Bomarc missile) on Canadians among others. Who would buy the Arrow if it went on the production line in this new economic environment? The shift back to loyal subordinate in this changed relationship proved to be as painful in the new situation as it had been in the old. It was perhaps representative of Canada's military history that when Defence Minister Harkness resigned over the Bomarc policy he should stress Canada's obligation and loyalty to the alliance (by which he meant the American military and their politicians). Lester Pearson seems to have realized the deep need that Canada had to move under the mantle of a protective state. By 1965 the uneasy alliance situation was politically masked when the policy of unification of the now starved services went ahead.

Somewhat ironically, during the period that an expansive military posture gave way to retrenchment, the popular interest in war revived. Renewed by the conviction that World War Two was a "just" war, it was fed by an enormous international outpouring of military writing of indifferent quality and dubious intent. Encouraged by the burgeoning war games mania and the complementary activities of the film industry, the resulting books have increased the general public's interest in military affairs on the one hand, and added significantly to the pile of published junk on the other. In Canada the military themselves have produced a number of commentators, some rigorously trained in the use of evidence and some not. They are supported by a few dedicated ex-servicemen and enthusiastic amateurs. However, while overall interest in military matters has grown, the proportion of serious writers concerned with military history remains small; the number of professional military historians even smaller. Canadians may read war stories and reminiscences, but Canadian interest in policy or defence-related subjects is not great in peacetime except when things military become a political football. It is no coincidence that the best-known Canadian commentator of international stature, Gwynne Dwyer, lives and works in England.

Nevertheless, as political support for Canada's armed services diminished, a growing number of analysts, often academics, began writing on defence policy. They did not greatly alter the attitudes of the government toward financial support for the services, but surprisingly this new generation of writers began to question long-standing assumptions. This questioning has been partly a response to the growing apprehension with regard to nuclear weapons, an apprehension that has sparked debate and protest. It also resulted partly from the fact that the members of one political party have advocated the withdrawal of Canada from NATO in contrast to what the Americans seem to want.

III

The attitudes that have sprung up have also much to do with the groundwork laid by the military historians. Basic policy questions have been carefully treated, so that there is a corpus of sound information to direct thinkers and scholars. First there was Stacey's history of Canadian foreign policy.[51] Along with that there are James Eayrs' five volumes on defence policy, *In Defence of Canada*.[52] Desmond Morton and Jack Granatstein have immeasurably enriched our understanding of modern key decision-making, especially in the two world wars, and have set the stage for some evaluation of modern policy, following in the Stacey-Stanley-Graham tradition. There is, in short, a growing literature in both political science and historical circles dealing with government military and defence policy.[53]

Laudable as this situation is, it would be idle to pretend that much that is being published is not under the influence of the military establishment, either directly by the Department of National Defence or indirectly (in one of their funded supporting groups, now called "strategic studies"). The close relations between the huge institutes and centres in the United States and the Pentagon is mirrored in a smaller way in Canada. The potential danger to sound scholarship is obvious, if Canada chooses to use its available funds in strategic studies to promote government or pro-American policies. There are plenty of volunteers. A second problem lies in the focus and direction of strategic studies. The slow emergence of dependable material concerning the navy, for example, has meant that the idea of a naval-oriented defence policy causes much uneasiness. Indeed, an attempt to produce a naval policy after so many years produced a sharp reaction: for a moment the military and the politicians seemed to be subscribing to a policy the new "big-brother" did not want. Still, a few submarines in the North Atlantic could be useful to the alliance, and so the debate returned to normal. Canada wants to fulfill its alliance obligations. Such attitudes certainly satisfy traditions; they are in many ways almost involuntary "historical" reactions. The nature of those reactions is conditioned, in substantial measure, by the approaches and assumptions of those who have written, and continue to write, Canada's military history.

Endnotes

1.   Names and numbers of units were changed as the century advanced; the unification of the three services begun in 1965 was regarded by many in the military as a direct attack on their traditions.

2.   Alfred Thayer Mahan, *Influence of Seapower on History* (Boston 1890); Henri Jomini, *Summary of the Art of War*, ed. J.D. Hittle (Harrisburg, PA, 1917).

3.   For a representative biography of an outstanding individual, see R.H. Roy, *For Most Conspicuous Gallantry: A Biography of Major General George A. Pearkes, V.C., Through Two World Wars* (Vancouver, 1977). However, even Canada's Great War ace, William Avery Bishop, V.C., did not have a proper biography until after World War Two: viz., William Arthur Bishop, *The Courage of Early Morning: A Son's Biography of a Famous Father: The Story of Billy Bishop* (Toronto, 1965).

4.   Even though it was not a part of Canada, Newfoundland suffered singularly heavy losses. See G.W.L. Nicholson, *The Fighting Newfoundlanders: A History of the Royal Newfoundland Regiment* (St. John's, 1964).

5.   Arthur F. Duguid, *Official History of the Canadian Forces in the Great War, 1914-1919*, Vol. 1 (Ottawa, 1938).

6.   Canada, Department of National Defence, General Staff. *Official History of the Canadian Army in the Second World War*, 3 vols. (Ottawa, 1955-60).

7.   The word "military" here connotes army. In the essay generally the word "military" refers to the two or three services unless indicated to the contrary.

8.   Among these others were J.B. Conacher, G.W.L. Nicholson, Eric Harrison, J.M.S. Careless, Donald Kerr, David Spring, and J.W. Spurr. See Carl Berger, *The Writing of Canadian History* (Toronto, 1976), 172: "From the forties onwards, even where Canadian historians did not themselves actually write military history, their work was to show a greater awareness of military and strategic consideration that affected the country's past."

9.   Gilbert N. Tucker, *A History of the Royal Canadian Navy*, 2 vols. (Ottawa, 1952).

10. Charles Stacey, *Canada and the British Army, 1846-1871: A Study in the Practice of Responsible Government* (London, 1936).

11. G.F.G. Stanley, *The Birth of Western Canada: A History of the Riel Rebellions* (London, 1936).

12. Desmond Morton, *A Military History of Canada* (Edmonton, 1985), 268. Morton's book is a useful starting place for students of military history, offering balanced judgments in a readable style; it includes a bibliographical note that is among the best available in published form.

13. W.J. Eccles: *Frontenac: The Courtier Governor* (Toronto, 1959); and *France and America* (Toronto, 1972).

14. J.S. McLellan, *Louisbourg From Its Foundation to Its Fall* (London, 1918); and G.R. Rawlyk, *Yankess at Louisbourg* (Orono, 1967).

15. Guy Frégault, *Canada and the War of Conquest* (Toronto, 1969), 320-26, 334-35. First published in French in 1954, Frégault's was the first history by a francophone to deal with the conquest using the documents of all sides. The most recent and balanced account is George Stanley's *New France: The Last Phase, 1744-1760* (Toronto, 1968).

16. Frégault, *Canada and the War*, 219.

17. Julian S. Corbett, *England in the Seven Year's War* (London, 1907).

18. W.C.H. Wood. *The Logs of the Conquest of Canada* (Toronto, 1909), Preface. For the fact that Wood and Corbett had met at Quebec, see Donald M. Schurman, *Julian S. Corbett* (London, 1982), 106.

19. Gerald Graham also edited *The Walker Expedition Against Quebec* (Toronto, 1953).

20. Charles Stacey, *Quebec, 1759: The Siege and the Battle* (Toronto,1959).

21. Gerald Graham, *Empire of the North Atlantic* (Toronto, 1950).

22. Stanley,*New France*, 249; Frégault,*Canada*, 278: referring to the *Lowestoft*, Frégault noted: "One swallow does not make a summer."

23. G.F.G. Stanley, *The War of 1812: Land Operations* (Toronto, 1983); Pierre Berton, *The Invasion of Canada* and *Flames Across the Border* (Toronto, 1981,1982); J.M. Hitsman, *The Incredible War of 1812* (Toronto, 1965).

24. A.T. Mahan, *Sea Power in its Relations to the War of 1812*, 2 vols. (London, 1905).

25. Kenneth Bourne, *Britain and the Balance of Power in North America, 1815-1902* (London, 1967). Much of the work covered by Bourne was also covered by Hitsman in *Safeguarding Canada, 1763-1871* (Toronto, 1968). Hitsman's survey is a insightful account of Canada's strategic realities.

26. Presumably by blockade and/or depredations against selected targets along the coast.

27. Desmond Morton, *A Military History of Canada* (Edmonton, 1985), 106.

28. Richard A. Preston, *Canada and "Imperial Defence": A Study of the Origins of the British Commonwealth's Defence Organization* (Durham, N.C., 1967).

29. Roger Sarty and Donald M. Schurman, "An Historical Perspective on Canadian Naval Policy," *Argonauta* 4:31 (March, 1987), 6-13.

30. We are inclined to forget that people in that age did not anticipate the savage cataclysm that World War One turned out to be — such sustained savagery was unthinkable.

31. Donald M. Schurman, *Julian S. Corbett, 1854-1922: Historian of British Maritime Policy from Drake to Jellicoe* (London, 1981), 99-100.

32. Julian S. Corbett, *The Official History of the Great War: Naval Operations*, 3 vols. (London, 1920); for the general argument see Vol. 1, Ch. 1.

33. There is no doubt that Canadians at 3rd Ypres (Passchendale) did what *they thought* other troops such as the British and the Australians, could not accomplish.

34.   G.W.L. Nicholson, *The Canadian Expeditionary Force, 1914-1919* (Ottawa, 1962). Nicholson's volume forms part of the Official History of the Canadian Army in the First World War, 1914-1919.

35.   S.F. Wise, *Canadian Airmen and the First World War* (Toronto, 1980).

36.   Desmond Morton, *A Peculiar Kind of Politics: Canada's Overseas Ministry in the First World War* (Toronto, 1982).

37.   R.H. Haycock, *Sam Hughes: The Public Career of a Controversial Canadian, 1885-1916* (Ottawa, 1986), especially 288-304.

38.   Eric Maria Remarque, *All Quiet on the Western Front* (London, 1929); Vera Brittain, *Testament of Youth* (London, 1933).

39.   There were other Canadian writers and poets, but there were no opponents of the war, except in French Canada. Among the Anglo-Saxon majority they were "scarce heard among the guns below."

40.   J.L. Granatstein and J.M. Hitsman, *Broken Promises: A History of Conscription in Canada* (Toronto, 1977).

41.   To understand the different aspects of the war's challenges to industry and manpower, see W.A.B. Douglas and Brereton Greenhous, *Out of the Shadows: Canada and the Second World War* (Toronto, 1977).

42.   Wise, *Canadian Airmen.*

43.   G.N. Tucker, *A History of the Royal Canadian Navy*, 2 vols. (Ottawa, 1952).

44.   The Historical Section of the R.C.A.F., *The R.C.A.F. Overseas*, 3 vols. (Toronto, 1944-49).

45.   Noble Frankland and Sir Charles Webster, *The Strategic Air Offensive Against Germany, 1939-1945* (London, 1961).

46.   It takes time to develop a naval escort force, and Canadian sailors learned on the job. See Marc Milner, *North Atlantic Run: The Royal Canadian Navy and the Battle for the Convoys* (Toronto, 1985).

47.   It will be interesting to see how the forthcoming volume from the Directorate of History deals with this problem. There has been no mention of fighters here. The Canadian Air Force's role as protectors of England and British shipping was straightforward, brilliant, and dangerous, but the Canadian effort in fighters was less massive than in bombers.

48.   J. Layton Ralston had commanded the 85th Infantry Battalion in World War One.

49.   C.P. Stacey, *Arms, Men and Government: The War Policies of Canada, 1939-1945* (Ottawa, 1970); and J.L. Granatstein, *Canada's War: The Politics of the Mackenzie King Government, 1939-1945* (Toronto, 1975). These writers and their books are not responsible for the comments that follow in the text.

50.   W.A.B. Douglas, "Conflict and Innovation in the Royal Canadian Navy, 1939-1945," in *Naval Warfare in the 20th Century*, ed. Gerald Jordan (London, 1977), 210-232, especially 221 and 228.

51.   C.P. Stacey, *Canada and the Age of Conflict*, 2 vols. (Toronto, 1981).

52.   James Eayrs, *In Defence of Canada*, 5 vols. (Toronto, 1964-83).

53.   For a review of recent publications, see Richard A. Preston, "Canadian Military History: A Reinterpretation. Challenge of the Eighties?", *American Review of Canadian Studies* 19 (Spring, 1989), 95-104.

APPENDIX
Historiographical Chronology

Only principal publications mentioned in this book of essays are included under Historiographical Events. Multi-volume publications are listed by year of first volume.

HISTORICAL EVENT	YEAR	HISTORIOGRAPHICAL EVENT
Confederation	1867	
	1868	"Canada First" group formed
Riel Rebellion	1869	
Organized labour launches Nine Hour Movement	1872	Dominion archives established
Pacific Scandal	1873	
	1874	New Brunswick Historical Society founded
Canadian National Association formed	1875	
	1876	Women's Literary Club founded
Grand Trunk Railroad strike	1877	
	1881	Royal Society founded
Canadian Pacific Railway completed	1885	J.C. Dent, *The Story of the Rebellion*
	1888	Historical Society of Ontario founded
Royal Commission on the Relations of Capital and Labour	1889	Dominion Women's Enfranchisement Association founded
Campaign for "unrestricted reciprocity"	1891	A.T. Mahan, *The Influence of Seapower Upon History, 1660-1793*

251

HISTORICAL EVENT	YEAR	HISTORIOGRAPHICAL EVENT
	1893	F.J. Turner, "The Significance of the Frontier in American History"
	1895	J.G. Bourinot, *How Canada is Governed*
Manitoba School Crisis	1896	
Klondike gold rush	1897	G.M. Wrong begins annual *Review of Historical Publications Relating to Canada*
	1898	Francis Parkman, *France and England in North America: The Old Regime in Canada*
Boom in western settlement and immigration began	1901	
	1905	Champlain Society founded
Industrial Disputes Investigation Act	1907	Historical Manuscripts Commission appointed
Naval Aid Bill defeated	1913	Charles Beard, *An Economic Interpretation of the Constitution of the United States*
World War I began	1914	Gustavus Myers, *A History of Canadian Wealth*
Federal suffrage extended to women	1918	W.L. MacKenzie King, *Industry and Humanity*
National Progressive Party established	1920	*Canadian Historical Review* founded
First woman elected to Parliament	1921	O.D. Skelton, *Life and Letters of Sir Wilfred Laurier*
	1922	Canadian Historical Association established

HISTORICAL EVENT	YEAR	HISTORIOGRAPHICAL EVENT
	1924	L.A. Wood, *History of Farmers' Movements in Canada*
Imperial Conference accepted equality of status Doctrine	1926	Beginning of colony-to-nation school
	1927	Edmund Bradwin, *The Bunkhouse Man*
	1928	Harold Logan, *History of Trade Union Organization in Canada*
Beginning of the Great Depression	1929	Founding of *Annales d'histoire économic et sociale* as journal of *Annales* school
Defeat of Mackenzie King government	1930	Publication of Harold Innis, *The Fur Trade in Canada* established staples approach to Canadian economics
Co-operative Commonwealth Federation formed	1932	*Canadian Frontiers of Settlement* series launched
Bennett "New Deal" launched	1935	W.A. MacIntosh, *Economic Problems of the Prairie Provinces*
		Lloyd Reynolds, *The British Immigrant in Canada*
		Canadian Journal of Economics and Political Science began publication
	1936	Harold Innis, *Settlement and the Mining Frontier*
		C.P. Stacey, *Canada and the British Army*
		G.F.G. Stanley, *The Birth of Western Canada*
Royal Commission on Dominion-Provincial Relations appointed	1937	D.G. Creighton, *The Commercial Empire of the St. Lawrence*
		H.A. Innis, *Labor in Canadian American Relations*

HISTORICAL EVENT	YEAR	HISTORIOGRAPHICAL EVENT
	1937	Beginning of the "Laurentian" school
	1938	A.F. Duguid, *Official History of the Canadian Forces in the Great War*
World War II began	1939	G.E. Britnell, *The Wheat Economy*
		N. Gras, *Business and Capitalism*, set framework for business history
Social Science Research Council established	1940	*Journal of the History of Ideas* begun
	1941	G.V. Haythorne, *Land and Labour*
		Fred Landon, *Western Ontario and the American Frontier*
	1944	Donald Creighton, *Dominion of the North*
Atomic Bomb dropped on Hiroshima	1945	Historical section of Army General Staff re-established
	1946	V.C. Fowke, *Canadian Agricultural Policy*
		R.L. Jones, *History of Agriculture in Ontario*
		A.R.M. Lower, *Colony to Nation*
		Institut d'histoire de l'Amérique-français founded
Mackenzie King retires	1948	Harold Logan, *Trade Unions in Canada*
		P.F. Sharp, *Agrarian Revolt in Western Canada*
		Launching of the People's History project
	1950	Gerald Graham, *Empire of the North Atlantic*

HISTORICAL EVENT	YEAR	HISTORIOGRAPHICAL EVENT
	1950	W.L. Morton, *Progressive Party in Canada*
Report of the Massey Comission	1951	Jean Burnet, *Next-Year Country*
	1952	D.G. Creighton, *John A. Macdonald*
		G.N. Tucker, *History of the Royal Canadian Navy*
St. Lawrence Seaway begun	1954	J.M.S. Careless, "Frontierism, Metropolitanism, and Canadian History"
		J.R. Mallory, *Social Credit and the Federal Power in Canada*
	1955	H. Ferns and Bernard Ostry, *The Age of Mackenzie King*
	1956	W.T. Easterbrook and Hugh Aitken, *Canadian Economic History*
Canada Council created	1957	Stuart Jamieson, *Industrial Relations in Canada*
		W.L. Morton, *Manitoba: A History*
		V.C. Fowke, *The National Policy and the Wheat Economy*
	1958	R.M. Dawson, *William Lyon Mackenzie King*
	1959	J.M.S. Careless, *Brown of the Globe*
		A.H. Hill, *Three Centuries and the Island*
Expansion of Canadian universities begins	1960	Stanley Ryerson, *The Founding of Canada*
		Frank Underhill, *In Search of Canadian Liberalism*
		Work starts on *Dictionary of Canadian Biography*

HISTORICAL EVENT	YEAR	HISTORIOGRAPHICAL EVENT
	1962	Canadian Forces' Directorate of History established
Royal Commission on Bilingualism and Biculturalism;	1963	W.S. MacNutt, *New Brunswick: A History*
Betty Friedan, *The Feminine Mystique*		W.L. Morton, *Kingdom of Canada*
	1964	R.C. Brown, *Canada's National Policy*
		James Eayrs, *In Defence of Canada*
		Frank Underhill, *The Image of Confederation*
	1965	S.F. Wise, "Sermon Literature and Canadian Intellectual History"
	1966	Carl Berger, "The True North Strong and Free"
		J.B. Brebner, *North Atlantic Triangle*
		D.G.G. Kerr, *Historical Atlas of Canada*
		Charles Lipton, *Trade Union Movement in Canada*
		Fernand Ouellet, *Histoire économique et sociale du Québec*
Centenary celebrations	1967	R.A. Preston, *Canada and Imperial Defence*
		G.A. Rawlyk, *Yankees at Louisbourg*
		Ramsey Cook suggests "limited identities," a way of approaching Canadian history
"Trudeaumania"	1968	Stuart Jamieson, *Times of Trouble*
		Histoire Sociale/Social History and *B.C. Studies* begun

HISTORICAL EVENT	YEAR	HISTORIOGRAPHICAL EVENT
October Crisis; Royal Commission on the Status of Women	1970	Carl Berger, *Sense of Power*
		Donald Creighton, *Canada's First Century*
		Louise Dechêne, *Habitants et marchants de Montréal au XIIIe siècle*
	1971	Richard Allen, *The Social Passion*
		Ramsay Cook, *The Maple Leaf Forever*
		Morris Zaslow, *The Opening of the Canadian North*
		Acadiensis founded
Canadian content regulations enforced by CRTC	1972	Richard Simeon, *Federal Provincial Diplomacy*
		Harold Troper, *Only Farmers Need Apply*
World oil crisis	1973	Harry Baglole and David Weale, *The Island and Confederation*
	1974	Ramsay Cook and Craig Brown, *Canada 1896-1921: A Nation Transformed*
		Terry Copp, *Anatomy of Poverty*
Wage and price controls introduced	1975	R.T. Naylor, *History of Canadian Business* Peter C. Newman, *The Canadian Establishment*
		C.P. Stacey, *Arms, Men and Governments*
Parti Québécois government elected	1976	Carl Berger, *The Writing of Canadian History*
		Donald Creighton, *Canada 1939-1957: The Forked Road*
		Launching of the *Generation Series*
		Labour/Le travail founded

HISTORICAL EVENT	YEAR	HISTORIOGRAPHICAL EVENT
Bill 101 passed	1977	David Bercuson, *Canada and the Burden of Unity*
		J.L. Granatstein and J.M. Hitsman, *Broken Promises*
		A.B. McKillop, *A Disciplined Intelligence*
		D. Monière, *Le Développement des idéalogies au Québec*
		Allison Prentice, *The School Promoters*
		C.P. Stacey, *Canada in the Age of Conflict*
		S.M. Trofimenkoff and Allison Prentice, *The Neglected Majority*
		Reg Whitaker, *The Government Party*
	1978	John H. Thompson, *Harvests of War*
		Publication of *Rural History* begun
	1979	Donald Avery, *Dangerous Foreigners*
		Robert Bothwell and William Kilbourn, *C.D. Howe*
		E.R. Forbes, *The Maritimes Rights Movement*
		Larry Pratt and John Richards, *Prairie Capitalism*
		Tom Traves, *The State and Enterprise*
National Energy Policy announced	1980	Greg Kealey, *Toronto Workers Respond to Industrialism*
Quebec referendum held		*Myrna Kostash, All of Baba's Children*
		John McCallum, *Unequal Beginnings*

HISTORICAL EVENT	YEAR	HISTORIOGRAPHICAL EVENT
	1980	Desmond Morton, *Working People*
		Doug Owram, *Promise of Eden*
		Donald Paterson and William Marr, *Canada: An Economic History*
		Richard Simeon and David Elkins, *Small Worlds*
		Veronica Strong-Boag and Beth Light, *True Daughters of the North*
	1981	Pierre Berton, *The Invasion of Canada*
		David Gagan, *Hopeful Travellers*
		A.G. Sunahara, *The Politics of Racism*
Constitution officially adoped	1982	Irving Abella and Harold Troper, *None Is Too Many*
		Carol Lee Bacchi, *Liberation Deferred*
		Eugene Forsey, *History of Trade Unions in Canada*
		J.L. Granatstein, *The Ottawa Men*
		L.D. McCann, *Heartland and Hinterland*
		J.M. Nyce, *The Gordon C. Eby Diaries*
	1983	Bryan Palmer, *Working Class Experience*
		P.A. Linteau, *Quebec: A History*
		James Struthers, *No Fault of Their Own*
		S.M. Trofimenkoff, *Dream of Nation*
Mulroney government elected	1984	Donald Akenson, *The Irish in Ontario*

HISTORICAL EVENT	YEAR	HISTORIOGRAPHICAL EVENT
	1984	William Coleman, *The Independence Movement in Quebec*
		Duncan McDowall, *Steel at the Sault*
	1985	Sylvia Bashevkin, *Toeing the Lines*
		Michael Behiels, *Prelude to Quebec's Quiet Revolution*
		Ramsay Cook, *The Regenerators*
		Allen Greer, *Peasant, Lord and Merchant*
		Desmond Morton, *A Military History of Canada*
		Wendy Owen, *The Wheat King*
		J.H. Thompson and Allen Seager, *Canada, 1922-1939: Decades of Discord*
Federal government attempts to control pornography	1986	Ben Forster, *A Conjunction of Interests*
		J.L. Granatstein, *Canada 1957-1967: The Years of Uncertainty and Innovation*
		Craig Heron and Bob Storey, *On the Job*
		D.C. Jones, *We'll All Be Buried Down Here*
		Doug Owram, *The Government Generation*
		Bryan Palmer, *The Character of Class Struggle*
		Gordon T. Stewart, *The Origins of Canadian Politics*
		Veronica Strong-Boag and A.C. Fellman, *Re-thinking Canada*

HISTORICAL EVENT	YEAR	HISTORIOGRAPHICAL EVENT
	1986	Douglas Verney, *Three Civilizations, Two Cultures, One State*
	1987	David Bercuson, *Canadian Labour History*
		Michael Bill, *Northern Enterprise*
		Clio Collective, *Quebec Women: A History*
		C.E.S. Franks, *The Parliament of Canada*
		Susan Zeller, *Inventing Canada*
		R. Cole Harris and G.J. Matthews, *The Historical Atlas of Canada*
Free Trade Agreement	1988	Christopher Armstrong and H.V. Nelles, *Monopoly's Moment*
		V. Lindstrom-Best, *Defiant Sisters*
		Allison Prentice, et al., *Canadian Women: A History*
		Veronica Strong-Boag, *New Day Recalled*
		Paul Voisey, *Vulcan*

INDEX

263

M

McCall-Newman, Christina, 11, 21 n.38
McCalla, Douglas, 43 n.36, n.39; 137 n.2; 139 n.16; 140 n.21
McCallum, John, 42 n.34, 114 n.26
McCann, L.D., 41 n.19, 93 n.28
McConica, J.K., 68 n.19
McCusher, John T., 138 n.9
McDairmid, O.J., 44 n.53
Macdonald, Sir John A., 176, 183
  biography of, 6, 73
Macdonald, L.R., 40 n.15, 139 n.16
MacDonald, Martha, 199 n.69
Macdonald, Norman, 112 n.11
MacDowall, Duncan, 139 n.11, 140 n.24, 141 n.26, 142 n.33
McGillvray, Don, 141 n.24
McGinnis, David, 117 n.57
McGowan, Don, 115 n.37
Macgregor, F.A., 159, 172 n.60
McInnis, R. Marvin, 41 n.22, 114 n.26, 116 n.49
Mackay, Douglas, 141 n.32
McKay, Ian, 96 n.60
Mackenzie King, William Lyon, 6, 24 n.72, 169 n.13, 189
  biography of, 159
  as labour historian, 149-50
McKillop, A.B., 62-64, 68 n.22, 69 n.32, 70 n.41, 168 n.3
Mackinnon, Neil, 95 n.53
Mackintosh, W.A., 27, 29, 40 n.3, 112 n.9, 113 n.13, 123
Maclachlan, Morag, 119 n.73
McLaren, Angus, 198 n.53, 199 n.68
McLaren, Arlene Tigar, 194 n.1, 198 n.53, 199 n.68
McLellan, J.S., 246 n.14
McManus, J., 43 n.35, 44 n.51
Macmillan, David R., 138 n.3, 140 n.21

McNally, David, 138 n.10
McNaught, Kenneth, 5, 20 n.10, 119 n.72, 159, 161, 172 n.59
MacNutt, W.S., 91 n.3
Macphail, Agnes, 189
Macphail, Margaret, 200, n.82
Macpherson, C.B., 16, 21 n.34, 24 n.76, 168 n.8
  Social Credit, 10-11, 18
MacPherson, Ian, 117 n.54, 118 n.61, 119 n.75
McPherson, K., 199 n.55, 200 n.79
McRae, Kenneth, 12, 17, 22 n.49, 24 n.86
McRoberts, Kenneth, 13, 23 n.54
Mahan, Alfred Thayer, 246 n.2, 247 n.24
Mahon, Rianne, 14
Mallory, J.R., 11, 21 n.36
Mandrou, Robert, 114 n.27
Manzer, Ronald, 14, 23 n.60
Marchildon, Gregory, 127-28, 139 n.17
Maritime History Project, 38
Maritime Provinces
  colonial history of, 85-86
  entrepreneurial failure, 37, 38
  ethnic research, 84-85
  mercantile capitalism, 37
  myths and stereotypes, 88
  regional history, 75
  Scottish emigration to, 85
Maritime Rights Movement, 75, 81
Marr, William, 39 n.1, 40 n.6, 116 n.48, 137 n.1
Marsh, Leonard, 153, 170 n.32
Marshall, David, 70 n.44
Martgens, Hildegard, 228 n.49
Martin, Chester, 113 n.13
Martin, W.S.A., 171 n.40
Martin, William, 156

metropolitanism, 74
migration studies, Ontario, 84
myths and distortions, disproving, 87-88
Ontario, 84-85
political economy, variations in, 78-79
Prairie, 76
Quebec, 72, 82-84
region, defining, 79-80, 81
regional journals, new, 75-76
western, 75-76
Reid, John G., 71-96 (essay), 93 n.26
Reid, Stanford, 224, n.17
Religion, 61-62
decline of, 63-64
of immigrants, 213-14
secularization, 62-63
Social gospel and, 62-63
Remarque, Eric Maria, 248 n.38
Report of the Royal Commission on the
Status of Women in Canada (1970), 192
Resnick, Philip, 18, 25 n.87
*Resources for Feminist
Research/Documentation sur la
recherche feministe*, 182
Reuben, Grant L., 168 n.8
Reuther, Victor, 157
Revue d' histoire de l' Amérique française,
110
Reynolds, Lloyd, 153, 170 n.30
Rich, E.E., 43 n.37, 141 n.32
Richards, John, 11, 21 n.35
Robert, J.C., 118 n.70, n.182; 196 n.19
Robertson, Norman, 7
Roby, Yves, 43 n.45
Romantic love, 187-88
Rooke, Patricia, 196 n.24
Rosenberg, Nathan, 139 n.19
Rosenthal, Star, 197 n.34
Ross, Douglas, 15, 24 n.70
Ross, Victor, 142 n.32
Rotstein, Abraham, 43 n.37

Rouillard, Jacques, 167
Roy, Patricia, 44 n.49, 92 n.18
Roy, R.H., 246 n.3
Royal Commission on Bilingualism and
Biculturalism, 201
Rudin, Ron, 41 n.19, 140 n.22
Rudnyckyj, J., 223 n.2
Rueschmeyer, D., 19 n.7
Ruggles, Richard I., 118 n.67
Rural demography, 97, 105
Rural history
Annales school, influence of, 98
Canadian Papers in Rural History,
(CPRH), 103
folk technology, 108
frontier thesis rejected, 99-100, 104, 113
n.15
future agenda for, 110-12
government policy decisions, effect of,
109
Hs/SH, significance of, 102-103; 114
n.28, n.29
local, studies of, 104-105
metropolitanism, 100
microstudies of, 105-106
neglect of, 97-98, 101
new, 103
social science contribution to, 100
Russell, Peter, 13, 23 n.59, 69 n.28
Ryan, John T., 116 n.53
Ryan, William F., 43 n.43
Ryerson, Stanley, 154, 155, 170 n.35, 178

S

Sacouman, R.J., 45 n.60
Safarian, A.E., 42 n.28
Sage, W.N., 91 n.7
Sager, Eric W., 41 n.19, 45 n.63, 92 n.15,
94 n.44
Sangster, Joan, 197 n.34, 228 n.55
Sarty, Roger, 247 n.29